Lord Leverhulme's Unknown Venture

Lord Leverhulme's Unknown Venture

The Lever Chair and the Beginnings of Town and Regional Planning 1908–48

The 1st Lord Leverhulme
Sir Charles Reilly
Stanley Adshead
Sir George Pepler
Sir Patrick Abercrombie
Lord Holford

Myles Wright

Hutchinson Benham
London

Hutchinson Benham Limited

An imprint of the Hutchinson Group
17-21 Conway Street, London W1P 6JD
London Melbourne Sydney Auckland Wellington
Johannesburg and agencies throughout the world

First published 1982

Wright, Myles
    The Lever Chair.
    1. University of Liverpool. *Department of*
    Civic Design—History
    I. Title
    711′.07′1142753   LF375
    ISBN 0-09-150340-X

Photoset in Century Schoolbook by V & M Graphics Ltd, Aylesbury, Bucks
Printed by Anchor Brendon, Tiptree, Essex.

CONTENTS

ACKNOWLEDGEMENTS

I am most grateful for help in preparing and publishing this book from Lord Leverhulme, the Leverhulme Trust and Unilever. The Leverhulme Trust provided funds for the three years of investigations on which the book is based. Lord Leverhulme and Sir David Orr, on behalf of Unilever, enabled publication to go ahead during a period when every publisher has been compelled to be very cautious in accepting books, of what can only be called, this kind.

I am also indebted to the University of Liverpool for permission to use the Holford papers, which are now in the University's possession, to Mr Michael Cook, the University Archivist, and to Professor Gerald Dix, sixth Lever Professor. Professor Dix was kind enough to provide accommodation for me and my assistants on what – for this book – is the sacred ground of the Department of Civic Design. He also generously answered my many questions about Sir Patrick Abercrombie whose papers he holds, and whose life he is writing.

Miss Susan Baker was my research assistant for one year, and Miss Elizabeth Bradford for two, and so it was Miss Bradford on whom fell the labour of checking references and events – a few of the latter having been invented by the eminent men of whom I was writing. Nothing that was real escaped her.

I owe special gratitude to the late Richard Wyndham Gray. He was Lord Holford's partner and friend for thirty years and my friend, too. From 1975 to his death this year he encouraged studies of Holford's life and times and collected information about them, especially of Holford's early life and his time in Italy. He may be said to have suggested this book.

I am indebted to the following for granting me interviews, writing to me of people and events, sending letters or other documents for allowing me to quote from material in which they hold the copyright or for giving help of several of these kinds: Adrian Allan, Victor Basil, Mrs Jessie Birss, Professor Ivan Boileau, Mrs Mark Bone (Mary Adshead), Derek Bridgwater, Monte Bryer, Sir Colin Buchanan, Julian Budden, Herbert Burchnall, F. Henry Carr, Professor Gordon Cherry, Professor John Cooper, T. C. Coote, Mrs Elfreda Cotton, E. A. Duley, Mrs E. F. Foster, E. Maxwell Fry, Emeritus Professor R. Gardner-Medwin, Race Godfrey, Emeritus Professor Denis Harper, Peter Harrison, Professor John Haskell, the late Lord Hinton, Neil and Gwen Holford, Sir Geoffrey Jellicoe, Emeritus Professor Rolf Jensen, Richard Jones, Roger Johnson, Professor Roy Kantorowich, Emeritus Professors Lewis Keeble and Tom Kelly, Mrs Ann Kempe, Emeritus Professor R. T. Kennedy, Lord Leverhulme, Dr Josephine Lomax-Simpson, the late Helen McCrae, John Macdonald, *The (Manchester) Guardian*, the late Howard Mason, Lady Matthew, Mrs Sheila Morgan, Emeritus Professor Jack Napper, Sir John Overall, Mrs Jo Pattrick, Lady Pepler, Mrs Lenore Rathbone, Lord Reilly, Professor Gareth Roberts, D. C. Robertson, Eugene Rosenburg, W. J. L. Rushworth, the late Dr Thomas Sharp, the late Ward Shennan, Michael Shippobottom, David Spreull, H.M. Stationery Office, Emeritus Professor Gordon Stephenson, Frank Stower, Sir John Summerson, Dr Michael Thompson, *The Times*, S. N. Tomkin, Mrs Madge Velarde, Dr W. N. Vellacott, Gavin Walkley, the late Sir Clough Williams-Ellis, the late K. M. Whitfield and Emeritus Professor Denis Winston.

I am also indebted to the following persons, or organizations, for permission to reproduce illustrations in which they hold the copyright: *The Architectural Review*; Stewart Bale Ltd; Professor Gerald Dix; E. Chambre Hardman; Holford Associates; Lord Leverhulme; Liverpool County Museums; the University of Liverpool; Meridian Air Maps; Lady Pepler; and Lord Reilly.

PREFACE

In 1977, it was suggested that I should write about the life and times of Lord Holford, who was probably the best known town planner of the period 1945-1970. I did not accept the suggestion then but when thinking about it, and of some of the events in Holford's career, I realized that an important phase in the history of British planning had come to an end.

For half a century town planning – town, country and regional planning – had been seen by most practitioners and students as the art and science of guiding the use, sometimes the conservation, of all land, and the layout and relationship of everything placed on the land. Town and country planning was thought to be concerned mainly with form and design. This view provided the foundation on which a new profession was built, and some of its achievements received worldwide recognition.

There is no doubt that this creative era began with Willial Hesketh Lever, 1st Lord Leverhulme's decision in 1908 to found the world's first university school of town planning at the University of Liverpool. It is very probable that his decision was then considered eccentric, by many academics and perhaps by many others. But Lever was almost the only man in the world at that time who would have done such a thing.

From this modest seed grew a great tree. A large part of the creation of the new profession, its education and its recognition by the public was the achievement of the first three Lever professors, Adshead, Abercrombie and Holford, and their three friends and allies – Lever, the patron, Reilly and Pepler – whose lives are told in the following chapters. Of these exceptional men Abercrombie and Holford were also the authors of the best known plans for cities and regions. They greatly influenced the provision, and the handbooks, for post-war physical planning and set the stage for the best post-war achievements, from National Parks to New Towns. They also worked as planning consultants in a dozen countries abroad.

For the time being, a belief in the power of design to improve and safeguard town and countryside has, at best, become dormant. Nearly all the attention of town planners today goes to legal, administrative, social and economic matters, and such a very different view may have value. However, a belief in the power of design will return in due course. The present lull provides the opportunity to look back, and to set down the considerable achievements of the first forty years. The pause also provides the chance to repay a debt and tell what great things resulted from *Lord Leverhulme's Unknown Venture.*

Myles Wright

June 1982

INTRODUCTION

In 1910 a deed of gift from William Hesketh Lever, later the 1st Viscount Leverhulme of the Western Isles, to the University of Liverpool contained the words:

> *It is the opinion of the Donor that it will be a boon*
> *to future generations that there should be an*
> *opportunity of training men to a full knowledge of*
> *the best possible methods of Town Planning and*
> *Civic Design and that the establishment of such a*
> *School will be found to fill a useful place even if*
> *its only result is to direct the attention of and*
> *educate Public Authorities to and upon the subject*
> *and that ... the permanent establishment and*
> *endowment of the School should in due time*
> *receive the careful consideration of the Council of*
> *the University.*

The Council of the University agreed to the establishment of what was to be called the Department of Civic Design, for which Lever provided at first £800 a year and later £1,200. It was the world's first centre for university studies of town planning and associated subjects.

The Department of Civic Design was one of the scores of departments concerned with a wide range of arts and sciences which were founded in Britain's new universities in the twenty years before 1914. To a contemporary writer on higher education the subject of study in this new venture at Liverpool must have seemed odd if not downright eccentric within a university; but a part-time professor and one full-time lecturer suggested an experiment that might come to nothing. The new department was however to begin to publish a quarterly journal at once; that was unusual, and might have aroused mild interest.

The pages that follow tell the story of how the Department came to be founded and of how Lever's gift had in the end consequences of national and international importance. The story is not told as a normal history, either of the Department or of town planning, but broadly and indirectly through the lives and influence of six remarkable men, and mainly concerns the years between 1908 and 1948. The chief events took place in those forty years, although the youth of the older men before 1908 and wider consequences after 1948 are also described. Four of these men – Lever himself, Reilly, Abercrombie and Holford – worked in or near Liverpool for periods of between ten and thirty years. Perhaps one should say Liverpool and Merseyside were their base and training ground; for Lever, after founding Port Sunlight, became an MP and travelled round the world building up his international business; Abercrombie and Holford both moved on to London for the works that brought them greatest fame; and Reilly, though at Liverpool till he retired as professor, also became something of a national figure and, in the architectural world, a national institution.

Adshead and Pepler were different. Adshead was the first Lever professor, a Lancashire man who had made his reputation in London as a brilliant architectural draughtsman. He was a sensitive architect and produced half a dozen town planning reports between the two world wars. Having begun his professional career in London he returned there in 1914 to become the first professor of town planning at University College, and to private practice. Yet Liverpool greatly influenced him. No one could work for half of five years with Reilly and the young Abercrombie and near to Lever without being influenced. Adshead and his students produced schemes for rebuilding run-down portions of Liverpool, for which Lever offered prizes. Adshead visited Thornton Manor (Lever's home) a number of times and no doubt took his students to Port Sunlight. Liverpool and Merseyside redirected and extended Adshead's energies and powers, but they could not claim to have formed him.

Pepler is the real exception. Save as a welcome visitor, examiner and friend of Abercrombie, he had no connection with the Department of Civic Design or with Liverpool. A pernickety reader, even one mildly so, may therefore ask why he has been chosen as one of the six great characters of this book – why indeed he is in the story at all. The answer is that in a story told mainly through the lives, times and influence of people, Pepler usefully represents, in fact personifies, the non-Liverpool history of town planning between the wars. His good-humoured, indefatigable work, his position as the Government's chief adviser on planning, his steady encouragement of the Town Planning Institute, and the influence of his friends, including Lord Milner and Clough Williams Ellis, were all of the greatest consequence in the inter-war years. They were years of feeble legislation and slow progress. Abercrombie was discouraged by nothing, and steadily enhanced his reputation in those twenty years. Adshead received fewer commissions than Abercrombie and was sometimes discouraged, and Holford only received his first major planning commission two years before the Second World War.

Pepler, in his central position, could see all that was going on between the wars. He was at the peak of his powers (aged forty-eight in 1930), and was able to guide the Ministry's small patronage to the people and places who would use it best. He was a John the Baptist. He made converts, and prepared the way for the real planning that began with the bombs of 1940–41; and helped all the Lever professors, from the first to the fifth, down the years.

After the chapters on the lives and influence of the five men who founded or occupied the Lever Chair and, with Pepler, prepared for post-war planning, two more chapters have been found necessary. The first describes the actual preparations for post-war planning from 1940 onwards. The account is needed to justify the claim that the Lever professors and their former students played a great part in that work; and since many people were involved, Chapter Eight has necessarily left biography and become a brief general account of a few important years.

Finally, the Epilogue tells of what happened afterwards, up to the Department of Civic Design's Jubilee in 1959, when the Minister for Town Planning, then called Minister for Local Government and Planning, came to Liverpool to help celebrate the fifty years. *The Times* and the (then) *Manchester Guardian* and other journals published articles about Lever's small venture of 1909 which had grown through the work and influence of six men into an institution that was famous and had drawn students to it from, in all, over fifty countries.

1

THE BACKGROUND

A man or woman who is interested in a professional innovation or sequence of events in the past century must resist the inclination to think that the social and economic background at the time of the innovation was, broadly, the same as that with which he or she is familiar: poorer and more smokier perhaps, and no TV, but roughly the same. He or she can then turn to the narrower professional matters that really interest them.

A large part of the interest of the Lever Chair however is that it was founded when Britain's social and economic circumstances were totally different from those of the 1980s, and Lever's gift was the more astonishing. Though town planning (the phrase was only three years old in 1909)[1] by local authorities had been in use abroad for thirty or forty years, it was unknown in Britain, and Lever's foundation was a true pioneering venture in a land where the study and practice of town planning were greatly needed, along with many other reforms. It is therefore useful to show the greatness of the need in 1909 by a background sketch of how things were in Edwardian Britain – divided into the national scene, and that on Merseyside.

Britain 1905-10

The outstanding difference between now and then was the poverty and harshness of life for the poor in the 1900s, and their appalling dwellings. The poor were then about two-thirds of the population. Booth's studies in London (1902–3), Rowntree's in York (1901) and the rejection rate of would-be recruits in the Boer War had made the facts plain, but the middle classes and the wealthy of any social class either did not want to know or thought the situation was irremediable, even natural.

Good steady workers then received *Round about a Pound a Week* and a classic study under that title was soon to be published.[2] Eighty-seven per cent of the population earned less than £100 a year, and between a third and a half of all workers in the biggest industries earned less than 25s (£1.25) a week.[3] In 1910 over a million people were listed as paupers in *Whitaker's Almanac*. From 1900 unemployment grew and had reached 8 per cent in 1913; although Winston Churchill's Bill establishing Labour Exchanges was passed in 1909, and by 1914 a million jobs were being filled by the Exchanges. Until after 1908 there was no health or unemployment insurance and no old age pensions. If the wage-earner of a family died or became unable to work the family's position became truly desperate.

The housing of the poorest third of the population, and perhaps of more than a third, was to us almost incredibly bad. Overcrowding of more than two people to a room and often a small room, was suffered by 9 per cent, so that about four million men, women and children lived thus. It was common for families to have to live in two rooms, and in large districts of big cities five or six families shared one water tap in the street and two privies in an alley or court. This was despite the sixteen Housing (of the labouring classes) Acts which had been passed between 1851 and 1909. Illness was of course rife and a doctor's visit was supposed to cost a minimum of 2/6d, although it is to the credit of the medical profession that they often did not press for payment from the poor.[4]

When one realizes that only about 40 per cent of men, and no women, had votes, there must have been much desperation around, and arousal of the famous 'middle-class conscience' certainly contributed to the Liberal landslide victory of 1906.[5] Liverpool had built the first local authority dwellings in Britain in 1869, yet the new London County Council – a progressive body – built only 10,000 dwellings between 1894 and 1914: a number it exceeded in the single year 1927.

If a thirty-five-year-old of 1981 were transported back to Liverpool (or Manchester or Birmingham) as it was in 1909, he or she would be struck first of all by the smoke and the dirt. The aerial sewage, as Professor Reilly called it, descended from forty million chimneys and coated everything and to some degree everyone. The second big impression would almost certainly be of the electric trams and horse transport. Within a mile or two of a city centre little moved faster than a boy could run. Apart from the railways, people moved by tram or on foot, the lucky few in cabs or carriages. Motor vehicles were then only 1 for every 200 to be seen in 1981.

The third unexpected sight would be the swarms of ragged, barefoot, half-starved children that darted about carrying or selling newspapers or picking up horse dung or worse. They were often bow-legged from rickets, a disease of malnutrition. The most splendid British achievement in the last seventy-five years has surely been the transformation of almost every aspect of the care of children.

Another most obvious aspect of a 1909 street scene that needs to be mentioned is the black or dark clothes commonly worn. To some extent the women's dark clothes were a hangover from Queen Victoria's forty years of exaggerated widowhood, but the main reason for their popularity was that dark clothes did not show the dirt. Dirty clothes were the daily wear of much more than half the population. Soap had fallen in price over a long period – partly owing to Lever – from 6d a pound to 2d or 2½d.[6] This was a low price even then, but for 2½d a poor housewife could buy two pairs of kippers or a 2 lb loaf of bread for a hungry family: so for a large part of the population it was starve or stink. Their choice was obvious in public transport in hot weather. So was the prevalence of fleas, because of which the middle classes preferred hard wooden seats in local transport.

These were the realities of urban life in Britain, for the majority, in 1909. Of course there was pomp and glitter, and a sunset glory about the British Empire. It was the greatest empire ever – almost a quarter of the map of the world was coloured red – and the valuable imports and captive markets for exports gave a rather deceptive feeling of strength. In fact both the United States and Germany had already surpassed Britain in industrial output and were cutting into her markets. And in military terms the countries of the Empire – apart from Canada – had either internal problems (India, South Africa) or small populations in big countries living with the punishing drawbacks of great distances (Australia, New Zealand) or were just a wide-spread scatter of multi-racial splodges and splinters. Against this, Germany was a compact mass of almost 65 million people, with the biggest and best army in the world.

The great Liberal electoral victory of 1906 (comparable with the Labour victory of 1945) at last gave liberal ideas a chance and led to some improvements in the lives of the poor. Between 1906 and 1912 measures were passed that introduced old age pensions, health and unemployment insurance, Employment Exchanges, school meals and a school medical service, and an eight-hour day for miners.

In Edwardian times life was pleasant for most of the middle classes (estimated at 5 million) and luxurious for the rich.[7] A family with £500 a year was very comfortable, and £1,000 a year opened up the full range of middle-class recreations: reading; attending lectures; musical, religious and charitable activities; tennis, bicycling and holidays abroad; and charades, musical parties and dances at home – and probably motoring as well. Domestic electric lighting and gramophones were also becoming quite common. Theatres were rather suspect for young people and their seniors carefully vetted the plays on offer.

A large proportion of the middle classes, who for the most part ran the country, were serious minded, and took pains over their careers and good works. The young men would work from 9.0 am till 6.30 pm (12.30 pm on Saturdays), often went to improving societies in the evenings and to two services at church or chapel on Sundays. Satan seemed to have little chance: and opportunities for young men and women to be innocently alone and talk about life were very few, but family stories suggest that one man in every three or four families took to drink.

The lifestyle of the rich and powerful Edwardians has been sufficiently publicized, but must be mentioned here just because they *were* powerful in a way very difficult to believe in 1981. Out of a population of 45 million 120,000 people owned two-thirds of the wealth of Britain, and 40,000 persons owned four-fifths of the land of England and Wales. Five hundred had more than £100,000 a year and 30,000 had more than £10,000 (which was still within the 1/2d per £1 band of tax).[8]

The luxury of life in the greatest houses is read of today almost with incredulity and, it must be confessed, with some goggling envy. At least most of us would like to have experienced an Edwardian weekend party; say, twice. Fifty guests might each bring two or three of their own servants, meals ran up to twelve courses and boredom was kept at bay by slaughtering 2,000 or more birds and hares a day, by ladies changing their clothes five times daily and by judicious arrangements of who had adjacent bedrooms. Yet political discussions and even decisions of great consequence took place in some of the great houses. Relatives and nominees of about twenty peers held 150 or even 200 seats in the House of Commons.[9]

To us the fears of the wealthy that the radicals would seize their wealth seem absurd, even though Lloyd George gave them a nasty turn when, in his Peoples' Budget of 1909, he announced a 20 per cent tax on land values every time land changed hands.[10] Lloyd George was as much a bogy to the rich at that time as Mr Tony Benn and his close associates are in 1981. Lloyd George's most famous rabble-rouser was his statement that 'a fully equipped Duke costs as much to keep up as two Dreadnoughts, and is far more difficult to scrap'. Even the King – usually level-headed in matters political – wrote to the Prime Minister in April 1909 (just as the first Lever professor was being chosen):

> The Income Tax which has always been regarded
> as a war tax now stands so high for unearned
> incomes over a certain amount that any increase
> would have a disastrous effect.
>   The intolerable burden of tax ... was levied at 1/8d
> in the £ on incomes over £18,000 per annum.[11]

Communications other than transport would also have astonished the 1981 time-traveller back in 1909. There was no television or domestic radio of course. 'Wireless telegraphy' was just being developed, mainly for messages from ships to shore, and telegraph cables ran to most bigger countries. In big towns there were several postal deliveries each day and one on Sundays. It was quite possible to post a letter to someone in the same city and receive a reply the same day. Nearly all commercial and domestic messages went by letter, supplemented by telegrams. Telegrams cost 6d for twelve words (the minimum) and ½d for each additional word. Eighty-six million inland telegrams were sent in 1908, and when Winston and Clementine Churchill were separated they usually telegraphed to one another every day.[12]

For news, everyone depended on newspapers. The cheaper and sensational national daily newspapers – like the *Daily Mail* – were gaining readers among the first generation of Britons who could (almost) all read simple stories. But it was the local newspapers that were the mainstay of most adults. Little attention was paid in these to London events except politics, or to foreign affairs, but local events were reported in tiny print and at stupefying length. Politics were given specially full treatment and political meetings were numerous and crowded; understandably, since the meetings were free and exciting, and the topics dealt with might mean the difference between semi-starvation and something better for poorer citizens of any big town.

Not all was gloom, however, in 1909. Cheerfulness broke through even for the poor; too often in the numerous public houses, but also by means of street bands, church tea parties, processions, fairs of the roundabout and side-show kind, football matches, and excursions by rail and steamer, which were cheap, well organized and extremely popular. The better paid and more thrifty workers could sometimes manage a long weekend at Margate or Blackpool, although few of the working classes received holidays with pay. There were also cheap seats in the upper circles of music halls and theatres, and, for those better off who also had the energy, there was pigeon and whippet breeding and racing, or working on one's own allotment. An interest in horse-racing was shared by many of all classes, and in our great year of 1909 King Edward himself won the Derby with his horse Minoru.

The middle and upper classes who read or went to plays could choose between Thomas Hardy, Henry James, H. G. Wells, Mrs Humphrey Ward, Marie Corelli, Elinor Glyn, Edgar Wallace and Max Beerbohm; and of contemporary playwrights remembered today there were Chekhov, Ibsen, Bernard Shaw, Oscar Wilde and Somerset Maugham.

Amidst laborious lives and rare holidays the mass of Britons had little time for rumours of war; or even for new dangerous inventions, though Louis Bleriot flew the Channel in 1909 and Zeppelins were undertaking long flights. John Galsworthy protested vigorously in 1911 (*The Times*) against defiling the air with engines of destruction. No one heeded him. Politics to most people meant Home Rule for Ireland, National Insurance or suffragettes chaining themselves to railings as part of their campaign to achieve votes for women. To a minority of thoughtful people, however, including the King and the Foreign Secretary, the situation in Europe was very worrying. Of the five great powers there (if Turkey could be so called), only Germany was politically stable, and half a dozen Balkan countries continued to fly or try to fly at each others' throats. In the midst of all this, the neurotic Kaiser Wilhelm of Germany made warlike speeches whose only acceptable aspect was the impartiality with which he annoyed Britain, France and Russia in turn.

Whether the dangers and irrational behaviour of statesmen in 1909 were greater than in 1981 we cannot tell, but at least our horrors are no longer in fancy dress. In 1909, the armies clanked in spiked helmets, breastplates and a hundred uniforms of every colour; and France's much admired Zouaves wore, even, briefly, in war, brilliant scarlet baggy trousers.

The ghastly marching, naval manoeuvres, boasting and pageantry went on, mostly ignored in Britain, where for the five years to 1914 the incompetence of the army in the Boer War was forgotten,

and things were a little better for the poor and a paradise for the rich.
Winston Churchill put it all majestically in the first volume of *The
World Crisis*:

> *Nations and Empires crowned with princes and
> potentates rose majestically on every side, lapped
> in the accumulated treasures of the long peace ...
> The two mighty European systems faced each
> other glittering and clanking in their panoply, but
> with a tranquil gaze ... The old world in its sunset
> was fair to see.*
>
> *But there was a strange temper in the air ...
> Almost one might think the world wished to
> suffer.*[13]

Edwardian Merseyside

Liverpool – by which Britain meant Merseyside in general – had the
importance in 1909 which Greater Birmingham has today if one
were to add in London Airport; and Liverpool meant the sea and
overseas trade in the way that the whole of the west Midlands now
means motor cars. Next to London, Liverpool was the largest port in
the Empire. One third of all Britain's imports came to Liverpool and
a quarter of all exports left the Mersey, even more than left the
Thames.

The docks stretched for seven miles, and for more than ten if one
included those on the Birkenhead side of the river. There were
twenty-six miles of quay space. Shipping lines like Cunard, White
Star and Canadian Pacific were as familiar to the public then as
British Airways and Pan-American are today. Blue Funnel, Elder
Dempster and Ellerman were also household words to all concerned
with shipping. All the growing trans-Atlantic passenger traffic
came or left Princes Landing stage at Liverpool's Pierhead, and
many passengers for South America, West Africa and the Far East
also sailed from Liverpool. The VIP passengers boarding at
Pierhead were not conscious of the emigrants, packed into the
steerage the night before, of whom about half left through Liverpool
each year, with no very kind feelings for their native land.

The population of Liverpool itself was 746,000 in 1911 and
Merseyside contained about 1¼ million with a hinterland containing
another 4½ million in the rest of Lancashire and Cheshire. The
populations on either side of the Mersey were closely linked. In 1911
30 million passengers used the ferries across the river. (See map in
illus.) It was a trading area, and manufacturing industries were
mainly linked with the sea: shipbuilding and repairs, flour milling,
sugar refining, and of course soap with its principal raw materials
from West Africa.

In many ways Liverpool was a typical part of the national big city
scene: smoke, dirt, poverty, dreadful housing for the poor, horse
transport and smells. On the other hand Liverpool had made great

efforts to improve itself. Its water supply, sewerage, paving and street lighting were highly regarded, and Liverpool had inaugurated Britain's Medical Officers of Health, district nurses, public bath houses and dwellings built by local authorities, though only 2,000 had been built by 1907. Its electric tram service was considered the best in the country, and its suburban railway under the Mersey to Birkenhead and the Wirral had been electrified in 1903.

The state of dock labourers remained very bad. The work being casual, it was thought the labourers had to live close-packed near the docks, and that regular employment was impossible. Eleanor Rathbone, who had studied dock workers' living conditions,[6] became the first woman member of the City Council in 1909.

Bessie Braddock described scenes and attitudes just before our special year of 1909, that seem today almost impossible:

> *I remember the faces of the unemployed when the*
> *soup ran out. I remember their dull eyes and their*
> *thin, blue lips. I remember blank, hopeless stares,*
> *day after day, week after week, all through the*
> *hard winter of 1906–7, when I was seven years old*
> *... the wharves and the dock roads silent. Of the*
> *city's seven hundred thousand people, a thousand*
> *were dying of starvation and tens of thousands,*
> *men, women and children, were hungry and cold*
> *and sick. Meanwhile, in the fashionable suburbs,*
> *the civic leaders, the bankers, the merchants and*
> *the captains of industry sat, well-fed and well-*
> *housed and well-clothed, and made no serious*
> *effort to ease the distress.*[14]

The lines of byelaw and pre-byelaw dwellings along Scotland Road were generally of very poor quality. Charles Reilly wrote of the slums on his arrival in 1904:

> *Miles of narrow streets of such buildings, with*
> *separate families living in the basements and in*
> *each room of the three or four floors above, with*
> *every other window, it seemed, broken and stuffed*
> *up with sacking, every doorway worn shiny and*
> *darker still with the grease and dirt of the*
> *inhabitants and their clothes, every other child*
> *with bare feet, that was what this dockline of*
> *slums was like nearly as far as the docks*
> *extended.*[15]

Merseyside differed in its social pattern from that of the nation as a whole. Its interested nobility was confined to the Earls of Derby, though the Earls of Sefton and the Dukes of Westminster from Eaton Hall near Chester, took an occasional part in good causes.[16] Its resident aristocracy was therefore upper middle class: the Rathbones, Holts, Glynns, Bibbys and perhaps a score of other wealthy families, who considered it their duty to do voluntary work for their city, in medical and educational and other ways. Across the Mersey the new great man, Lever, did the same.

Below the great families, and several hundred other trading families of substantial wealth, there were perhaps 20,000 or 30,000 professional people and managers, chief engineers, clerks, shop keepers, tugmasters, officers of merchant vessels, and the officials of local authorities, the port and other institutions – together with their families. Below the 30,000 was the mass of the population, mainly divided into those with regular work and those without; and a great deal of work associated with the port was intermittent, or 'casual' as it was called until recently. Liverpool was not a peaceful place: the quotation from the Braddocks' book makes one surprised that mob violence was not constant and bloody. Besides national strikes, like that on the railways in 1911 (in Liverpool troops fired on a mob and two were killed), there was always the prospect of sectarian violence.

Since at least the time of the famines in the 1840s, the Irish had been forced to emigrate in large numbers. For most of these Liverpool was the great emigration centre, and having reached Liverpool many stayed there and competed for the scarce jobs. As the Irish were nearly all Catholics, the Orange Lodges (Protestant and anti-Catholic groups of Northern Irish origin) received many new recruits, and they organized anti-Catholic processions that nearly always led to violence. Indeed Orange-*versus*-Irish fights were liable to occur at any time. Perhaps because the wretched Irish forced standards down, poverty was specially severe in Liverpool. Eleanor Rathbone's studies of dock labourers described a grown-up girl who was unable to seek work as she had no boots, and no girl could get work without them.

Ramsay Muir wrote that in Edwardian times Liverpool was 'full of fizz and go'. It had its own university, its own repertory theatre and other theatres, a philharmonic orchestra, the William Brown and Picton Libraries, a museum and the Walker Art Gallery which had a high reputation.[17] In 1908 W. B. Yeats was in Liverpool to see Mrs Patrick Campbell in *Electra*. She also played in *Hedda Gabler*. The docks were still expanding and in 1908 Liverpool's first (Anglican) Cathedral was being built and so were the Cotton Exchange and the Liver Building. It was an inward-looking city, and paid little attention to London. Government interference with the life and revenues of big cities was then small. It also (as was common for big cities) thought little of its rivals. 'Manchester man and Liverpool gentleman' must surely have been thought of in one of Liverpool's clubs – the Athenaeum, Lyceum or the rest. The four local daily newspapers and twenty-three weekly newspapers kept national and foreign news on back pages.

Small contemporary word pictures of Edwardian Liverpool show very different facets of life. One firm of carting contractors stabled 200 horses in central Liverpool, and the family that owned it took servants, a pony and trap, two cats and two dogs to the Isle of Man for their holidays.[18] The wealthier citizens lived mainly to the south of the city, from Sefton Park to Mossley Hill where the Rathbones had entertained at Greenbank since 1787. 'Poor' relations of the Rathbones had six children but managed to keep five servants too. The well-to-do who had not migrated southwards still lived in Abercromby Square and its nearby streets. These were part of the Corporation Estate and had been well laid out in the 1830s. University staff lived near Abercromby Square till the Second World War, and it is now the centre of the university.

Mrs Elfreda Cotton records that although a young lady of good family could not be seen alone with a young man, she could, despite the awful conditions of the poor, travel alone to and from the university and almost anywhere in Liverpool by tram or on foot without any fear of molestation.[19] Also, subscription dances at the Mount Pleasant Assembly Rooms were so exclusive that ivory admission tokens were dropped into a velvet bag held by a footman.

The university had used its six years of full independence to good effect as is described in Professor Kelly's history of the university.[20] In 1909 it had about 40 professors and 1,150 students, and despite squalid surroundings – jammed in between a huge Workhouse, the Royal Infirmary and a former Lock Hospital, and straddling a railway line – it had attracted well-known men to its staff. Among those who were teachers in the period 1900–14 were Ronald Ross, Oliver Lodge, Charles Sherrington, Cyril Burt and Bernard Pares (all later knighted, as were Reilly and Abercrombie). And in 1907–08 the former Professor of Physiology, Richard Caton, became Lord Mayor of Liverpool.

In 1909 the 17th Earl of Derby, that famous King of Lancashire, was installed as University Chancellor and so remained till his death in 1948; and Vice-Chancellor Dale (who was to become Sir Alfred in 1911) kept a sharp eye on the new university's course from the robust Waterhouse Gothic of the Victoria Building.

Liverpool was an exciting attraction in those days – a kind of northern London – so much so that the great Bass brewery at Burton-on-Trent took their employees to Liverpool for an annual outing in seventeen special trains (starting at 4 am) and prepared a ninety-six-page booklet about Merseyside, with nearly as many illustrations, of which each excursionist received a copy. Bass employees were then made of strong stuff. If any of them did one quarter of the things they could have done in their thirteen hours in Liverpool, they must have slept the whole way back to Burton.

Such was Liverpool about the year 1909 when Lever, who had been a progressive Liberal MP since 1906, agreed with Reilly that town planning needed studies and a publication that could only be undertaken in a university. It was a vast smoky thrusting city, really a group of cities, with 24,000 ships paying dock dues each year for the use of the Mersey. The greatest liners – including the much-loved *Mauretania* (in which Lever sailed to America in 1910), the

Lusitania and *Titanic* (both of which came to tragic ends) – were known to most British schoolboys, and one or another seemed to enter or leave almost daily.[21] The ferries ran ceaselessly to and fro from Pierhead to Wallasey, New Brighton, Woodside and elsewhere on the western side of the Mersey, where Port Sunlight unloaded the raw materials for soap. Wars seemed far away, although fourteen battleships of the Channel Fleet reassuringly entered the river to celebrate the seventh Centenary of Liverpool's first City Charter in 1907. The Second World War was then beyond anyone's imagination, but it did happen that a man called Adolf Hitler spent some months in Liverpool in 1912-13.[22] He did not like it.

NOTES AND REFERENCES

1   The term was first used by John Nettlefold in his speech as Chairman
     of the Birmingham City Council Housing Committee, 3 July 1906.
     Josephine Reynolds, *Thomas Coglan Horsfall 1841-1932 Pioneer of
     the Town Planning Movement in England* (MA Thesis Liverpool
     University 1953) 58.

2   Maud Pember Reeves, *Round About a Pound a Week* (Virago,
     London, 1979).

3   Robert Cecil, *Life in Edwardian England* (B.T. Batsford, London,
     1969) 51.

4   Leslie S. Hearnshaw, *Cyril Burt, Psychologist* (Hodder & Stoughton,
     London, 1979) 3.

5   'Other changes ultimately to revolutionize the world were germi-
     nating in the national conscience during this Indian summer ... A
     deepening sense of the necessity for 'social progress' mobilized much
     voluntary effort. A general awakening of all classes was taking place
     to the terrible consequences of environment in the slums. The scienti-
     fically guided Christian aspirations of such men as Canon Barnett
     and his wife; Charles Booth's statistical investigations into the ugly
     facts of London life; the civic patriotism of the new London County
     Council; and in the political field, the Women's Suffrage movement,
     were beginning to transform the familiar Victorian landscape.'
     Christopher Hussey, *The Life of Sir Edwin Lutyens* (Country Life Ltd,
     London, 1950) 119.

6   According to Henry R. Aldridge, *The National Housing Manual*
     (published by the National Housing and Town Planning Council in
     1923), soap cost 6d per lb. in 1839 (p. 100). Seventy years later Eleanor
     Rathbone in her report on *How the Casual Labourer Lives* (Northern
     Publishing Co. Liverpool, 1909) records that soap cost 2d-2½d per lb.

7   'Although the one was already an age of steam, it was still an age of
     horses. It was an age of well regulated economy of leisure, and rigid
     class distinction, an age of accepted sexual inequality, political expan-
     sion and unctuous platitude; of righteous indignation over very small
     matters, and apathy over great ones.' Robert Lutyens, *Sir Edwin
     Lutyens: An Appreciation in Perspective* (Country Life Ltd, London,
     1942) 28.

8   Paul Thompson, *The Edwardians* (Weidenfeld & Nicolson, London,
     1975) 12, 13. Peter Laslett, *The World We Have Lost* (Methuen & Co.
     Ltd, first published 1965 second edition 1971) 228.

9   The author regrets that he has lost the authoritative reference for this
     statement. But a similar impression is given in: Wilhelm Guttsman
     (Ed) *The English Ruling Class* (Weidenfeld & Nicolson, 1969); Ray
     Lewis and Angus Maude, *The English Middle Classes* (Phoenix

House, London, 1949); Peter Mauger and Leslie Smith, *The British People 1902-1975* (Heinemann, London, 1972); and Brian Masters *The Dukes* (Blond & Briggs Ltd, London, 1975).

10　This particular threat was not carried out; like the 1947 proposal to buy up the development rights in all land for the benefit of the public, it just faded away.

11　Giles St Aubyn, *Edward VII: Prince and King* (Collins, London, 1979) 349-50.

12　Mary Soames, *Clementine Churchill: By Her Daughter* (Cassell, London, 1979).

13　Winston Churchill, *The World Crisis 1911-1914* (Thornton Butterworth, London, 1923) 188.

14　Jack and Bessie Braddock, *The Braddocks* (Macdonald, London, 1963) 1-2.

15　Emeritus Professor Charles Reilly, *Scaffolding in the Sky* (George Routledge & Sons, London, 1938) 81.

16　Lords Sefton, Salisbury, and Derby together drew £345,000 a year in ground rents from Liverpool and contributed nothing to the City's expenditure. P. Mauger and L. Smith, *op. cit.*, 22.

17　Edward Prior wrote in The *Architectural Review* after referring to the new Cathedral:

　　'Liverpool has ... grown to be one of the greatest cities of the Empire ... with the good fortune of a striking and characteristic architecture. Its commercial building of sixty years ago, much of it stamped with the genius of Cockerell, gives its streets a dignity rare in modern cities, and above all Elme's St George's Hall stands pre-eminent as the most satisfactory Public Hall of the nineteenth century.'

The Architectural Review Vol. X (1901) 143.

18　Mrs Charles Wells letter to author, 19 January 1978. Mrs Wells was a daughter of the family in question.

19　Interview with Mrs Elfreda Cotton, 24 January 1978.

20　Emeritus Professor Thomas Kelly, *For Advancement of Learning* (Liverpool University Press, 1981).

21　The impressiveness of the great liners and importance of a maiden voyage and the passengers is portrayed in contemporary and rather florid notes by Dixon Scott on the Lusitania's first departure:

　　a monstrous series of leaning scarlet towers - four huge columns that overwhelmed the traffic and the buildings, and made even the lattice-work of the Overhead Railway seem a mere unimportant stain ... It was a public function. The trains

began to arrive from London; the crowd grew denser; it began
to assume that cosmopolitan complexion which is Liverpool's
native hue. There were splendid autocratic males who looked like
noblemen, and were probably commercial travellers; there were
frowsy plebeians who looked like commercial travellers and
were probably noblemen; there was a recognizable millionaire
or so; there were eager American women, heavily be-tulled,
carrying precious boxes labelled 'Maison Louise'; there were
their menfolk with clean tired faces and preposterous hats;
there were their self-possessed spirits and accents ... The thing
that thrilled them, that filled their imagination, was the fact
that they were about to embark on the swiftest and most
voluptuous voyage ever attempted by mankind.'

Dixon Scott, *A Number of Things* (T. N. Foulis, London and
Edinburgh, 1917) 189, 192–3.

22   William Stephenson, *A Man called Intrepid: The Secret War
      1939–1945* (Macmillan, London 1976) 120–21.

2

THE MAN WHO PAID FOR IT

1st Viscount Leverhulme of the Western Isles: 1851-1925

William Hesketh Lever was a great man who created one of the world's greatest businesses. He also initiated, guided and himself designed in part a host of building and landscape works, including new towns in several countries, and assembled a famous collection of furniture and works of art. He has been the subject of at least three books and a valuable unpublished study, on which most of the facts in this summary are based.[1-4]

This chapter is concerned with what must have then seemed a small incident, at one of the busiest times of Lever's life: the founding of the Department of Civic Design in the University of Liverpool in the year 1909. It was a venture, once begun, which received his continued interest and support and eventually had great consequences - including the shaping of the British town planning system after the 1939-45 war. One must therefore write briefly of Lever's youth, work and broad interests, to explain why a wealthy, famous man undertook so bizarre a venture, in 1909, as the endowment of university studies in town planning, a subject then unrecognized as a desirable field of study save by a few enthusiasts. No doubt there were smiles in Oxbridge Common Rooms among those who noticed the announcement.

Lever first became closely concerned with the University School of Architecture (of which Civic Design was to become a part) in 1908, when Charles Reilly, the ebullient Professor of Architecture at Liverpool, appealed to Lever for help in saving the old Bluecoat School, the City's best eighteenth-century building. This appeal is described in the next Chapter.

Lever, in 1908, was at the peak of his career.[5] He was very rich and famous as the creator of Sunlight Soap, built up by American advertising methods: 'We want to have this hypnotic effect with soap ... The whole object of advertising, is to build a halo round the article ... [6]

He had done this by gift coupons, and even by the then astonishing back projection of slides on to hoardings in public places - until the police stopped it because of the crowds it attracted.[7] The now almost standard television advertisement ploy - the worn housewife; the kind, bright visiting friend; the new product suggested; all well again - was all old hat to Lever ninety years ago. Nor did he forget to cash in on the rampant snobbery of the time[8] or the younger generation - a Sunlight Year Book was sent to schools. He also annoyed W. P. Frith, the current Victorian artist, by buying his picture of a little girl admiring her new white apron and then using reproductions of it for advertising soap. He had created the garden city of Port Sunlight around the factory that produced most of Sunlight Soap and allied products. As early as 1900 Lever had factories in seven countries.

In 1908 Lever had been a Member of Parliament for two years. He had been elected after five attempts, all made from a sense of duty as a wealthy Liberal and not from any wish to be an MP. Typically he suggested, almost at once, improvements to the buildings of Parliament.[9] These were not agreed. He was a forceful determined Victorian, with Victorian standards, and expected his employees to be obedient, sober, conscientious and respectful and only give opinions when asked.[10] He was also very un-Victorian in holding that workers should have good housing, good pay and eventually (he hoped) a six-hour working day. In 1907 he introduced a private member's Bill to pay everyone a pension at the age of sixty-five. He had also introduced at Port Sunlight – at the firm's expense – many of the services now grouped under 'health and social welfare'. In addition to old age pensions, he favoured votes for women and holidays with pay, and he was a pioneer of holiday camps. He thought that women should serve on his factory committees; and one finds, without surprise, they did.

Lever was short, about 5 feet and 5 inches, sturdily built, with small feet. His son said his hair was light brown, and his eyes were, according to one account, blue-grey. Reilly has, as usual, a different story. At his first visit to Lever he calls him 'a short, red, fiery little man with opalescent eyes changing from green to red if you dared to disagree with him, and fair hair standing up on end.[11] His hair did certainly stand up in something of a quiff, and this gave newspaper caricaturists an easy start when Lever became famous.

Sir Angus Watson, of Skipper Sardine fame, described him as being:

> short and thickset in stature with a sturdy body
> set on short legs and a massive head covered with
> thick upstanding hair; he radiated force and
> energy. He had piercing blue-grey humorous eyes,
> which however flashed with anger when he was
> angry. A strong, thin-lipped mouth set above a
> slightly receding chin, and the short neck and
> closely set ears of a prize-fighter. He possessed
> great physical strength and a gift of sleep which
> was always available at his command ... Dress
> always the same, grey tweed suit ... tall grey hat,
> white silk shirt and black shoes on his small
> shapely feet. Hands carefully attended to, which
> were also small. An expression always alert but
> rather strained because of the slight deafness,
> which increased as he grew older: a man who
> would have been singled out anywhere.[12]

He took great care of his health, and of his methods of work. He rose at 5 am in an open-air bedroom with a glass roof, sometimes with the bedspread powdered with snow; did twenty minutes of exercises, had a cup of tea and then worked until breakfast at 7.30 am.[13] His care of himself produced good results, as he could still run upstairs two at a time when over seventy.[14] He never liked being helped on with his coat or having his bag carried. Attendance of guests at a 7.30 am breakfast was not compulsory but earned them a good mark. He was usually in his office at Port Sunlight by 8.30 am. There, he did a lot of his work standing up at a high desk. He did much of his thinking when standing or walking, so he liked straight paths, or at least fairly level walks in his gardens. He dictated at a fast pace to several stenographers at once, relying on at least one to pick up something the others had missed. He is said to have left 30,000 files of letters. Until he became a national figure with evening engagements, he liked to be in bed early, and retained a youthful affection for a high tea.[15]

His recreations included, or had included, walking, swimming, riding and driving, and he later took up dancing at the age of sixty-nine. He had given up shooting about ten years before[16] but still provided shooting for his guests with the pawky comment: 'up goes ten shillings, bang goes twopence and down comes half a crown.[17] He was also an early convert to motoring, cleverly using two cars at a time in order to insure against the inconvenience and delay of the then common breakdown and to be able to call from the second car people with whom he wished to discuss business.[18]

There is no doubt, however, that his favourite recreations were visiting exhibitions, collecting works of art and, above all, altering and enlarging his homes and gardens:

> Architecture was always an absorbing study for
> him and one can safely say that no single man - at
> any rate in modern times - has ever built a larger
> number of houses and buildings and constructed a
> greater mileage of roads.[19]

He laid out and at least partly built ten new towns.[20]

In youth and early manhood he was a devotee of Samuel Smiles's *Self Help* and other improving books, a non-smoker and a teetotaller. His son records, rather to the reader's relief, that these abstentions were not rigorously kept to later on, but, as the result of a challenge, he finally stopped smoking when forty-five, and never cared for spirits or played cards.[21]

By 1908 Lever's business had already taken him several times to the United States, Canada, and South Africa, and twice around the world. Soap manufacturers had been going through bad times for several years, caused mainly by the rise in price of raw materials and intense competition in sales. In 1908 the manager of the Liverpool branch of the Bank of England went so far as to say that Lever Bros were 'in very great straits'.[24] Lever had had, in addition, to endure newspaper attacks in the autumn of 1906 which might be called vicious, and the firm had suffered substantial losses. In 1907 Lever had counterattacked, suing for libel and damages. Lever was never a man to turn the other cheek to continued and unearned slaps, and in deciding to sue he was strengthened by the opinion of Mr F. E. Smith (later the 1st Earl of Birkenhead but then a bright young barrister in Liverpool). According to one of the most frequently told stories about barristers, F. E. Smith was called in one night, faced with a stack of papers four feet high and told that an opinion was needed by nine o' clock the next morning. Smith sent out for a bottle of champagne and two dozen oysters, and next morning wrote: 'There is no answer to this action for libel and the damages must be enormous.'[25] Stories that seem too good to be true sometimes are true, and this one seems to be among them.

The case was heard at Liverpool in July 1907 with a wonderful turnout of leading counsel[26] and, because of the many preceding newpaper attacks on Sunlight Soap and Lever, there was great public interest. Partly because of Lever's unshakable performance under cross-examination by Rufus Isaacs (later Lord Reading, and reckoned most brilliant in cross-examination) the newspapers withdrew all allegations, and offered £50,000 in damages. Though this was then the greatest sum ever awarded in a libel action, subsidiary actions against other newspapers raised it to £91,000 or about £84,000 net of costs.[27]

Fortunately for the University of Liverpool, and British town planning, Lever regarded this sum as being wholly his own to dispose of as he wished, since he owned all the Ordinary shares, and even in the bad times the Preference shareholders had received their dividends. Yet it was the firm which had been materially damaged, as well as Lever's reputation. It was later calculated that the firm's losses from the various libels amounted up to the end of 1908 to £367,000 and £500,000 by the end of 1909.[28] Economies had been forced on it and building work stopped.[29] Probably most of the directors and even the employees thought that Lever, who had borne most of the stress and had triumphed over the several hostile newspapers, was entitled to the damages; all the more so when he gave them all to deserving causes.

It may well be regarded as astonishing that a man so burdened with great responsibilities and worries and Parliamentary duties, should have decided to finance university studies in what was an almost unknown subject. Town planning – or Civic Design as it was and still is called at Liverpool University – was then being much discussed and was vaguely thought to be necessary, but the boundaries of the subject were even more vague, and the phrase 'town planning' was itself only two years old. Perhaps the majority view was that town planning ought to be some kind of organized corrective action, probably taken by local authorities, for the bad aspects of town development during the previous hundred years, particularly the dreadful housing of the poor. As has been stated, the idea of a university meddling with such a subject was regarded with ridicule in some academic circles. One may remember that a Dr

Mayo said at Cambridge in 1917 'the teaching of foreign languages is futile and to be deprecated in the highest degree.[30] The Cambridge chairs in French and Spanish were established in 1919 and 1933.

Further enquiries make it certain that only Lever would have provided funds at that time for the study of town planning, at least in Great Britain.[31] It was one of those events of ultimately great consequence that depend on a particular man, certain special circumstances, and (thanks to the libels) the money, all being together at the right time and place. The certainty that only Lever would have founded the Department of Civic Design emerges from a study of his career and major interests and Lancashire loyalties; and is strengthened by the fact that, apart from a daughter school at University College, London, which the first Lever professor returned South to establish in 1915, no other university department of town planning was established in Britain for nearly twenty-five years; and the ill-advised scamper up to 120 courses in town planning and closely associated studies only really started in 1946.

Lever's Early Life

Lever was born into a strict Nonconformist family at Bolton in Lancashire in 1851. He was the first of two boys and the seventh of ten children. He may therefore have received the special favour which some parents show to a long-awaited first son, however much they may try to conceal it. The name of Lever is not uncommon in Lancashire and three villages near Bolton include the word.[32] At the age of six Lever went to a dame school across the road where he became close friends with Jonathan Simpson and Elizabeth Hulme. The strength of Lever's attachments and loyalties to early friends is shown by his lifelong friendship with Jonathan Simpson (and later with his son, James Lomax Simpson) and by his continued affection for Elizabeth Hulme, who became his wife in 1874. He also did much for Bolton in later life. Two other features of these early friendships may also be significant. Simpson and his son were both to become architects, and his best friend's profession and talk and their joint visits to famous old buildings, may have given Lever the first push towards his lifelong interest and achievements in what is now sometimes called 'the built environment' plus landscape design on any scale up to 1,000 square miles.[33] Secondly, as has been most shrewdly remarked, finding his future wife and best friend so early in life relieved Lever of some, perhaps most, of the tensions and sorrows of adolescence and young manhood. He could stick to work with an easy mind.[34]

Lever left school at fifteen and entered his father's wholesale grocery business in Bolton at a wage of one shilling a week and all found. He proved to be exceptionally industrious and sharp-witted, despite long hours, long Nonconformist church attendances on Sundays, and improving books. It is pleasant to learn of his clandestine correspondence with Elizabeth Hulme, whose mother, then a widow, had removed her, in the unfeeling way of girl-friends' mothers, to live at Southport. Lever spent much time in feeling unworthy, and in coaxing his family to make trips to enjoy the bracing air at Southport. Quite a lot of these suitable teenage activities may have been wasted since, as Professor Jolly remarks,[35] Mrs Hulme must have thought young Lever had possibilities as a son-in-law or she would have intervened long before – and in those days decisively. Lever and Elizabeth Hulme were married in April 1874, when Lever was twenty-three; and then lived happily ever after till death parted them in 1913, 'neither having remembered a world without the other in it'.[36]

In 1870 Lever had become a commercial traveller for the firm, widened its sales area and, at twenty-one, became a partner at the then large salary of £800 a year. After his marriage, Lever's Dick, Whittington-type success story gained in pace, and by the time he was thirty-three he and his brother had built the firm into one of the biggest wholesale groceries in the north-west of England. This was just a beginning: *Soap* then came into the story. From all the smoke belching from ten million houses, factories, foundries, steam engines and steamers, large parts of Britain had become filthy, and for the first time many families could afford to buy soap.

Soap at that time commonly reached retail shops in long bars and was cut to the customer's needs, rather as big cheeses are today. Lever determined to make, package and market his own soap and, with the help of W. P. Thompson and Co., then, as now, leading trade-mark and patent agents in Liverpool, he decided on the name *Sunlight*. For two years the soap was made at Warrington, and by strenuous salesmanship, advertising, gift tokens and improvements of the product, the firm did so well that Lever and his brother decided in 1887 to look for a site for a brand-new factory.

Port Sunlight

The result was Port Sunlight. Lever had already altered houses and built one new one, but Port Sunlight offered quite new opportunities for the great part of his talents and energy that throughout his life demanded an outlet in building or planning.[37] One might say his second career really began at Port Sunlight. He always had a drawing-board and T-square available and collaborated with his architects rather than employed them.[38]

He and his first architect, William Owen, searched for land which had all the advantages: cheapness, access by rail and from the sea and a supply of labour nearby. They found what they wanted in (at first) fifty-two acres of dreary, marshy land on the Wirral peninsula, on the west side of the river Mersey, a few miles upstream from the centre of Liverpool.[39] It was also far enough upstream to escape Liverpool Dock and Harbour dues.[40] Lever and Owen must have had great faith in their own judgement.[41]

Mrs Lever cut the first sod for the new factory in 1888, and at a celebratory dinner that night Lever announced that he and his brother hoped to build comfortable houses for their work people.[42]

There was no delay; Lever was never one for delay. By the next year William Owen was designing the first twenty-eight cottages and an entrance lodge. This first block was reproduced at the Brussels exhibition of 1910 and was awarded a Grand Prix.

Although Lever Brothers became a world-wide organization before Lever died and now, as Unilever, is one of the world's greatest companies, Port Sunlight was the biggest factory for many years, and is still the best known town and works associated with Lever. When he began to build houses for his workers Lever had almost certainly heard of other industrial villages, from Robert Owen's work at New Lanark in 1800[43] to the village then being built by the Cadburys at Bournville.[44, 45] He may have been aware of Roebuck's struggles from 1828 onwards to enable towns to buy land on their outskirts, and for taxes on increased land values around towns – perhaps the first mention of the great 'betterment' question of World War II and afterwards.[46] He also fully realized that good houses for his workers would make them healthier and more contented,[47] and held that the devotion of a portion of the firm's profits to what he called 'prosperity sharing' – good houses, social services, community buildings, parks – was better than any profit-sharing scheme. He held for a long time, like W. L. George,[48] that the latter schemes were somewhat bogus. In a bad year extra payments might not be made to workers, but no one could expect them to bear part of big losses. Nevertheless by 1909 Lever introduced his own version of profit-sharing which he called Co-partnership. He was not afraid to change his mind when he saw good reason.

There is some doubt about the origin of the first plan for Port Sunlight, which was extended and filled in over many years. By 1909 the firm owned 221 acres.[49] Lever claimed on two occasions that he himself made the plan. In a letter to T. H. Mawson[50] he gave the date of the plan as 1890:

> *I made the plans so that as the land was acquired*
> *the streets would run where, at the time I planned*
> *Port Sunlight, I had no power to run them. It*
> *always seemed to me that the life of the people in*
> *town planning must be the first consideration ... I*
> *believe ... that the convenience and life of the*
> *people can be achieved without any sacrifice to*
> *(of?) beauty or inspiring vistas.*

At a later date, Lever spoke of the plan as having been thought of during a voyage round the world in 1892.[51] The probability is that the original plan, now lost, was sketched out by Lever and modified in discussions with his architects.

The main part of the site lay between the railway line and Greendale Road on the west and the New Chester Road on the east. The chief features of the plan are wide roads with houses built on one side only. In the centre of each larger group of houses were allotment gardens. Almost every dwelling had views over open space or wide roads on one side and allotments on the other. And this is still so, save that some of the allotments have gone. When W. L. George was writing in 1909 the population of Port Sunlight was 3,500 in 720 houses, and Lever had had almost twenty years of experience in the practice of town planning. The houses themselves were as superior to the general run of working-class housing of that time as were their outlook and surroundings. There were no basements or coal cellars. Every house was well lighted and equipped with hot and cold water, a gas supply and a bathroom. Every house had at least three bedrooms.[52] The rents were appreciably less than would have had to be paid for similar accommodation elsewhere (no profit was made from them) but they came to between one-quarter and one-fifth of the workers' weekly wages. Mr George was firm in 1909 that such a proportionate expenditure on rent was too high 'but it is one that is frequent everywhere'.[53] It remained frequent up to 1939. The appearance of the houses, or style of the designs, was very varied. (See Illustrations.) House agents today might well call many of them Tudor, half-timbered, or Cheshire black-and-white half-timber. There are also traces of what might be called Norman Shaw Dutch here and there. The houses were all carefully designed and grouped to achieve variety, and were well built. Some of the bronze door furniture may become collectors' items in the 1980s. One feels sure that Lever carefully discussed every design with the architects.

Buildings to serve the whole community began to be provided from 1891, some of them under the prosperity-sharing scheme already mentioned, by which Lever provided community buildings rather than bonuses. These included the church, social clubs, halls, technical institute and gymnasium, and in 1914 the Lady Lever Art Gallery was begun.[54] Here again one may be sure that Lever was involved in the design and siting of each public building, and as the town grew new ideas were sought by holding competitions for the layout and design of some extensions. There were shops at Port Sunlight, though their apparent absence has astonished those who studied the layout plans. The reason is that the few shops were situated under the Collegium, or Girls Institute as it was formerly called, and were therefore not marked on the plans. The first shop had been built in 1898 and by 1902 there was a Post Office, a grocery and provision shop, a drapery and millinery shop and a butcher's shop, all of which were controlled and financed entirely by the Employees' Provident Society.[55] There were three or four competitions for buildings and groups of buildings[56] and up to his death Lever offered prizes in the School of Architecture and Department of Civic Design for the layout of dwellings or redevelopment of parts of Liverpool. Lever continued to take a special interest in expansion of the factory, as is shown by a plan of 1912 covered with his notes.

It is impossible for an ex-architect writing of Lever not to feel sure that at times he was a sore trial to his architects, of whom Mr Shippobottom lists a total of over thirty employed at Port Sunlight and others elsewhere. Not all the designs were carried out. The firms were all from Lancashire and Merseyside. There is no mention of Norman Shaw, Scott, Waterhouse or other top architects of the 1880-1910 period; and none of Lethaby, Voysey, Lutyens, C. R. MacKintosh and a few others who are now regarded as the most valuable architectural pioneers of the time. It is equally probable that some of the architects were a sore trial to Lever.[57] Reilly sublet portions of Bluecoat Chambers without telling Lever (who was the owner) and had to appeal for Lever's help in paying some bill; and Edwin Lutyens when - at long last - he was summoned to Lewis in the Western Isles in 1919 about the design of a hotel wrote, according to Lady Sackville, rather acidly of his meeting with his client.[58] But of course by that time it was Giant meeting Giant. They did not take to one another.

Port Sunlight, which today still contains about 3,000 inhabitants, was a memorable achievement, constantly improved for the benefit of the employees under the eye and firm hand of the master, up to 1914 and beyond. Lever was the first employer in the district to reduce the working day to eight hours, and in 1905 he introduced a pension fund and a holiday club which had an initial membership of 2,000.[59] He also 'rounded off' Port Sunlight by buying 800 acres of adjoining land, with a mile and a half of deep-water frontage, and in 1908 - this same year in which Lever is introduced to the reader - a company was formed to develop the land, called the Bromborough Estate Company. Until 1930 nearly all the works built at Bromborough were connected with Lever Bros. By further purchases the firm came to control the foreshore between the New Ferry pier and the entry to the Manchester Ship Canal, and thus held all the remaining land adjoining the deep-water channel. It is now owned and managed by a Unilever subsidiary.[60]

Lever's Houses, Gardens and Landscape Designs

Lever's twenty years' experience of 'Civic Design' by 1908 was by no means confined to Port Sunlight, though that was the greatest work of the team of architects and others whom he had directed. Since moving his factory to the Wirral he had bought, altered and occupied for part of each year three houses, all different in kind and location. In all Lever built, rebuilt or altered twelve houses and for the last thirty-five years of his life he never lived in a completed home. Of these Thornton Manor is the most important to our story in that it was his principal home and that of his son and grandson, the centre before long of a large estate, and to it came at various times three major participants in the foundation, salvation and development of the Department of Civic Design: Reilly, Adshead and Patrick Abercrombie. These three are described in later chapters.

In 1888 Lever moved to Thornton Manor near to the village of Thornton Hough, which is about ten miles from Liverpool, on the Wirral peninsula, rather nearer the Dee than the Mersey.[61] The original form and design of the house matters little, as Lever's

Above: 'Pierhead', the Liverpool landing stage in 1890. At this time almost all transatlantic passages, and many others, began and ended at Liverpool. *Below:* Transport and warehouses near the Liverpool docks.

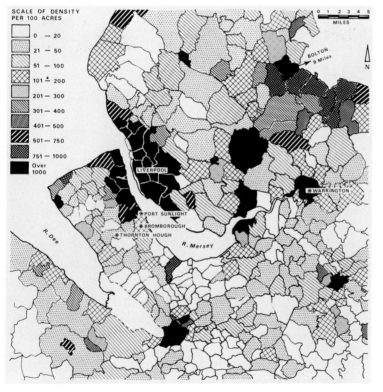

Above: Washing day
in the Liverpool
slums, which ran for
7 or 8 miles
alongside the docks.
Below: Population
map of Merseyside in
1911. The population
was densely grouped
on either side of the
Mersey, and towards
what is now Greater
Manchester.

SCALE OF DENSITY
PER 100 ACRES

0 — 20
21 — 50
51 — 100
101 — 200
201 — 300
301 — 400
401 — 500
501 — 750
751 — 1000
Over
1000

0 1 2 3 4 5
MILES

BOLTON
9 Miles

N

LIVERPOOL

WARRINGTON

R. Dee

PORT SUNLIGHT

BROMBOROUGH

THORNTON HOUGH

R. Mersey

Above: A famous photograph in maritime history, the first *Mauretania* which from 1909 for nearly 20 years was the fastest vessel on the transatlantic run to New York. The small vessel alongside is the *Turbinia. Below:* Traffic converging on the Liverpool docks below the former Overhead Railway.

Above: Lever was created a Baronet in 1911, and this portrait by George Hall Neale was executed the same year. Lever was 60 years old and had then created a worldwide business. *Opposite page, above:* Aerial view of Port Sunlight in 1979. The Lady Lever Art Gallery is the large building with two domes. The broad tree-lined streets were a new feature in a village designed for occupation by manual workers. Port Sunlight was begun in 1888. *Opposite page, below:* A street in Port Sunlight.

Opposite page, above: Air view of Thornton Manor, upper centre, and its grounds, woods and radiating drives or rides. The village of Thornton Heath is on the left. *Opposite page, below:* One of the drives at Thornton Manor. *Above:* Part of the village of Thornton Hough which was almost wholly rebuilt by Lever. The Congregational church in the photograph was Lever's gift. *Below:* The Green at Thornton Hough and some of the rebuilt houses. Dwellings which front direct on to a public open space look attractive and this layout was much repeated after 1945. Such dwellings are much disliked by most occupants.

Above: The west elevation of Charles Reilly's design in the 1901 competition for an Anglican Cathedral at Liverpool. *Below:* 'Reilly's Cowsheds'.

Above: Reilly, determined and a little dashing.
Below: Liverpool's Anglican Cathedral completed
in 1979.

Above: Reilly as he actually was in the 1930s. A painting by Marjorie Brooks, later Lady Holford. *Below:* The Bluecoat School, which was rescued by Reilly in 1908 with funds provided by Lever. It housed the School of Architecture and Department of Civic Design for 10 years.

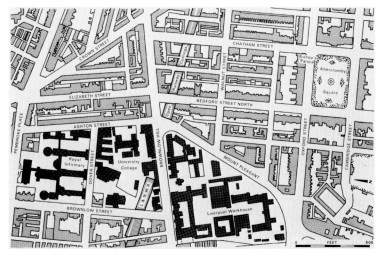

Above: Reilly's design for Liverpool Cathedral. Perspective of the interior by Stanley Adshead. *Below:* The area around the University of Liverpool as it was when Reilly arrived in 1904. Situated between a workhouse and a hospital, adjoining a railway cutting which belched smoke, Reilly said it was a queer site on which to build a University.

Above, left: Another drawing by Stanley Adshead of Reilly's design for Liverpool Cathedral. *Above right:* One of the six-hour sketch designs, which Reilly required from all his students each week. This one was drawn by Holford when a second-year student. Stanley Adshead's reputation as a fine draughtsman was one of the reasons for trying to recruit him as the first professor of Civic Design. *Below:* Stanley Adshead when aged about 50.

Above: Adshead's best work as an architect was in the design and layout of small houses such as those built for the Duchy of Cornwall's estate at Kennington in South London. The houses, built in the early 1920s, were photographed in 1979.

Above: George Pepler as
he was in the early 1930s,
aged about 50. *Below:* The
plan for a new layout for
central Dublin prepared
mainly by Abercrombie in
1914. The plan and
accompanying report were
published and established
Abercrombie's reputation
as a town planner.

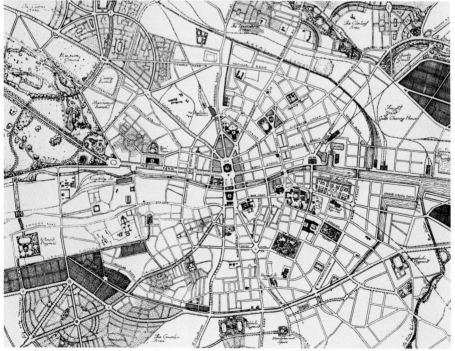

Above: Patrick Abercrombie when aged about 45. A famous photograph
by E. Chambré Hardman.

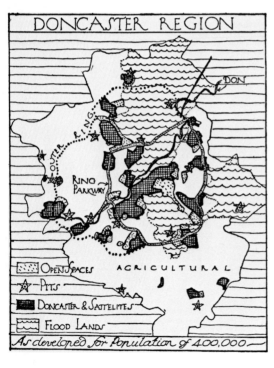

Above: The well known 'eggs in a basket' drawing from Abercrombie and Forshaw's *Country of London Plan*, 1943, which showed London divided into zones of special activities in the centre and villages around. It was proposed to encourage reconstruction and development around these local centres. *Below:* A diagram of Abercrombie's proposals in 1922 for the expansion of the Doncaster area to take account of the opening of new collieries. This plan for the Doncaster Region enhanced Abercrombie's reputation.

attitude to any newly acquired property reminds one of the story of the then chairman of Rolls-Royce on being shown the very early jet aircraft engine designed by Whittle. Its great virtue, he was told, lay in its simplicity. 'You leave that to us' he is alleged to have replied, 'we'll soon take the simplicity out of it!' And so it was with Thornton Manor, and Lever's other houses. Thornton Manor was altered a number of times, only reaching its present form in 1914. Thomas H. Mawson, the most prominent British landscape architect of the day,[62] helped Lever to lay out the large gardens and park, including lakes. As has been said, Lever always liked straight and more or less level walks, as he used gardens mainly for walking and, according to his son, discussed and solved a lot of his problems while walking.[63]

Mawson's designs enabled Lever to indulge this taste to the full. Mawson was a terrace and axial line man, and his plans for gardens, and larger landscaping, are, at least to some modern eyes, rather crude and unsympathetic.[64] No doubt his great knowledge of plants and trees enabled a softening process to be quickly begun and sometimes achieved. Lever then bought nearly all of the village of Thornton Hough, about half a mile from the Manor. Many of the cottages were insanitary and before long Lever and his architects were at work creating an ideal village with cottages like those at Port Sunlight, a village green, a smithy with *two* chestnut trees, a Post Office and butcher's shop, some larger houses for his family, and a substantial Congregational church in the Norman style.[65] Most of the buildings, apart from the Church, are solidly built in variations of brick and half-timber, sometimes on a stone base. The craftsmanship is of a high standard. Apart from a distressing recent public lavatory in a corner of the green, the village remains in appearance almost as it was in 1908, pleasing and unusual to the passer-by in the absence of private gardens and the linking of houses in short terraces.

Soon after his arrival in the area, Lever decided to buy land near Thornton Manor as it became available, and at one time he owned 8,000 acres in Cheshire of which by far the greater part was on the Wirral.[66] Equally in the Lever spirit, he planned tree-lined roads, one of which was to have three carriageways, the central one for fast traffic and eventually another on each side for slow. Several of these intended roads were planted with what are now fine trees, and though some remain as rides, the furthest flung reached out over three miles from Thornton Manor, and the public portion is now suitably called the Lever Causeway.

With such great works going on in building and in moulding the landscape – added to his huge business and other duties – Lever had to push people hard. There is a story that once, when driving with an agent down one of his new roads, then being fenced, he asked if the ends of the posts below ground had been thoroughly tarred to prevent rot. The agent took a chance and said 'Yes'. Unfortunately, although no undriven posts were in sight, a labourer with a spade was only too near. He was induced by Lever to dig up a post already in place, it was untarred, the agent was sacked, and left to walk home. That this story, heard from more than one person, is true is quite probable; yet anyone who studies Lever's life as patron, builder, town planner and helper of good causes will doubt whether the agent remained sacked for very long. As is the way of good stories, this one seems to have grown in the telling. The present Lord Leverhulme says that his grandfather's agent at Thornton Manor, Mr Frank Clarke, served for many years, unsacked. The man concerned was probably the foreman of the fencing contractors.

Lever was forceful, determined, pugnacious, litigious and doubtless irritable at times, but he did not bear grudges for long. Certainly he did not do so towards Reilly, the University of Liverpool, or the inhabitants of the island of Lewis, all of whom - in ascending order of magnitude - gave him good reason for being angry. And though at one time he dismissed T. H. Mawson (rightly) for neglecting the work he was supposed to be doing for Lever,[67] he soon took him back. When Mawson no longer lectured in Civic Design, Lever wrote at once to ask ahy, and later offered to supplement Mawson's remuneration.[68]

By 1908 Lever had two other houses besides Thornton Manor, and lived part of the year in each of them. These were The Bungalow on the Rivington Estate about six miles from Bolton, and The Hill at Hampstead. Lever had bought the Rivington Estate in 1900, and it included a large area of moorland running up to Rivington Pike (1,200 feet) which had been well known to him as a boy. The land drained into some reservoirs in the valley which served Liverpool, and for that reason Lever offered the City of Liverpool the chance to buy the estate. The offer was refused. Lever then built a simple wooden bungalow - designed by his old friend Jonathan Simpson - just below the ridge, and began on forty-five acres his most ambitious and even eccentric schemes of garden-making and changing the landscape. The rest of the estate he offered to Bolton as a public park.[69]

Liverpool afterwards changed its mind and promoted a Bill to buy the estate. After a lawsuit Lever was left free to improve the parkland at his own expense, and it is now called Lever Park. He made roads - always a favourite occupation - and restored and converted buildings to serve as a tea house and museum. He then built on the shores of a reservoir a replica of the ruins of Liverpool Castle, which at one time had defended the port of Liverpool. This odd venture - one of the last of the architectural follies and a small foreshadowing of Disneyland - was supported as a tourist attraction by the first of the British Safari Parks.[70] He fenced in certain fields and placed in them herds of deer, Indian cattle, wallabies and even emus. These excitements were supplemented by the works and plantings within Lever's own gardens.

Thomas Mawson was again called in, and, fighting indefatigably against the limitations of a piece of bleak exposed moorland 1,000 feet above sea level, the Lever-Mawson alliance created Japanese gardens, a look-out tower, lawns, lakes, terraces and waterfalls; and a bridge entirely designed by Lever that has a decidedly Roman appearance. Since the bridge's roadway and parapets slope downward as it crosses the road below, the lowest arch conveys an impression of struggling hard to bear its load. Second thoughts bring reassurance: while Lever lived that arch *dared not* collapse. It never has.

The original wooden bungalow was burnt down, allegedly by suffragettes, on a night in July 1913 when Lever and his wife were dining with King George V and Queen Mary as guests of Lord Derby at Knowsley, just outside Liverpool. It was a strange act if supporters of women's suffrage were responsible, as is very probable.[71] Lever had long supported votes for women, but on a clear night the blaze must have been visible for a long way, and the royal visit doubtless increased the publicity. Lever rebuilt the bungalow in stone and concrete within a year. This time it was designed by James Lomax Simpson, Jonathan's son who had studied at the Liverpool School of Architecture.[72] It eventually contained, as additions, a ballroom with musicians' gallery, a telescope house, and another open-air bedroom.

When The Bungalow (also called Roynton Cottage) and its grounds and Lever Park were all at their best, perhaps in the early 1920s, they must have made an astonishing sight – or rather a whole series of astonishing sights, views and glimpses: impressive, beautiful in parts, exciting wonder that they had been made at all, and also perhaps a little disturbing. A suggestion of Hollywood, even of megalomania, must have been enhanced by distant views over stretches of mill towns and the smoke of Lancashire, and by thoughts of the hard lives, the unemployment and extreme poverty then endured by most of those on the land within view.

Today (at least in October 1980) Rivington is a haunting and moving place. One cannot continue to call it The Bungalow, since no trace of the house remains save a little tiled paving. But out of the woods on the ridge above Lever Park there emerge here and there curiously Roman-looking pavilions, nearly all constructed of ten-inch cubes of millstone grit. There are flights of steps up from Lever's bridge that divide several times to enclose pavilions overlooking the park, and Lancashire, from successively higher levels. Between pavilions the flights merge again into a single stairway and bring the visitor to a path along a contour, passing shrunken lakes and tangled gardens. There are several roads, all solidly bottomed with cubes of millstone grit. And then over the tangled clumps of rhododendrons one sees again the lookout tower in vaguely Scottish Baronial style, with upper windows still glazed: alone, forlorn and exactly like the tower in which in old books for children the beautiful princess awaited rescue.

Perhaps no other place gives such an impression of Lever's strength and grandeur of conception and determination. It was very odd to want to build on a bleak and rather grimy Lancashire ridge, but having decided to do so, Lever coaxed, encouraged and probably drove Thomas Mawson, Jonathan Simpson and the multitude of workmen until they created an impressive and unique assembly of buildings, roads and gardens.[73]

Lever's London house, where the family lived for part of each year from 1904, was called The Hill and was on the edge of Hampstead Heath with views towards Harrow-on-the-Hill and the Welsh Harp. It was a rich man's house of no great architectural attraction. Lever and Mawson at once got to work on the grounds, forming two level lawns instead of a slope towards the Heath. There was also a lily-pond, and of course terraces and curved steps. A big pergola with stone columns and timber trellis screened most of the upper lawn from any of the public who were walking on the Heath, and there were adverse comments made about the pergola for a time. Lever allowed the garden to be used for charitable purposes including pastoral plays and classical dancing[74] and, by the time he and Mawson had finished, visitors must have been quite bemused by the arts and crafts of garden-making displayed for their delight.[75] Lever bought and demolished an adjoining house and its grounds were linked with those of The Hill by a bridge over a public footpath. The controversial pergola was extended into the new grounds and ended in a belvedere. This part of the design was Lever's, according to Mawson.[76] In 1914 Lever bought the house on the other side of The Hill and was about to pull it down too, and extend his grounds even further; but the project was postponed on the outbreak of the 1914–18 War, and not resumed.

Lever's passion for building and altering houses, and for landscape design on any scale, was accompanied by strong views on internal design and decoration, and the purchase of works of art and antique furniture on a vast scale. A substantial portion of his purchases are now in the Lady Lever Art Gallery at Port Sunlight, and were shown at a special exhibition at the Royal Academy in April and May 1980. With these last this study cannot be concerned, though once one has learnt quite a lot about this extraordinary man it needs a real act of will to stop exploring further. As one would expect, Lever's views on interior decoration were highly personal. He wrote to T. H. Mawson in 1910: ' ... I prefer Georgian dining rooms as the rooms in which to give large dinners; for small dining-rooms I prefer Tudor ... '[77] It was within Lever's power to ensure that all the furniture was genuinely of the right period. It probably was. There is no record of his having transported and re-erected an entire period interior: walls, ceiling, floors, panelling, fireplace and all – though he did something like this in the Lady Lever Art Gallery. One has, however, a sneaking hope it will be found in due course that on at least one occasion, instead of moving the furniture to a carefully prepared building,[78] he moved a building to the furniture.

In addition to collecting works of art – latterly through agents who told him when pictures, furniture and porcelain likely to interest him were on the market – Lever had his own portrait painted at least three times. The best-known one was by Augustus John in 1920.

Lever disliked John's portrayal of his face so much that he cut it out of the painting, of which the remainder was accidentally returned to Augustus John. This naturally caused John great annoyance and he told the story to the newspapers; and painters in Italy were reported to have held a one-day strike in support of their brother artist. Eventually the head was put back in the portrait. It is easy to understand why Lever and his family had no more affection for the painting than Winston and Lady Churchill felt for the now destroyed Graham Sutherland portrait of Churchill.

In 1908 Port Sunlight and the three houses of Thornton Manor, The Bungalow at Rivington, and The Hill were all in Lever's possession, being improved and occupied at various times of the year.

Mrs Lever was of course overshadowed by her formidable mate. There is little about her in her son's book about his father, and not very much in Professor Jolly's. She must, however, have been a woman of great forbearance, as well as devotion. Knox refers to her as gracious, kindly and gentle: 'Mrs Lever was asked once, after the Old Man had bought The Hill ... how she liked it. She replied, "It's very nice, but it is like having two houses and no home".'[79]

T. H. Mawson writes:

> *Mrs Lever was a perfect complement to her*
> *husband, quietly interested in all his wonderful*
> *projects, but not a little anxious to know when it*
> *would all come to an end so they might be able to*
> *enjoy their home in peace.*[80]

She travelled with Lever to places where few white women had then been and the risks of illness were high, and, according to Lever, however early he breakfasted – and, my word, how early! – she was there to see that all was well. Her forbearance over building works at close quarters makes it plain she was no ordinary woman. She seldom lived for long free of building works[81] and the trial for her and daytime visitors of knocking, banging and builders' dust week after week, and year after year, must have been great.

Once they had three houses, the Levers could no doubt sometimes escape the noise and mess of building near one house by occupying another,[82] and a world voyage must have come in very handy if begun at the same time as a big building alteration. But for the most part, Mrs Lever just put up with it all, while her William marched on to greater things. They had come a long way together since that dame school at Bolton. She devoted herself to good causes and especially to the children of Port Sunlight. Lady Lever, as she had then become, died suddenly of pneumonia in 1913. The blow to Lever was as great as one would expect, and his son suggested that some of Lever's later ventures – not all successful – might not have been undertaken had his wife survived.[83] Her principal memorial is the Lady Lever Art Gallery at Port Sunlight, in which Lever placed a large portion of his great collection of works of art.

Before leaving Lever's houses, however, one other demands mention. Lever bought the lease of Stafford House which lies between St James's Palace and Buckingham Palace. It was his intention for the building to be used in part to house the collections of the London Museum and, in part, as a government entertainment centre. He asked for a change of name to Lancaster House, both as a Lancashire man and because the King (or Queen) holds the title of Duke of Lancaster. Insinuations were made that the gift was a concealed bribe to obtain favourable treatment over Lever's colonial plantations, but these were refuted, and Asquith, then Prime Minister, accepted Lancaster House for the nation.[84] It is today the centre for the British Government's official hospitality, with almost no one aware of who it was that foresaw the now essential need, recognized the ideal position for its fulfilment, and made the gift.

In the seventeen years after 1908 Lever was to continue town building on his plantations, to plan and begin improvements to towns and landscaping, with 1,000 square miles as a special challenge on the island of Lewis to the west of Scotland. 1908, however, was the year of his life of most interest to this study.

The Year of the Decision: 1908

This summary account of Lever's achievements and interests, worries and responsibilities up to 1908 has, it is hoped, shown why Lever was almost certainly the only man who would have agreed immediately – or at all – to Reilly's request for funds to found a chair of Civic Design in the University of Liverpool, and to provide for research in the new subject and the publication of results.

There is plenty more evidence for Lever's interest in all aspects of town planning, civic design, housing and new towns, if more were needed. He had seen the Chicago Exposition of 1893 just before it opened and had been much impressed by this starting point of the City Beautiful movement;[85] and, as a reminder, a City Beautiful Conference had been held in Liverpool in 1907, and another two on housing and garden cities in London. He had been a member of the Board of Letchworth, Britain's first independent new town, a guarantor of Hampstead Garden Suburb,[86] and his travels around the world had shown him how inferior were the British to the French in the planning of their colonial towns.

Lever was perhaps all the more ready to found the chair because he had carefully examined the 1908 Bill and was a warm supporter of Clause 50 which enabled local authorities to buy land near their boundaries:

> For a town to have the powers of acquisition
> and to exercise those well in advance is for a town
> to acquire its fringe at a very little over
> agricultural value, and entrenched in this strong
> position a proper scheme of town-planning can be
> brought forward, the development under town-
> planning can be controlled, lines of trams can be

laid to benefit the land owned by the town,
building operations would follow in the same
direction, and the whole transaction be far
removed from any possibility of speculation, so far
as the town is concerned.

There is no sounder or safer investment than land
at or near its agricultural value in close proximity to
a growing town ... [87]

Lever had therefore not only a great interest in the subject and personal experience of what had been done in several countries. He had himself initiated and guided many schemes of building, planning and landscape design, both at home and abroad; in all, he said, ten new towns.[88] He was very willing to respond when Reilly apporoached him with his new idea in May or June 1908; and thanks to the successful libel actions of the previous year, money was available for a good cause.

The deed of gift made by Lever in 1910 describes why Lever decided to give £800 a year towards the foundation of the Department of Civic Design. The actual words have been quoted in the preface to this study. He increased the annual income to £1,200[89] in 1914 - and this was then a considerable sum and, as is told in a later chapter, Lever came out firmly in support of the department when there was a possibility of its being closed down because of the drastic fall in the university's income during the 1914-18 War. A quarrel with the university[90] was also forgotten as time went on, and he kept to his promise to pay for a new School of Architecture for the university, although for various reasons the actual building was postponed till after his death, and it was his son who saw the new school opened in 1933 and paid for nearly all of it. He added £5,000 to his father's gift.

The Last Years

Towards the end Lever rose earlier than ever, and in a letter to a colleague written at the age of seventy-two he gave a Victorian, but rather appealing, reason why:

I ask myself what has caused me to begin work at
4.30 in the morning in the last two or three years
and work laborious hours and have only one
absorbing thought, namely my own efficiency and
the maintenance of my own health for the task I
had to perform; and I am bound to confess ... it
has been the gnawing fear in my heart that Lever
Bros. would have to pass their dividends (i.e. fail
to pay dividends because of insufficient funds). I
had placed myself in this position by accepting
money from all classes of investors including
widows, spinsters, clergymen ... and that to forego
their dividends ... would probably mean

curtailment of what they depended on for their
day-to-day food, rent, clothing etc. Candidly this
has been my great fear, and this is what has
caused me to get up at 4.30 in the morning.[91]

Lever died in May 1925 as the 1st Viscount Leverhulme of the Western Isles,[92] at the age of nearly seventy-four. His best-known memorial is the great international company of Unilever into which Lever Bros. changed and grew.[93] Even by 1949 Unilever owned 500 companies all over the world and held a majority of shares in another 55.[94] The Leverhulme Trust Fund, which disburses annually £3½ millions to support scholarship and research is, in different circles, an equally famous memorial.

Yet Lever's second career of patron, initiator and collaborator in a great variety of town planning, town building and extension, housing and landscape design may also be held to have had as lasting, important and worldwide an influence; and to have done so mainly because of his decision to found the Department of Civic Design in the University of Liverpool, the first university depart-ment of its kind. It must have seemed at the time a very small decision during one of Lever's busiest years, and the new foundation was a feeble thing to start with. Lever may merely have thought – perhaps as he began work at 6 am at Thornton Manor – 'this is one of Charles Reilly's better ideas! I suppose I've really been interested in these things all my life, and I can afford another £800 a year for a a good cause' ... and then perhaps he moved on to weightier problems.

The decision was taken in May or June of 1908,[95] and perhaps in his open-air bedroom on the roof of Thornton Manor. Later chapters describe some of the consequences, which can reasonably be held to have been momentous and almost world wide.

NOTES AND REFERENCES

1   In this book it seems simplest to refer throughout to William Hesketh Lever as 'Lever', since *The Lever Chair* and its holders and their influence is the central object of study. Lever became Sir William Lever, Baronet, in 1911, Baron Leverhulme of Bolton-le-Moors in 1917, and Viscount Leverhulme of the Western Isles in 1922, but all who examine the life of this remarkable man are likely to end by thinking of him just as Lever. He probably thought of himself that way. He was not at all pompous. 2nd Viscount Leverhulme, *Viscount Leverhulme* (George Allen and Unwin, London, 1927).

2   Professor William P. Jolly, *Lord Leverhulme: a Biography* (Constable, London, 1976).

3   Michael Shippobottom, *A Study of an Architectural Patron and his Work* (MA Thesis, University of Manchester, 1977).

4   Charles Wilson, *The History of Unilever* (Vol. I) (Cassell & Co., London 1954).

5   According to Charles Wilson (*op. cit.*, 48) he was just past the zenith period of 1894-1907.

6   Letter from Lever to John Cheshire 13 June 1909. (Quoted in C. Wilson *op. cit.*, 21).

7   2nd Viscount Leverhulme, *op. cit.*, 72.
      from 'Lady Gwendolin's Lament':

          'Twill make your brow a snowy white,
          As free from grief and care,
          As when with youth your eyes were bright
          And cheeks beyond compare.
          This article, if you but try,
          Will realize each hope,
          Go send your maid at once, and buy
          A box of Sunlight Soap.'

8   C. Wilson, *op. cit.*, 40.

9   W. P. Jolly, *op. cit.*, 67.

10   A severe rebuke to a secretary who offered advice unasked is quoted in C. Wilson (*op. cit.*, 49).

11   Emeritus Professor Charles H. Reilly, *Scaffolding in the Sky* (George Routledge, London, 1938) 93.

12   Angus Watson, *My Life* (Ivor Nicholson & Watson, 1937) 140-41

13   2nd Viscount Leverhulme, *op. cit.*, 269.

14 Nigel Nicolson, *Lord of the Isles: Lord Leverhulme in the Hebrides* (Weidenfeld & Nicolson, 1960) 63.

15 2nd Viscount Leverhulme, *op. cit.*, 270.

16 2nd Viscount Leverhulme, *op. cit.*, 101.

17 2nd Viscount Leverhulme, *op. cit.*, 103.

18 W. P. Jolly, *op. cit.*, 61.

19 2nd Viscount Leverhulme *op. cit.*, pp. 75, 86.

20 Lever's speech at Liverpool University's Annual Exhibition of Architectural drawings *The Builder* Vol. CXXV, July 1923, p.63.

21 2nd Viscount Leverhulme *op. cit.*, pp. 102-103.

22 Sidney Pollard and John Salt (ed), *Robert Owen, Prophet of the Poor* (Macmillan, 1971).

23 James Murphy Robert Owen in Liverpool, *Transactions of the Historical Society of Lancashire and Cheshire* Vol. 112 (1960) 79-103.

24 C. Wilson, *op. cit.*, p. 119.

25 2nd Viscount Leverhulme, *op. cit.*, 136 et seq.

26 For Lever: Sir Edward Carson, Mr Horridge, F. E. Smith and E. G. Hemmerde. For Associated Newspapers (Lord Northcliffe): Rufus Isaacs, H. E. Duke, Norman Craig and Mr Branson. Six of these eight were to be translated in due course into a Marquess, an Earl, a Law Lord, two High Court Judges and a Recorder.

27 Letter from Lever to Reilly 4 October 1909 *Univ. Archives*

28 C. Wilson, *op. cit.*, 119.

29 W. P. Jolly, *op. cit.*, 57.

30 Harold Wright, *Cambridge University Studies* (Nicholson and Watson Ltd, 1933) 257.

31 In the USA the great development since 1893 of the "City Beautiful" movement and the great prestige of landscape architects (who did some town planning as well) makes it mildly surprising that a Rockefeller or Pierpoint Morgan did not lead the way. But only midly. Rich men's gifts to universities usually go to the oldest and richest and for the most obvious purposes- such as adding one more College to a score already there.

32 2nd Viscount Leverhulme, *op. cit.*, p. 11.

33 'And now allow me to explain, in order that you may understand my

position and work better, that I have always wished that I had been an architect. I have been building since when, at nine years of age, a lean-to rabbit hutch absorbed all my spare time for that year ... The third year saw a further development in carrying out a startling idea, that of covering the roof with soil to the depth of about 6 in, and planting oats therein, with the object of raising food for the ever-increasing stock of rabbits. But alas! ... although the corn grew luxuriantly in the early spring, it all withered away in the summer heat, and so this economy of space, which, had it proved practicable, might have done so much for distressed agriculture, had to be abandoned.'
W.H. Lever Dwellings erected at Port Sunlight and Thornton Hough, *The Builder* Vol. 82 (March 1902) 316.

34   W. P. Jolly, *op. cit.*, 6.

35   W. P. Jolly, *op. cit.*, 13.

36   2nd Viscount Leverhulme, *op. cit.*, 15.

37   'After his marriage, my father lived in thirteen houses and ... (with one exception) ... he built, rebuilt or, to some extent, altered all of them.' (2nd Viscount Leverhulme, *op. cit.*, 290).

38   2nd Viscount Leverhulme, *op. cit.*, 86.

39   Walter L. George in *Labour and Housing at Port Sunlight* (Alston Rivers, 1909) describes just how dreary the site was when first seen, 6-7.

40   C. Wilson, *op. cit.*, 34.

41   And this was justified in other places besides Port Sunlight (2nd Viscount Leverhulme, *op. cit.*, 152).

42   'It is my hope and my brother's hope, someday to build houses in which our work-people will be able to live and be comfortable - semi-detached houses, with gardens back and front, in which they will be able to know more about the science of life than they can in a back slum, and in which they will learn that there is more enjoyment in life than the mere going to and returning from work and looking forward to Saturday night to drawn their wages.' W. P. Jolly *op. cit.*, p. 27.

43   Robert Owen, *A New View of Society* (republished Dent & Co., London, 1927).

44   A few semi-detached houses had been built near the factory at Bournville as early as 1879 but the village proper was not begun until ten years later, at the same time as Port Sunlight. Charles B. Purdom, *The Garden City* (Dent & Co., London, 1913) 15.

45   Lever's library eventually contained many books on architecture and town planning, painting and furniture (2nd Viscount Leverhulme, *op. cit.*, 273) though not all had arrived by 1908.

46 Francis Hyde 'Utilitarian Town Planning 1825-1845', *Town Planning Review* Vol. XIX (1943-47) 153-159.

47 If the difficulties of building garden cities were infinitely greater than I have ventured to point out, they are very small compared with the prize to be won by the production of a physically superior, and contented and happy people ... We cannot attain any finer object, and it will be the means of placing our nation, as a nation, far ahead of any of our competitors. Charles B. Purdom, *The Building of Satellite Towns* (J. M. Dent & Sons Ltd, 1925) 135.

48 W. L. George, *op. cit.*, 9-15.

49 W. L. George, *op. cit.*, 7.

50 Letter from Lever to T. H. Mawson in 1918 (2nd Viscount Leverhulme, *op. cit.*, 86).

51 Lever's vote of thanks to the President of the Royal Institute of British Architects, Mr P. Waterhouse, after his address to the students on the subject of clients. *Journal of Royal Institute of British Architects* Vol. XXX (1923) 204.

52 W. L. George, *op. cit.*, 72 *et seq*.

53 W. L. George, *op. cit.*, 87.

54 M. Shippobottom (*op. cit.*, 65) names the architects of fourteen of these buildings. Five firms were involved.

55 W. L. George, *op. cit.*, 121. W. H. Lever, *op. cit.*,[33] 313.

56 Apart from competitions limited to students there were a number of open competitions. According to M. Shippobottom (*op. cit.*, 65), the earliest competition was in October 1890 for the design of cottages and a dining hall which was won by W. Owen. Owen was asked to build the dining hall and two blocks of cottages while Grayson and Ould were to build a shop block and a further block of cottages.

57 They included a few eccentric characters. Naseby Adams, a well-known local architect, designed some houses for Lever and asked to be paid in golden guineas. At the Sandon Club he opened the wash-leather bag and exclaiming 'all my life I have wanted to do this!' poured the contents over his head. Roderick F. Bisson, *The Sandon Studios Society and the Arts* (Parry Books Ltd, 1965) 77.

58 M. Shippobottom, *op. cit.*, 187. Quoted from the diary of Lady Sackville, 25 September 1919.

59 2nd Viscount Leverhulme, *op. cit.*, 84.

60 Charles Wilson, *Unilever 1945-1965* (Cassell, 1968) 159.

61 2nd Viscount Leverhulme, *op. cit.*, 50. The house was actually bought in 1891.

62   Mawson, a considerable character, is further mentioned on pp 84/6 His manner of writing has period charm. He writes of Lever: 'At our first meeting he struck me as a veritable Napoleon in his grasp of all the factors dominating any problem he tackled, in his walk and pose, and in his speech, which contained the concentrated essence of thought.' Thomas H. Mawson, *The Life and Work of an English Landscape Architect* (Richards Press, London 1927) 116.

63   2nd Viscount Leverhulme, *op. cit.*, 291-92.

64   Mawson was engaged in the formal *versus* informal garden argument which was then going on. This is mentioned in the note about Mawson and his work in Chapter Four.

65   The Church was designed by J. Lomax Simpson, the son of Lever's old friend. M. Shippobottom says (*op. cit.*, 105) that Simpson and a craftsman called Griffiths were sent on an extensive study-tour of Norman Churches so that every detail might be right. The result is painstaking.

66   One of Lever's many far-sighted views was that towns should buy land around their borders in order to control future development, as in several continental countries they were entitled to do by law. In view of this he later offered his Storeton estate to Birkenhead at a bargain price. The offer was refused because a government loan was refused (2nd Viscount Leverhulme, *op. cit.*, 298).

67   T. H. Mawson, *op. cit.*, 190-91. The day before Mawson was due to sail to America for the fourth time he received a letter of dismissal from Lever. In return Mawson sent a letter to Lever giving his reasons why junior partners should share more of the work. Within a fortnight he had received a letter from Lever asking him when he was returning. Later Mawson visited Roynton Cottage and made a report of the Island of Lewis for Lever.

68   Letter from Lever to Reilly 12 September 1914 (*Univ. Archives*) Letter from Lever to Abercrombie concerning Mawson's salary, 30 September and 9 October 1914 (*Univ. Archives*)

69   2nd Viscount Leverhulme, *op. cit.*, 127 *et seq.*

70   Chillingham and Woburn and other places where grandees kept herds of unusual animals were not then open to the public, not even in the restricted manner allowed at Chillingham.

71   Phoebe Hesketh in her *My Aunt Edith* says it was burnt down by her aunt. Phoebe Hesketh, *My Aunt Edith* (Peter Davies, London 1966) 74.

72   2nd Viscount Leverhulme, *op. cit.*, 176-77.

73   Rivington is now owned by the City of Bolton who can spare at present very little for conservation and repair. Volunteers have cleared the stone stairs and pavilions and stiles here and there guide visitors. Great crowds come at holiday times to Rivington and the park below.

74   2nd Viscount Leverhulme, *op. cit.*, 294.

75   The Hill is mentioned on pp. 374 and 379 of Thomas H. Mawson's *The Art and Craft of Garden Making* (B. T. Batsford Ltd. London 1912).

76   T. H. Mawson, *op. cit.*[62], 179, 189.

77   2nd Viscount Leverhulme, *op. cit.*, 295.

78   As at Rivington Hall (2nd Viscount Leverhulme *op. cit.*, 31).

79   Andrew M. Knox, *Coming Clean* (Heinemann London 1976) 45.

80   T. H. Mawson, *op. cit.*,[62] 116–117.

81   2nd Viscount Leverhulme, *op. cit.*, 289.

82   2nd Viscount Leverhulme, *op. cit.*, 88. For example in 1896 and 1897 Lever lived at Port Sunlight in Bridge Cottage which faces the stone bridge across the dell, while alterations were being made to Thornton Manor.

83   2nd Viscount Leverhulme, *op. cit.*, 179.

84   W. P. Jolly, *op. cit.*, 145–46.

85   We spent a few days in Chicago visiting the World's Fair, and as far as one could judge in its present incomplete state the Americans have every cause to feel proud of this monument to their energy. For picturesqueness of situation, beauty and extent of buildings, arrangement, conception and general execution it leaves nothing to be desired, and it ought to be the finest Exhibition the world has ever seen. The site is unique, extending over 700 acres of park land on the shores of that beautiful inland sea, Lake Michigan. W. H. Lever, *Following the Flag* (Simpkin Marshall & Co. Ltd, London and Edward Howell, Liverpool 1893) 7.

86   2nd Viscount Leverhulme, *op. cit.*, 258.

87   Letter from Lever quoted in *Garden Cities and Town Planning* Vol. III (April 1908) 47.

88   In 1910, having carried on this second career for over twenty years, he was tapped on the shoulder at a town planning lecture by someone well known, who exclaimed 'Hullo, Lever! I had no idea you took an interest in these recondite subjects!' 2nd Viscount Leverhulme, *op. cit.*, 256.

89   Letter from Lever to (Vice-Chancellor) Dale, 16 September 1914 (*Univ. Archives*).

90   Letters between Reilly and Hugh Rathbone, 17 - 27 January 1922 (*Univ. Archives*), see note (54) Chapter Three.

91   C. Wilson, *op. cit.*,[4] 291.

92 The title of Leverhulme was obtained by Lever's joining his own surname to that of his wife, born Elizabeth Hulme. It is said that the College of Arms demurred over the innovation, but Lever of course had his way, and so anticipated by some forty years the now almost universal practice by which a new peer retains in his title the name by which he became famous. Lever simply could not stop being a pioneer.

93 Lever has been quoted as saying 'My happiness is my business. I can see finality for myself ... but none for my business. There one has room to breathe, to grow, to expand and the possibilities are boundless. Gordon Read, *Lancashire History Makers* (E. P. Publishing Ltd, Wakefield Yorks 1975) 73–80.

94 C. Wilson, *op. cit.*,[4], xviii.

95 The Rt Hon. John Burn's speech introducing a Bill that contained town planning powers was made on 12 May 1908. The Bill was later reintroduced and passed in 1909.

3

THE MAN WHO HAD THE IDEA

Sir Charles Reilly: 1874-1948

The second parent of the Lever Chair – the man who had the idea of
founding a department for the study of town planning and civic
design in the University of Liverpool – was Charles Herbert Reilly.
In 1908 he was thirty-four and had held the Roscoe Chair of
Architecture for four years.

Descriptions of Reilly by colleagues and former students always
refer to his abundant vitality, energy and tremendous enthusiasms.
They sometimes go on to say other things as well, but these qualities
are central. 'Reilly', writes Maxwell Fry,' [was] a personal vortex for
whatever was in the wind, a perambulating transmitter of rapidly
digested material that issued in waves of enthusism to whomsoever
was capable of receiving it: he was a culture in himself.[1]

According to Lionel Budden, Reilly's successor as Roscoe professor
and a colleague for twenty years:

> Reilly in no ordinary measure possessed vitality, a
> nervous restless energy that some found
> exhilarating and others exhausting. For a great
> majority of students he was a stimulating force: he
> heightened their sense of the importance of
> architecture, and by infecting them with his own
> enthusiasms he made life seem fuller, richer and
> altogether more exciting.[2]

> He made all architecture seem terribly important
> and in his Monday morning 'crits' could discover
> merits in your own design which you had never
> seen for yourself ... he was a professor-friend to all
> students.[3]

There were other things said of him. Lionel Budden also wrote (and
who knew him better?):

> He was formidable in controversy ... for it was his
> custom to throw everything into the fray. When it
> was all over and he had won – as in most cases he
> did – he freely forgave the luckless victims of his
> invective in a manner that took away their breath
> ...[4]

He could be very trying. There was an

> occasion when all the staff at the School of
> Architecture resigned in protest at a Reilly
> decision, had their resignations calmly accepted,

and then returned en masse, *exasperated still but*
unable to resist the Professor's magnetism.[5]

He gave most generous help to chosen good causes and to all ex-students of his school – to aid talented ex-students he would stop at (almost) nothing; and yet he could be mean in small matters. Mimics of their fellowmen often re-enacted the scene of Reilly, having emerged from a cab with a companion, raising his ivory-nobbed stick to point out the beauties of the building opposite, while the other man paid up.

His enthusiasms were many and lasted till his death. The greatest of them was for the Liverpool School of Architecture, with himself as its head. Among the others was the saving of the old Bluecoat School, a fine Queen Anne (1717) building in the centre of Liverpool, which housed for nearly ten years the School of Architecture. He helped to establish the Liverpool Repertory Theatre (later the Playhouse), helped internees and refugees in both world wars, and expressed opinions in about a thousand articles in newspapers and journals on all and any subject on which editors would ask him to write, and probably on a lot on which they did not mean him to write.

He blew his own trumpet, and it was said that whatever the subject on which he started to write, the article always in the end contained a puff for his school or an ex-student. He made no claim to scholarship; and allegedly smiled with kindly indulgence if he saw a student reading a book. He was a man of action, and so acted that he raised the numbers of students in the Liverpool School of Architecture from 15 or 20 to 200, and made it during the 1920s into one of the best and easily the most publicized schools of architecture in the world. He was a remarkable man.

School, Cambridge and Apprenticeship

Reilly was born in 1874, the son of an architect and surveyor who did a lot of his work for the Drapers' Company, one of the largest among the City of London's Livery Companies.[6] He claimed descent from a prosperous Bath innkeeper and coach-owner in the late 1700s.

Reilly had three brothers and two sisters, and writes that he was a fair-haired, blue-eyed and rather weak-looking child. He went to a preparatory school at Brighton, which improved his health and then on to the Merchant Taylors School for five years. The school was then near the centre of the City of London, which called for a twice-daily journey, long and smoky, to and from his home in north London. Reilly did not think much of his school education. Some ingratitude creeps in here. What he was actually taught seems very odd – as do most school curricula – yet whatever it was it gained him a Cambridge scholarship, and the school then gave him another for getting the first one.

He moved to Queens' College, Cambridge in 1892 and managed to pay his way on £120 a year, of which his father was only called on for £50. Even this proved too much for the family finances. Reilly Senior, like a great many architects then and now, received fees at almost unpredictable intervals and in varying amounts. With supplies cut off for a year, Reilly was lucky enough to obtain pupils to coach in his own subject – the new Mechanical Sciences Tripos – and kept ahead of them to such good effect that he obtained a first class degree. Although in later life Reilly rather emphasized his lack of scholarship and, one gathers, used to smile a little at intellectuals, he certainly possessed that huge aid to a flying start in life – the ability to pass exams well and seemingly without too much effort. One may assume that having found a suitable role as man of action and propagandist, Reilly liked to poke a little fun at colleagues who had made other choices. It is a common habit.

Reilly thought even less of the tuition and supervision at Cambridge in his day than he had of his school, and with reason. Nevertheless,

I owe a great deal of my little stock-in-hand to Cambridge. I am not denying that. But I owe it in the first place to the Cambridge buildings, lawns and trees, and in the second place to certain of its undergraduates.[7]

The biggest event was when Reilly invited Keir Hardie, recently elected as one of the first Labour MPs, to address a public meeting in Cambridge. He accepted and the meeting was lively.

Reilly seems to have drifted into being an architect because it was an easy choice. His father's small office was there and unpaid work could be found for him. So he started the way a multitude have done before and since. During two boring years Reilly continued in this office. He mentions a few of the most prominent architects of the day, Norman Shaw, John Belcher and Aston Webb. Like his later patron Lever, he does not mention any of the architects of the 1890s who are now highly respected, save for Edwin Lutyens. He did not spot and back pioneers. Later, he preferred solidly established architects. In general, he liked influential, wealthy and titled people: a little perhaps for their being so, but mainly because they could help the Liverpool school, its head, reputation and students, to greater effect and with less effort than any pioneer.

When Reilly, at twenty-four, was trying to escape from his father's dull and cramped office he was no doubt full of ideals about his chosen profession, as a young man should be; and, as he was always an enthusiast, he took pains to decide which other office he should try to enter. It was a hugely prosperous time for architects who had established themselves. The Empire was still supremely confident, and wanted buildings in Britain's big cities worthy of the most world-wide empire ever known. It also needed country houses for men who had made much money in extending industry and commerce. There was a demand for new and better Town Halls, office buildings – then a fairly novel form of specialized building – hospitals, hotels, and also the plum jobs as they were then thought; country houses for the newly rich. Lever's house at Thornton Manor and his other houses and landscaping were impressive works, but Lord Armstrong's Cragside estates and the rebuilt Bamburgh Castle in Northumberland were even more so. There were plenty of clients.

Norman Shaw and Aston Webb had probably the dominant offices, and Reginald Blomfield (forty in 1896) had obtained some large commissions. Reilly and a friend, Lionel Detmar, had to avoid offices which could and did ask for premiums from pupils. They finally chose and managed to enter the office of John Belcher because they specially admired his accountant's building near Moorgate which is now attributed to Belcher and Beresford Pite. This building is still much admired, and today's architects will envy the marvellous craftsmanship then available at modest cost. It was in Belcher's office that Reilly first met 'the great gaunt figure of Stanley Adshead',[8] the first holder of the Lever Chair and the subject of the next chapter.

In the four years from 1898 Reilly made a great move ahead in professional skills, interests and achievements, as though during the dull unpaid years in his father's office a strong spring had been wound up and was now released. He became a lecturer in architecture at King's College London, and concurrently a student at the Architectural Association, also in London, where experienced architects criticized the designs of younger men. He also passed the final examination of the Royal Institute of British Architects, and became a partner of Stanley Peach, a little known architect. He seems to have faded out of John Belcher's office without ill-will. By 1901-02 he was earning £700-£800 a year, then a substantial sum. He went to Italy to draw and paint 'on proper architectural holidays'[9] and also first met Dorothy Pratt who was to become his wife, then still at boarding school. At his first proposal he found she regarded him 'as a kind of Uncle person, kindly interested in her drawings'.[10] She decided to study at the Slade School of Art: but all came right in the end.

Liverpool Cathedral

In 1901 the first event took place that led on to the Lever Chair, and all that followed. A competition was announced for a cathedral at Liverpool, which then (the reader should be reminded) had the importance and about twice the relative wealth of Birmingham today, plus London Airport. This new competition was the result of the driving force and persuasiveness of the new and diminutive Bishop of Liverpool, Bishop Chavasse.

The competition attracted about 100 entries. A design in concrete was submitted by W. R. Lethaby and others, and so called early attention to a material and methods of construction that were to sweep the world. Reilly submitted a design. Though it had been stated by the assessors, G. F. Bodley and Norman Shaw, that the Gothic style was not obligatory it was bound to be favoured: partly by the Victorian middle-class belief that Gothic was in the great

English tradition and that anything Classical was also Popish (as Liverpool had a large Irish population, strong Protestant v. Catholic feelings still existed.) and partly because neither of the assessors had designed neoclassic buildings.

Reilly's design was a classical one (see illus.), and receieved a favourable mention. The winner of the final competition – it was a two-stage affair – was Giles Gilbert Scott, aged twenty-one and grandson of the Gilbert Scott who built or rebuilt some 200 churches in the great Victorian church building period. Giles Scott's design was changed and remodelled by him and later by his partner F. G. Thomas and is today almost certainly the last cathedral to be built of stone in the traditional manner.

Big drawings were the thing in those days, and Reilly travelled up with his drawings and saw the smoky grandeur of Liverpool for the first time from a cart which he managed to hire, as the drawings were too big for a cab.[11] Reilly wrote that after delivering his drawings he went to see the site, a plan of which, he said, had not been issued with the conditions. Architects who have frequently entered for competitions for new buildings often say half-jokingly that it is a mistake to go to see the intended site before one submits one's design, but this omission, alleged by Reilly, strained credulity, as the site is long and narrow and on the edge of a cliff. It was assumed that this 'was just one of Reilly's stories', but the matter was investigated; and on this occasion at least Reilly's ghost is entitled to wag a reproving finger. The story is true. Several sites were being considered when the first competition was being organized, and although the final St James's Mount site was a slight favourite, the competitors in the first competition were at liberty to imagine their own site or presumably to choose one of those being discussed.[12] The first competition was to choose several suitable architects and not a building. By the time Reilly delivered his drawings, in June 1902, the final choice of site had been made, and Reilly saw that his design was unsuitable.

In 1903, Reilly felt confident enough to apply for the Chair of Architecture at King's College London and reached the short list of three. He was beaten by Professor F. M. Simpson who had held the Chair of Architecture at Liverpool for ten years. Reilly's ability to charm and impress people at short notice is often referred to by those who knew him. This time he used it to good purpose on Simpson while they shared a waiting room before being interviewed. In a manner mildly reminiscent of the famous Wellington-Nelson interview (also in a waiting room),[13] he so impressed Simpson that the latter said that if he was chosen for King's College he would do his best to help Reilly to replace him at Liverpool;[14] and he was, and did.

Reilly Comes to Liverpool

It was also in 1903 that Reilly heard he had been shortlisted to fill

Simpson's place as Professor of Architecture at Liverpool. He then travelled to Liverpool, and spent a weekend with the Dean of Arts and attended an alarming dinner party with a number of professors and doubtless some lay members of Council. He was successful, and was appointed. In the notice issued to the press Reilly's achievements to the age of twenty-nine were written up, as they were in *The Times*.[15] He was supported by Norman Shaw, Aston Webb, John Belcher and even the Bishop of Exeter, former Principal of King's College London. What the Bishop really remembered of a part-time lecturer at King's may have been minimal, but anyway he signed a letter of support.

Charles Reilly plunged, bursting with enthusiasm, into improving his small department and into the life of the university and city. In 1904 there were only about 800 students and less than 30 professors. The staff was small but of high quality in the period 1899–1909 and included, as has been stated, seven members of staff who were later knighted. In proportion to numbers, the present academic staff would have to contain, to equal the 1904 standard, about 100 future knights. The architects were tucked away in an attic full of plaster casts above the big Arts Theatre (lecture room) in the Victoria Building. In his autobiography Reilly is terribly rude about the university site as he found it. He had good reason. The site was adjoined by a great workhouse, what had been recently a lunatic asylum, the Royal Infirmary and a Lock hospital. Moreover, then and for the next sixty years, it was not only traversed by the main line railway tunnel and cuttings from Lime Street – Liverpool's largest railway station – but from a dozen openings smoke and steam belched out as the trains climbed a stiff gradient. Students of the 1920s comment on the continuing dirt.[16] Memories of his time spent in Cambridge must have made the site seem to Reilly a shocking choice for a university, as they did to another professor coming from Cambridge in 1954.[17]

Reilly, writing thirty-five years later, describes the state of the School of Architecture in 1904 as worse than it really was. His predecessor, Simpson, had established an Honours BA in Architecture – the first in the country – and by 1904 there were about twenty architectural students in the two-year course. Reilly was not satisfied with an Honours BA in Architecture and by 1906–07 changed it to the Honours Degree of Bachelor of Architecture. Augustus John had taught in the school for a brief period when it was still 'Architecture and Applied Art', and Liverpool later tried to cling on to John's coat tails, not always with dignity, as his fame grew. The Liverpool Academy once rejected all John's submissions, but at their 150th Anniversary Exhibition in 1960 they asked Augustus John to lend some works. He replied that he was too busy, 'but you can tell them I've forgiven them all long ago'.[18] The University has, however, named a public house after him. He would have liked that.

Reilly took the second step that led to the Lever Chair soon after he came to Liverpool. He sought out Mr W. H. Lever and asked if the architectural students could visit Port Sunlight. On the visit Reilly sent in his card to Lever and he and 'the short red fiery little man'[19] had a not very promising first meeting. The university were still so ignorant of the great man across the Mersey that the Registrar advised Reilly to write to the wrong brother (James D'Arcy Lever), who by then was taking only a minor part in the firm's affairs. At least this is Reilly's story of how he made a bad start.[20] Better things came later.

Having obtained a professorship, a young and beautiful bride in Dorothy Pratt and a house of some distinction at the Dingle, all in his thirtieth year, Reilly turned great attention to boosting his school.[21] In his second year, he published a portfolio of his students' measured drawings.[22] Its success is not known, Portfolios of famous classical style buildings were expensive to produce, but when Reilly became consulting editor of The *Builder's Journal* (later The *Architects' Journal*) he soon hit on the idea of publishing in the journal measured drawings and designs by his students. He was then able to buy the printing blocks at a low price and re-use them in an anual *Liverpool Sketch Book*.[23] The price was low; there were practically no rivals; and the publicity for the school and its professor was continuous and rewarding.

But before all these things happened, Reilly had turned to other matters. The first was some architectural work for himself, and since the university had several new buildings in prospect it seemed to him only proper that one of them – or perhaps more than one – should be designed by the University's own Professor of Architecture. In a matter which had about it a distinct flavour of self-interest other men might have adopted an indirect approach. Not Reilly. In a good cause, Reilly resembled Admiral Earl St Vincent, who is said by Carola Oman to have been 'untroubled by any feelings of nervous diffidence'. He was prepared to overlook the fact that he himself would be the beneficiary. In February 1906 Reilly sent to the Vice-Chancellor 'some reasons why the Professor of Architecture should not be passed over when a new University Building is required'. It was a good note.[24]

Having begun this campaign Reilly also tried again to win an open competition, that for the London County Council's County Hall, at Westminster Bridge. His design – fully classical with two domes – did not win, but one feature of it – the concave central portion of the river façade – appears in Ralph Knott's building as it is today.

Reilly then turned to the problem of finding better accommodation for his school than the attics of the Victoria Building, with their motley collection of plaster casts and ample smoke from the railway cutting. No solution emerged until early in 1908. It was then that he learnt that the Trustees of the Bluecoat Hospital, a pleasing early-eighteenth-century building near the centre of Liverpool, were putting it up for sale. Liverpool had few buildings of such

architectural quality, and at once Reilly's energy and enthusiasm –
at high pressure – were turned on to a work of what would now be
called conservation. With the help of Lascelles Abercrombie, brother
of Patrick and poet and man of letters,[25] Reilly drafted an appeal to
save the Bluecoat, apparently in mid-1908. This suggested that the
central portion of the building should be used for the University
School of Architecture – 'at present inadequately housed far from the
architects of the town' – and that the rest of the building should be
used as studios for painters, sculptors and other artists: as indeed it
had been for a year or more, and is to this day.

The price the Trustees had in mind was £30,000–£40,000, and
Reilly decided to approach Lever. Lever came to look, and of course –
given his great interest in buildings – was soon hooked. He agreed to
lease the building for five years, pay for repairs and give the
university the option to buy the building at a later date if they so
desired. Soon Lever agreed that if the university did not want to
retain the Bluecoat School, he would pay for a new School of
Architecture elsewhere. Lever allowed the university to use the
Bluecoat School rent free. [26]

Civic Design

It was towards the beginning of the save-the-Bluecoat campaign
that Reilly had the idea which, as far as this book is concerned, was
his most important, and led in the end to great results. In 1908 town
planning had been talked about for years as a necessary guide to the
expansion of towns and a corrective for slum housing, and at last the
Liberal Government, elected in 1906, was going to introduce a Bill.

Legislation that would have some effect was long overdue. The
housing of the poor in larger towns (and indeed almost everywhere)
was disgusting, despite Commissions of Inquiry and Housing Acts
going back sixty years; and a dozen examples of planned
settlements, large and small, had shown that immense improvements were practicable at a cost which great industrialists regarded
as moderate. Moreover, as was constantly pointed out, Belgium had
had town planning powers since 1836 and Sweden and Germany
since the 1870s.[27]

The previous year (1907) a City Beautiful Conference had been
held in Liverpool. It was attended by Reilly, and one may assume
that he saw that three professions would each try to obtain a major
share in the new field of work if an Act of Parliament were passed:
architects, civil and municipal engineers and surveyors. To Reilly it
was crystal-clear that architects should hold a commanding
position in the new art and science. He saw things very simply when
it suited his current enthusiasm. A town needed to be designed just
like a building or small group of buildings, and who could do that
save an architect? A simple idea tenaciously held by a man of
influence has great powers of survival. Men originally trained as architects held a majority of the most important posts in town planning in
Britain and the Commonwealth for the next half century.[28]

Reilly says[29] that he was given the idea of a University Department of Civic Design by the speech of the Rt Hon. John Burns when he introduced a Housing and Town Planning Bill which was subsequently withdrawn. Burns was President of the Local Government Board, the ancestor, via five or six changes of name and powers, of the present Department of the Environment. Reilly read the report of the speech and was indignant that architecture and amenity were never mentioned. Burns aimed 'at healthy homes ... and suburbs salubrious'; and to abolish, reconstruct and prevent slums. Britons now lived in big towns. Back-to-back houses must be abolished. Excellent examples of lay-out existed (Bournville, Hampstead Garden Suburb and Bournemouth were mentioned in the Debate). Half a million houses had been built in London in fifteen years, unplanned on 1,400 miles of streets, and there was no way of bringing all interests together to assure a good layout. The country had no right to allow half a million acres to vanish every fifteen years into unplanned towns. Legislation would be permissive but the Local Government Board would have reserved powers to compel.[30]

Reilly thought it essential to connect architecture and town planning in the public mind, and at once thought of a Chair at Liverpool. He also thought of Lever - that source for Reilly from whom most blessings flowed - and a man greatly interested in planning, housing, garden cities and landscape design. Reilly wrote to Lever and asked for money for a Chair of Town Planning and Lectureship and the publication of a journal on the subject. Lever responded at once and Reilly says it was all fixed up within a few days.[31] It is doubtful if it happened as quickly as that - not in a university; but Reilly had asked for money for a cause in which, as described in the previous chapter, Lever had always been greatly interested and - thanks to the libel damages - he had asked at the right time.

The net proceeds from the libel actions amounted to about £84,000, and Lever found time in 1908-09 to found what he called 'the Chair of Town Planning and Civic Design', plus a Research Fellowship and The *Town Planning Review*, to offer £24,000 for a School of Architecture in the Bluecoat School or elsewhere, and to help the Departments of Tropical Medicine and Russian studies. He fitted all this in during a period when his business worries world-wide responsibilities and Parliamentary duties were at their peak, or on their highest plateau. He was truly an astonishing man. The amount paid to the Department of Civic Design was £800 a year to begin with, and was raised to £1,200 in 1914.

The proposal that the new Department of Civic Design (as it was called in its first prospectus and ever since) should at once publish a journal - The *Town Planning Review* - was one of the two most opportune and fruitful of all Reilly's ideas.[32] It was probable that the new department would, to begin with, attract few students: and a journal would be a great help to the new professor in spreading his views, and enable him to invite other experts to help to mark out suitable boundaries for the new subject. It was Reilly who seemed to make all arrangements for the first issue of The *Town Planning Review* in April 1910.[33]

Town planning in 1909 - as stated earlier - was really unknown to the general public. A number of societies were asking for legislation, including the Garden Cities Association and the National Housing Reform Council and these two did not always agree with one another. Progressive local authorities were asking for greater control over new building and redevelopment, and greater powers to get rid of slums. Other bodies saw town planning as a means towards better public health, more parks and playgrounds, and a reduction of vandalism; and Ebenezer Howard and his supporters, including the Letchworth pioneers, wanted to build garden cities with ideal housing, shops, factories and amenities, in which all the land and rises in land and property values would eventually belong to the town's inhabitants. There were many other aims and examples. In some Continental cities the number of storeys allowed in buildings depended on their distance from the city centre; and in the United States the City Beautiful movement and landscape designers (who prepared many town plans) were modifying the rules, in an almost inexplicable way, for players in the country's greatest outdoor sport of land speculation. The three most interested British professions watched what was happening, and their members sometimes attended conferences and wrote articles, or even books.

John Burns's speech in May 1908 may have been the final spur to action for Reilly, but the idea of seizing hold of the new subject for Liverpool - that is for the School of Architecture and Reilly - had probably been suggested by the three conferences of the previous year. One of these, as has been stated, was the City Beautiful conference in Liverpool which Reilly almost certainly attended and may have helped to organize. The other two, held in London, were the conference of the Garden City Association and an International Housing Congress. Reilly's lively mind would certainly have thought about this group of subjects, closely or loosely connected with architecture, which seemed to need some form of permanent home.

By 1910 Reilly must have felt extremely pleased that he had seen this need and moved so swiftly to make Liverpool the academic home of the new studies, for there were two conferences held in that year. By far the more important was that held at the Royal Institute of British Architects in October. This, as stated in the next chapter, provided in its report a most useful summary of town planning as it was then seen. With the probable aim of ensuring that architects obtained the major share of work in the new town planning, the RIBA really let itself go. It must have surprised itself. HM the King was Patron. Everyone was there or lent support from Lord Kitchener of Khartoum (the contemporary equivalent of the late Lord

Mountbatten) who did attend, Lord Curzon and thirty-six others with titles, experts from nine countries, to almost everyone who had any reputation in British town planning between 1900 and 1930. The Royal Academy held a supporting exhibition and the *Transactions* of the conference, published in 1911, is a hefty volume of 800 pages and about 250 illustrations. The book is a splendid exposition of town planning and the history of town planning as they were seen in 1910, as well as of many problems still unsolved in 1981.[34]

Reilly, who gave a paper, must have looked round him with great and fully earned satisfaction. Four Liverpool men gave papers, his students had even designed the banquet menu card, and best of all, when these captains and kings had all departed, his school would still be the only centre for university studies of all these subjects.

But this great day was in the future. After Lever's agreement in 1908 to pay for the new department, Reilly's next tasks were to find a suitable first occupant for the Lever Chair (as it was to be called), and then to persuade the Faculty of Arts and the Senate to agree to the new project and the man. By 1908 several of men were beginning to be known, if not widely, as writers and propagandists on one or more aspects of the new subject, and even as practitioners. These included Ebenezer Howard, Patrick Geddes, J. S. Nettlefold, T. C. Horsfall and others. Of the practitioners only Parker and Unwin were architects, mainly of small houses, but they had had practical experience of town layout at Letchworth and Hampstead Garden Suburb.[35]

There is no evidence that Reilly considered any of these, or Thomas Adams (who became the most eminent of the early planners) or even T. H. Mawson, who was then working both as a landscape designer at Thornton Manor and on an improvement plan for Bolton, for both of which Lever was paying. Reilly was thinking of noble buildings in full neoclassical style, in noble streets and groups, and several of the proposals he put to Lever were for the redesign of run-down parts of Liverpool.[36]

There was a great gap between these visions and their realization, but one step forward was to be able to show them in perspective drawings of high quality, from the air and from the ground, and both plain and coloured. One man who was famous for architectural perspectives and also Reilly's friend was Stanley Davenport Adshead. Once Reilly had thought of Adshead it is very doubtful if he bothered to think of anyone else.[37] Reilly was always powerfully influenced by his current enthusiasm, which also seems to have given him the power to convince others of the rightness of his views. Two other possibilities of course exist: his colleagues may have thought their lives would become intolerable unless Reilly was allowed his way; secondly, Reilly's enthusiasms were usually such that he himself would have to live at very close quarters with the results, and so the consent of some of his colleagues may have been influenced by a little malicious hope. At any rate by January 1909, Adshead was writing to Reilly about what should be taught in civic design (see pp. 79-80), by March he had sent a *curriculum vitae*, and in the same month the Faculty of Arts recommended his appointment as a senior lecturer for three years, doubtless as a precaution against a wrong appointment in a subject of which little was known. The offer was accepted.

A second reason for Reilly's choice was probably the proposal by Reginald Blomfield that an advanced school of architectural design should be established. Blomfield had in mind that this should be at the Royal Academy in London, and as he, a formidable man (later Sir Reginald and designer of the new Regent Quadrant), had been chairman of the Board of Architectural Education for several years, Reilly no doubt kept himself well informed of what was going on. To Reilly there was only one place for an advanced school of architectural design, and to attract a famous architectural perspectivist to Liverpool would help to raise standards and help him to fulfil his aim. Results came soon.[38]

Yet a third reason for Reilly's advocacy of Adshead for the appointment was probably Reilly's desire to find a man who would accept gracefully the position of second-in-command in the School of Architecture, besides raising its standards of draughtsmanship, and generally agree with Reilly that civic design and town planning was, or ought to be, architecture writ large. Moreover, Reilly had several times employed Adshead to make perspective drawings in which Reilly's role had been that of patron towards an artist and a patron able to express firm views; and this probably gave him confidence that, in a very friendly way, their future relationship would be that of master and assistant. Indeed Reilly was not at all good at taking a back seat, but there are signs that in the next few years Adshead, stroking his Jack Hulbert chin with a huge hand, learnt to manage Reilly.

Later that summer at Lever's expense,[39] Reilly travelled for three months in the United States to study what was then being done there in civic design. Adshead, as described in Chapter 4, was to do the same on a trip to Europe, and did so. A great deal was then being done in the United States in what is still commonly called the City Beautiful Movement, which had been the chief result of the Chicago Exposition of 1893. Many American cities were improving themselves, or planning to do so, as has been mentioned earlier, by constructing fine public buildings and associated parks, 'parkways', and gardens. Landscape architects then played a specially important part in American planning, and joined with architects in preparing ambitious city improvement schemes.

When Adshead began work at Liverpool in October 1909 the new department, together with the School of Architecture, was settling into the repaired Bluecoat Building (see illustrations). The plan of part of the repaired building shows that civic design was, as Reilly intended, an integral part of the School of Architecture. Adshead was first known as Associate Professor, a title which Reilly may have brought back with him from American universities, as it was almost unknown in British universities for a further half-century, and is not much favoured by older university teachers to this day.

Reilly 1909 - 33

As far as the founding of the Lever Chair was concerned, Reilly's great deed was done by October 1909. He may be called the begetter, obstetrician, midwife and even nurse of the infant department, and did all save pay expenses. This was a very special achievement. Reilly had suggested to Lever a number of ways in which Lever could spend some of his great wealth on schemes of public benefit. We do not know them all, but in at least three of them (saving the Bluecoat School, helping the School of Architecture and taking shares in the proposed Repertory Theatre) Lever had assurance that others shared Reilly's views. The School of Architecture had been in existence for twenty years and a lot of influential people wanted to save the Bluecoat School or took shares in the Repertory Theatre. But the civic design project was quite new[40] and despite Lever's knowledge of and interest in related subjects, he must have relied greatly on Reilly for the academic possibilities of the new studies when he took his decision.

It is true that the time was ripe, Lever was an MP and the Bill of 1908 was modified and reintroduced and later became the Housing, Town Planning Act of 1909. But rich men often stay rich by keeping their money in their pockets until others have proved the ripeness of the times. Here Reilly may have been helped by Lever's impatience with the slow procedures of the House of Commons. As recorded earlier, Lever was an early advocate of old age pensions, women's suffrage, payment for MPs and a shorter working day. If, in his business, he decided that a project was worthwhile he had become accustomed to being able to order it to be carried out forthwith, and after the huge Liberal majority in the General Election of 1906, he doubtless expected legislation on worthy causes to follow rapidly. So his irritation at Parliamentary delays may well have inclined him to make an immediate decision over a town planning 'Act' that lay wholly within his own power.

Reilly believed to the end of his life that town planning was an extension of architecture, or at least all of that part of it that interested him, which he called civic design. He therefore incorporated the new Department of Civic Design within the School of Architecture and there it remained until Reilly retired. In the 1920s, Abercrombie (the second Lever professor) was forced by the rising number of architects to use two or three rooms round the corner, at 175 Brownlow Hill, for himself and the *Town Planning Review*. Architectural students were however free to attend civic design lectures whether or not they were enrolled as civic design students – or at any rate, a number did so attend – and some of these later became eminent professional town planners. The close relationship between architecture and civic design is emphasized by the first Prospectus of Civic Design where *School of Architecture* appears at the top and *Department of Civic Design* below it. Moreover, at the end of the Prospectus, there appears what may be called an advertisement for the School of Architecture.[41]

Once the new department was launched, Reilly could turn his abundant energies to writing about architecture, publishing the *Sketch Books* and generally making the school, and Reilly, better known. During his three months in the United States, Reilly had become greatly attracted by the new American neo-classical buildings, exemplified by the work of Carrere and Hastings, McKim, Mead and White and others. He decided this was the best and only style for buildings of consequence and impressed it on his students for a generation, although in the end his ex-students persuaded him to see merits in what in the 1930s was called Modern Architecture.

Reilly's successor, Lionel Budden, puts Reilly's views differently: 'English Palladian, late Georgian, Neo-Grec, American Beaux-Arts Classic, each of these modes of design in turn fired his imagination and claimed his allegiance.'[42] But in his own book Reilly is firm that from 1909 American work had a great hold upon him. 'I came back loaded with vast prize drawings which I had been given or managed to buy.'[43] As a number of leading American architects up to 1914 had studied at the École des Beaux-Arts in Paris, one may say that the French had a powerful influence on the Liverpool School *via* the roundabout route of Chicago and New York.

Up to 1914 Reilly's students numbered thirty to forty. He had two full-time and some part-time lecturers, and could thus spare time to help to edit the *Builder's Journal*, to design the first part of the Student's Union and to help to launch the Liverpool Repertory Theatre (now the Playhouse). After a trial season, the Old Star Music Hall was bought in 1911, Adshead was made architect for the alterations, and the foyer – made within an old beer hall – proved a great success, with plenty of room for the quality to move about and chat to friends.

Money of course ran short, and Basil Dean, then in almost his first job as a producer, accompanied Reilly to Thornton Manor, and once again Reilly obtained help from Lever, who pledged himself to take £500 worth of shares. Basil Dean tells of a procession of footmen bringing in silver tea things and makes mild fun of Mrs Lever's Lancashire accent. In those pre-BBC days Mrs Lever shared her regional accent with many, including the 17th Earl of Derby, 'the King of Lancashire'; and anyway Basil Dean's memory more than half a century later was not without its faults.[44]

The refurbished theatre had a memorable opening night with the great Lord Derby there both as Lord Mayor of Liverpool and Chancellor of its university, and Adshead's auditorium was coloured in ivory, crimson and gold.[45] The theatre, soon to be called the Playhouse, has played a part in Liverpool's cultural life ever since. Sadly, the Reilly-Dean alliance was broken up within two years, as too culturally ambitious and too unmindful of the granite hardness of theatrical finance in pre-Arts Council – or pre-Greater

London Council – days. Basil Dean departed to his later London triumphs.

When the British School at Rome was about to be established in 1911 – shockingly late in comparison with those of other nations – Reilly was asked to serve on its Faculty of Architecture,[46] and had the pleasure in 1913 of seeing one of his own students, H. Chalton Bradshaw, win the first British Rome Scholarship in Architecture. This triumph probably strengthened his belief in the École des Beaux Arts methods and outlook. Reilly also wrote a great deal for newspapers on architectural subjects and may have begun to feel he was the only proper judge of these matters on Merseyside, and perhaps more widely. At any rate, when Goscombe John, as sculptor, and Norman Shaw, as architect, proposed to place a memorial to King Edward VII at the south end of St George's Hall at Liverpool, Reilly started one more crusade: this time against the proposal, in which he was joined by Adshead. Norman Shaw had been one of Reilly's sponsors for the Chair of Architecture and found this insubordination hard to bear. 'Both of these men (Elmes and Cockerell, architects of St George's Hall) were as much superior to these tin-pot professors and so-called experts as light is superior to darkness. Oh, don't talk to me!'[47] Perhaps his indignation contributed to his death soon afterwards. This may have helped Reilly to win the battle. The statue was eventually placed at Pierhead, the great Liverpool landing place, which, as has been stated, was then as well known to trans-Atlantic travellers as London Airport is today.

During the Great War of 1914–18 Reilly was for most of the time an inspector of munitions. It was then that a company complained that their big shells 'costing fabulous sums were being passed by an architect, who employed a poet (Lascelles Abercrombie) and a painter (Henry Carr) to assist him'.[48] They might have added 'and a landscape architect' as T. H. Mawson also helped Reilly for a period.

Reilly returned to the School of Architecture in 1919, and for the ten years till his retirement devoted his great energies to building up the school in numbers and reputation and – as some saw it – to seeking all forms of publicity for the school, its students and himself.

He succeeded to an extent which most right-thinking academics naturally found distasteful. There were many difficulties, though he had Lionel Budden as his second-in-command.[49] The school had left the Bluecoat Building because of a quarrel between the university and Lever (see p. 39) and was accommodated in part of the former Lock hospital in Ashton Street, which comprised a two-or three-storey central block in gimcrack classical style with single-storey wards on either side. The latter became 'Reilly's cowsheds', first so called in mockery and later with pride. Certainly, Reilly and his staff and students were one more example of the truism that in education it is the staff, students and the spirit of the place that really matter. Few places could have looked more unpromising as the nursery of many distinguished architects and planners. The

Infirmary was just across the street, smoke still belched from the railway cutting and miles of slums and hordes of barefoot children surrounded the potential Christopher Wrens.[49] Reilly of course did his best to change things. In 1922 he wrote quite a sharp letter to Hugh Rathbone then President of the University Council pointing out that Lever had promised £24,000 for a new school in 1910 and that he (Reilly) had designed a new building in 1914, prices had since then greatly increased and, because of the University's quarrel with Lever, it was impossible for Reilly to ask Lever for more money. The school 'with a leading position' was thus housed unworthily. Rathbone replied as all men in such a position tend to reply for five or seven years after a war: no money.

The move to the old hospital from the Bluecoat Building appears to have been caused by Lever's belief that the university had treated Sir Ronald Ross (principal discoverer of the cause of malaria) rather shabbily when he left Liverpool. That there was some such quarrel is certain[50] but Lever never bore lasting resentments, and he and his son honoured his promise to pay for a new School of Architecture, built in 1930–33.

This, however, did not help Reilly in 1919. His first need, in his view, was to obtain the sole use of the old hospital and to justify this a big increase in student numbers was necessary. We may disregard the fable of the Egyptian student, looking for the School of Agriculture, who had a fatherly arm kept around his shoulder till he enrolled in the School of Architecture,[51] but the fifty Australians, all ex-service men with grants, whom he recruited almost in a day, were long regarded as having more substance – as one would expect of Australians.[52] Yet the university records refuse to reveal them, and Derek Bridgwater, later Reilly's son-in-law, who arrived at the school in January 1919, is quite certain that no more than three or four Australian or New Zealand students were there in 1919–22.[53] But Reilly's energies soon produced other ex-servicemen, and among them were Derek Bridgwater, Maxwell Fry, J. H. Forshaw and Wesley Dougill, who all became distinguished in various ways. The *Builder* reported in 1920 that 125 students were taking the full architectural course at the School of Architecture, of whom seventy-six came from outside Liverpool.

Later in 1919 Reilly was in Canada and the USA for six months, partly to secure treatment for his wife's tuberculosis. He then renewed his friendships with prominent American architects and prepared the way for his fourth-year students to spend six months in the best American offices. In all, Reilly visited the USA and sometimes Canada four or five times.

In the 1920s Reilly's students were rigorously drilled in the Classic Orders and in Classical designs. In this he was followed by the Architectural Association School in London (Liverpool's only serious British rival at that time). Reilly had been to Paris a number of times as a student, and with his own students, but he says nothing in his autobiography about direct contacts with the École des Beaux

Arts.[54] He seems to have relied on Beaux-Arts influences *via* the USA:

> *We imbibed the Renaissance as the architecture of*
> *humanism extolled by Geoffrey Scott, but it came*
> *to us monitored by America. Our professor was in*
> *touch with American architects and there were*
> *volumes of the works of the great men of that*
> *period when noble classical buildings were going*
> *up in every state, and New York was celebrating*
> *its wealth in apartment buildings, clubs and*
> *banks in the Renaissance manner, beautifully*
> *produced.*[55]

Reilly's own powers of design are shown in his scheme for Liverpool Cathedral, in his part of the Students' Union and in St Barnabas Mission Church at Dalston in north London (see pp. 51-2,54) by which, he wrote, that he would most like to be remembered as an architect. In the early 1920s he was consultant architect for Devonshire House in Piccadilly and later for Peter Jones's building in Sloane Square, the first 'Modern' department store in Britain.

His views on planning never changed much from 1908. Architects should lead, if not comprise, all planning teams. His views on towns are set out in an article called 'The Soul of Liverpool' in 1923 and in his Roscoe lecture in 1934. In a host of articles, he was one of the many to suggest taxes on increased land values, and that cities should be entitled to buy land needed for improvement and extensions and so take the place of the great ground landlords of the past – the best ones of course. The idea that he should stick to architecture, and allow his more expert colleague to talk and write about town planning, never crossed his mind. To him architecture and planning were just different aspects of the same field, and this view was shared by many of his students who turned from architecture to planning, or practised both without any idea of 'demarcation disputes'.

As has been stated, Reilly was no scholar and his gift as a teacher was to inspire enthusiasm. Every Monday in term-time some one-day design subject was set to the whole school, so that the youngest student could compete with the most experienced. The subjects were exciting, 'A Grand Staircase for a Palace' or 'A Bedroom for a Famous Courtesan'. All the staff no doubt took part in a private staff criticism, but Reilly alone usually gave the criticism before all the students. It was clearly a dramatic and enthralling performance.

Reilly loved competition of all kinds, and the highlights of the school year were the architectural competitions for the Rome Scholarship and its lesser companions such as the Victory Scholarship, the Soane Medallion and the Tite Prize. His students were expected to work hard and the discipline he imposed and the beautiful drawings he demanded would probably not be acceptable today. On the other hand, students and staff relaxed on occasions with a completeness, wit and ingenuity which seemed equally rare today: indeed, they have almost vanished. When Sir Edwin Lutyens, then designing New Delhi, arrived at Liverpool for an honorary degree, he was met by salaaming 'Indians' and his carriage, according to Reilly, was drawn up to theUniversity by architectural students. The annual Architects' Ball at the Bluecoat School was one of the biggest events of the year for the School of Architecture, the architects of Merseyside and anyone else who could obtain a ticket. As the main hall was surrounded by the Sandon Society's rooms and artists' studios, the goings-on were often wild; and the architectural students put on a floor-show in which Reilly quite frequently appeared as an emperor or in some similar such role.[57] The Sandon Studio's Society was to Reilly a privileged extension of the school:

> *Reilly wafted in and out of it as opportunity*
> *allowed, for he was a professor first and a*
> *Bohemian later, and kept too many balls*
> *balancing to devote more than the breathless*
> *moment to a Society that took its ease as this did.*
> *But he approved of my being there and it*
> *established me with him.*[58]

From 1923 to his retirement ten years later Reilly was in peak form, and built up the school's reputation until the majority of architects in practice probably could not think, off-hand, of any other school. One notes however that when the Royal Fine Art Commission was set up in 1924, Reilly was not a member. As there were then six or seven schools of architecture doing good work with less publicity than Reilly's, including, in London, the Architectural Association, the Bartlett and the Royal Academy, the omission at that time of any teacher was perhaps wise. In any case, several people would have tried to veto Reilly.

In his flat in Bedford Street South, Reilly had a smallish dining room with the walls painted with murals by Mary Adshead (Mrs Bone) where life-size figures and a tiger peered out of tropical jungle over the diners' shoulders. They made for conversation.[59] Each student was invited on at least one occasion to tea or dinner, but probably most guests were those whom Reilly wished to recruit for one of his 'schemes':

> *Mrs Reilly was very retiring but had a most happy*
> *disposition and exercised a considerable influence*
> *on all people who knew her, and was very highly*
> *regarded. Her husband did all the talking and was*
> *a much more boisterous and enthusiastic person.*
> *She just kept reasonably quiet in the*
> *background.*[60]

The students who mattered most for this book arrived in the years 1924 to 1926 when new entrants included William Holford,[61] Gordon

Stephenson and Robert Gardner-Medwin. Twenty to twenty-five years later these three became respectively chief planning advisers to the Ministry of Town and Country Planning (as it then was) and – under the divided British system – to its equivalent in Scotland. Oddly, two of the three paid little attention to planning as students, although Patrick Abercrombie was delivering his high-speed lectures in the school and building up an international reputation in nearby rooms. Gardner-Medwin enrolled for the Diploma Course in Civic Design (then open to fifth-year architects) and Holford for the less demanding Certificate Course. Holford thus achieved one of his astonishing feats, this time academically. Officially, he did not complete the course, and yet within six years he became Professor and head of that, by then famous, department, after some private studies in related fields.

Reilly certainly had favourites among his students and these were the ablest or the well-endowed – if possible both. Reilly was proud of two that went to Harrow, then to Oxford where they took good degrees, and *then* came to the Liverpool School to take a full five-year course.[62] But also among his favourites were Maxwell Fry, Bridgwater (his future son-in-law), Holford, Gardner-Medwin and Gordon Stephenson; and the private means of these ranged from *nil* to just enough.

Reilly would stick at little to push his favourites, himself and any Liverpool architectural student or graduate – in that order. Some said he would stick at nothing, and naturally his students loved him for it. A few of the stories of what he would do seem to be fiction or founded on facts still concealed: like that of his hearing, the day before, that the Rome Scholarship was going to the wrong man – presumably a non-Liverpool student; that he used his first-class season ticket to London to travel down overnight, and so charmed or bullied the judges that they changed their award. Fact did not follow very far behind this probable fiction, but in this case Reginald Blomfield was chairman of the adjudicators for the Rome Scholarship, and not even Reilly would have tried to bully him.

In 1930 both Holford and Stephenson were among the finalists for the Rome Scholarship. By a small margin Reilly preferred Holford, who in fact won the competition. But then Reilly cast about for a consolation prize for Gordon Stephenson. The Great Slump of 1930–33 was deepening quickly and causing great hardship to architects, as well as to the majority of the population. Reilly found there was a Chadwick Fellowship for the study of sanitary engineering, and somehow he and Stephenson convinced the principal adjudicator, an Oxford don, that this subject could best be studied in the office of Le Corbusier in Paris – Corbusier then being the darling of all right-minded young architects. So that gave Stephenson the means of living through two of the worst slump years.[63] Reilly also kept a sharp eye on Commonwealth Scholarships to the USA and between 1925 and 1939, the School of Architecture obtained eight, including that of Stephenson (later fourth Lever professor) in 1936.

In such matters Reilly usually got his way. One can see why some of his colleagues hated him. He also commanded the hard work, if not always the whole-time devotion, of his staff. That he gave the school an international reputation for excellence is beyond all doubt.

His Later Life

Reilly wrote articles for a wide variety of journals: the *Manchester Guardian, Liverpool Daily Post, Country Life* and the *Architects' Journal* and even the *Strand* magazine. He said he invented 'play streets' in slums by the closure of them to traffic, and chose the best Liverpool entrance to the first Mersey road tunnel. The latter is denied. He travelled to India with Lutyens in 1927, at Brendan Bracken's expense,[65] to write about New Delhi. To save the Bluecoat Chambers once again he organized the first public showing of Epstein's *Genesis*[66] – a huge statue of a pregnant woman which caused far more controversy then than all the Tate Gallery's purchases in recent years. He says that 50,000 visitors went to look, at sixpence a head.[67]

Reilly joined the Athenaeum Club, became Vice-President of the RIBA, and managed to coax various eminent people to visit the School of Architecture, including: Ramsay Macdonald, Gordon Selfridge, Lady Diana Cooper – then at the peak of her fame and beauty – and Erich Mendelsohn, one of the first of the flood of Jewish architect refugees from Germany.

It is therefore not entirely surprising that Reilly, who had had some heart trouble, felt that he must resign his chair in 1933. The event was celebrated by a dinner in Liverpool presided over by the President of the RIBA. Reilly had become a national institution. And a handsome *Book of the Liverpool School of Architecture* was published by subscription and dedicated to him.[68] His copy was printed on vellum.

After retirement, Reilly seems to have continued his journalism, and all other activities save teaching, as strenuously as ever. In particular, he lobbied for good jobs for his favourite ex-students, and then for any Liverpool man.

There is little doubt that he exercised influence over the appointment of William Holford as third Lever Professor at the age of twenty-nine, and that he persuaded Walter Gropius – perhaps the most famous of Hitler's refugee architects – to write a letter supporting Holford's candidature. It is quite possible that Gropius barely knew Holford's name.

Reilly wrote an annual review of British architecture in the New Year issue of the *Architects' Journal* until his death, and ex-Liverpool architects received the most praise. As has been said, Reilly in retirement had become an institution, and his favouritism was read with smiles, or at worst with amused cries of 'Oh No!' In his broad-brimmed black hat, black cloak and his silver- or ivory-topped ebony stick, he was recognized by all in the profession, and by many others, as he moved between the Athenaeum and the RIBA building in Portland Place. He was naughty as ever, and would sneak into the office of the secretary to the great Sir Ian MacAlister (Secretary of the RIBA and a most powerful influence in the profession in the 1930s), and dictate to this young lady, fresh from Somerville, 'important' letters that needed to be typed at once.[69] It was some time before she enquired into the precise rights of this imposing Mussolini figure.

During the Second World War and immediately afterwards Reilly took a great interest in planning. He prepared a plan for Birkenhead[70] that included 'the Reilly Greens', a layout in which most houses adjoined a miniature village green; and he and N. J. Aslan proposed a Wallasey Tunnel approximately on the route occupied by the Kingsway Tunnel, completed in 1971.

Reilly had disappointments, though probably not a fair share. One of the last was when he received his well-deserved knighthood, some years after his equally deserved Royal Gold Medal. And there was his name CHARLES HERBERT REILLY incised and gilded in the marble of the RIBA entrance hall. But just that: no SIR in front of it like twenty-six of the preceding Royal Gold Medallists. This upset him a lot, but the RIBA was adamant that it would not make any large reshuffle in the most expensive incised names, which followed one another fairly closely in long lines. The problem was solved by finding just enough space for a KT. after Reilly's name.

He worked to the last, and just as he helped others so he expected help. In the Holford papers there are a number of Reilly's letters – not easy to read – in which he asked for help on this or that. There need be no doubt that he got it, as Holford helped so many that one wonders how he found time for his own work, and 'The Prof' would certainly receive priority.

Reilly died in February 1948. He was memorable for many things in the world of architecture and associated arts. Here he is memorable – one hopes for ever – for three actions among his thousands. He had the idea, at just the right moment, of a University School of Town Planning – the first in the world – and thought out how it could be established. He went at once to perhaps the only man who would then have put up the money for so bizarre a venture, and persuaded him to do so.[71] And he was the anonymous member of the University of Liverpool who persuaded Lever (by then Lord Leverhulme) to write in 1915 to the Vice-Chancellor and avert the danger of the Department of Civic Design being closed down.[72] The consequences of these actions are set out in later chapters. They were great and lasting.

NOTES AND REFERENCES

1   E. Maxwell Fry, *Autobiographical Sketches* (Elek, London, 1975) 88.

2   Professor Lionel Budden, 'Charles Reilly An Appreciation' *Journal of the Royal Institute of British Architects* Vol. 55 (March 1948) 212.

3   Emeritus Professor Robert Gardner-Medwin, interview July 1978.

4   L. Budden, *op. cit.*

5   *Architects' Journal* Vol. 107 (12 February 1948) 146.

6   Emeritus Professor Charles H. Reilly, *Scaffolding in the Sky* (George Routledge London 1938). Most of the details of Reilly's early life are based on this autobiography, by permission.

7   C. H. Reilly, *op. cit.* 30.

8   C. H. Reilly, *op. cit.*, 49.

9   C. H. Reilly, *op. cit.*, 57.

10   C. H. Reilly, *op. cit.*, 62.

11   C. H. Reilly, *op. cit.*, 65.

12   See Vere E. Cotton, *The Book of Liverpool Cathedral* (Liverpool University Press 1964) and Professor Frederick M. Simpson, 'The new Cathedral for Liverpool: Its Site and Style' The *Architectural Review* Vol. X (October 1901) 138-146.

13   Carola Oman, *Nelson* (The Reprint Society London 1950) 522.

14   C. H. Reilly, *op. cit.*, 65.

15   *The Times* (17 February 1904) 7. 'At a meeting of the University Council today, Mr. C. H. Reilly was appointed to the Roscoe Chair of Architecture, vacant through Professor Simpson's resignation. Mr. Reilly was a scholar of Queens' College, Cambridge, and in 1896 was placed in the first class of the Mechanical Sciences Tripos. After leaving Cambridge he received practical training under his father, and in the office of Mr. John Belcher, A.R.A. Since then he has been in practice for three years. In the competition for Liverpool Cathedral the

assessors accorded his design honourable mention. Mr. Reilly has lectured for the past three years at Kings' College London.'

16   Emeritus Professors Robert Gardner-Medwin and Gordon Stephenson. Interviews July and June 1978 respectively.

17   The author of this book was appointed fifth Lever professor in 1954 when working as an architect and town planner at Cambridge.

18   Roderick F. Bisson, *The Sandon Studios Society and the Arts* (Parry Books Ltd, Liverpool, 1955) 17.

19   See p. 17.

20   C. H. Reilly, *op. cit.*, 93.

21   His income from his professorship rose from £671 in 1904-05 to £882 in 1909-10, (*Univ. Archives*).

22   Portfolio of Measured Drawings (Liverpool University Press 1905) price 12/6d, (*Univ. Archives*).

23   Measured buildings chosen for the 1910 *Sketch Book* included St George's Hall in Liverpool, the Custom House at Dublin, the Fellows' Building at Kings' College Cambridge, and St Mary-le-Strand in London. Reilly's own design for a public building is published as a frontispiece, in full Corinthian classic with an attic storey supported by chesty caryatids. Studies of the orders lean towards severe Greek Doric. 'Faith is needed,' says Reilly in the introduction, 'and it does not matter whether it is based on Gothic sentiment, Byzantine cleverness, or Greek purity of form.' *Liverpool Architectural Sketch Book* (published by the Proprietors of the *Architectural Review*, 1910) price unstated.

24   Most of the reasons in the note are valid seventy-five years later. A professor of architecture must practise, Reilly said, or he cannot be an efficient teacher. A building designed by him would be the best possible workshop for his students. If the professor is passed over, it implies that the Council do not think he compares favourably with other local architects. If this were true he is not a fit person to hold his chair.
Reilly also offered to get over the difficult point of 'double pay' by devoting an agreed proportion of the fees to a scholarship for his own students - so benefiting his own students and avoiding any charge of undercutting that might be made by other architects. In due course, Reilly was to be architect of the first part of the Students' Union building.
Letter from Reilly to Vice-Chancellor Dale 25 February 1906, (*Univ. Archives*).

25   Public Appeal. Drafted by C. H. Reilly and Lascelles Abercrombie, May 1908, (*Univ. Archives*).

26   Lever was excusably annoyed later on to find that Reilly was letting

off bits of the building which the university did not want, seemingly to the artists already mentioned. Whether he paid the rents to the university or to the School of Architecture funds is not clear. Thereafter the rents went to Lever.
Letter apparently from Reilly to Hugh Rathbone 21 August 1914, (*Univ. Archives*).

27 John S. Nettlefold, *Practical Housing* (Garden City Press Ltd. 1908). Chapter VII contains information on planning powers in other countries.

28 The architects in European and other countries also appear to have held a monopoly of planning posts for many years. In the early 1960s, Constantinos Doxiadis, a planner who practised all over the world, told the author that he could not recall offhand a planner in an important post anywhere who had not been originally trained as an architect.

29 C. H. Reilly, *op. cit.*, 125 *et seq.*

30 *Hansard*, 12 May 1908, Cole 947 onwards.

31 C. H. Reilly, *op. cit.*, 126.

32 The other was to build up a School of Architecture so famous that it would attract students from many countries. And in due course it was so, or at least students came from most English-speaking countries.

33 Letter from Lever to Reilly 18 November 1910, (*Univ. Archives*).

34 The Royal Institute of British Architects, *Town Planning Conference: London 10-15 October 1910. Transactions* (RIBA, London, 1911).

35 They were self-taught as town planners, as was then common and indeed unavoidable. Sir Raymond Unwin began his life as a mining engineer influenced by William Morris, and became in the end President of the RIBA and Royal Gold Medallist.

36 C. H. Reilly, *op. cit.*, 123-24; and also designs for Brownlow Hill in the *Town Planning Review* Vol. III (1912) 80.

37 Not even of E. A. Rickards, an equally able draughtsman, and as short as Adshead was tall. But probably, in 1908-09, Rickards was far too busy producing wonderful neo-Baroque designs for his firm of Lanchester and Rickards to consider any move, even if he had been asked.

38 Of the position in 1909 Blomfield later wrote, 'It is only fair to say that Professor Reilly and Adshead, who were in charge of the Liverpool school, were making strenuous efforts to rescue architectural training from the dull routine of training current at the time.' Sir Reginald Blomfield, *Memoirs of an Architect* (Macmillan & Co., London, 1932) 126.

39 Reilly says he travelled for three months for £80 and that Lever said he had never sent a traveller so far so cheaply (C. H. Reilly, *op. cit.*, 128). One hopes that the traditional and most generous American hospitality to visitors was not overstrained.

40 It is impossible to be quite certain that Civic Design at Liverpool was the first university department to devote itself entirely to town planning and related subjects, but, to say the least, it is highly probable. The *Town Planning Review* (1910) soon attracted subscribers in foreign countries, and a special issue was published in 1959 to celebrate the department's jubilee. No rival claims to priority have been made. In the École des Beaux-Arts in Paris young architects had been preparing grand layouts for grand buildings for the previous hundred years, but there was no research or detailed study of town planning in any wider sense.

41 This fraternal custom continued until 1971, when it became very difficult to continue to believe that prospective architectural students, aged sixteen to eighteen, would be guided to the school by a prospectus for a town planning department aimed at graduates – 90 per cent of them non-architects – aged between twenty-one and twenty-seven.

42 L. Budden, *op. cit.*

43 C. H. Reilly, *op. cit.*, 123.

44 He says that (in early 1911) he met 'the present Lord Holford then working with Reilly on the Prix de Rome' (Basil Dean, *The Seven Ages of Man*, Hutchinson, London, 1970, 83). The later Lord Holford was then in a house near Johannesburg, aged three and a half. (For Lord Derby's accent see Randolph S. Churchill, *Lord Derby: King of Lancashire*, Heinemann, London, 1959, 129, 148).

45 Grace Wyndham Goldie, *The Liverpool Repertory Theatre 1911–1934* (Liverpool University Press and Hodder & Stoughton London 1935) 62.

46 The Faculty of Architecture put a strong team of judges into the field. They included (Sir) Reginald Blomfield, W. R. Lethaby, (Sir) Robert Lorimer, (Sir) Edwin Lutyens, Ernest Newton, Reilly, Simpson (Reilly's predecessor at Liverpool), Leonard Stokes and Sir Aston Webb. When one thinks of the widely opposed architectural views of these men it is a wonder they ever agreed about anything.

47 Andrew Saint, *Richard Norman Shaw* (Yale University Press 1976) 395.

48 C. H. Reilly, *op. cit.*, 192.
    Reilly obtained his wartime job on the strength of his degree in Mechanical Sciences at Cambridge. It may also be that Reilly's heart trouble, which eventually caused his early retirement, was already perceptible, as he was never one to stand back if there was fighting to be done, although he was forty-two in 1916 when the real manpower shortage began to be felt. His son says it was mainly Reilly's defect of hammer toes that led to his rejection for active service.

49 Lionel Budden had kept the school going somehow during the war; and he told the author in 1956 that he loved administration and really did it pretty well. He did.

50 Reilly writes that there was an annual deposit of 600 tons of 'aerial sewage' in one district of Liverpool. (C. H. Reilly, *op. cit.*, 33.) And despite the efforts of Sir Lancelot Keay and his housing staff things had not changed so very much by 1956, when a Scandinavian student of civic design returned from his first walk in Liverpool and, indignant and shaken, told his professor that nowhere in Scandinavia did such slums exist; and implied that the Department had been wasting its time for half a century.

51 The university held that it must refuse 'the endowment of a Professor going elsewhere to better himself' as this would have led to other similar claims. There is a strong possibility that the professor concerned was Sir Ronald Ross. (Letters between Reilly and Hugh Rathbone 17 - 27 January 1922, *Univ. Archives*).

52 There is a large and well-known group of Veterinary Departments at Liverpool which run a big field station and a farm, but no Department of Agriculture.

53 C. H. Reilly, *op. cit.*, 204.

54 Derek Bridgwater, interviewed in April 1978, had a clear memory of his early days at the School of Architecture and drew correct diagrams of its layout including 'the cowsheds'.

55 Recently the work of the École des Beaux Arts has been splendidly described and illustrated by Arthur Drexler and others in *The Architecture of the École des Beaux Arts*. (Secker and Warburg, London, 1977).

56 M. Fry, *op. cit.*, 94.

57 Gordon Stephenson and others.

58 M. Fry, *op. cit.*, 94.

59 Most of these murals now hang in the Department of Civic Design as a memorial both to Reilly's suggestion that such a department should be created and to Adshead, the first professor.

60 Derek Bridgwater, *op. cit.*

61 There is an often repeated story that Holford with a portfolio of drawings and his mother visited Reilly about a year before he entered the school; and Reilly soon exclaimed 'If this young man comes to me he will win the Rome Scholarship within six years!' Neither Reilly nor Holford took much trouble to deny the story, which should be true, but isn't. Holford's first passport shows he came to Britain just before term began in October 1925.

62   C. H. Reilly, *op. cit.*, 234–35. One of the two, Anthony Minoprio, became a Rome Scholar.

63   G. Stephenson, interviews and correspondence 1978.

64   D. Bridgwater, *op. cit.*

65   Brendan Bracken's red hair, character and drive reminded Reilly of Lever (C. H. Reilly *op. cit.*, 266).

66   C. H. Reilly, *op. cit.*, 242–43.

   Reilly's powers of advertisement for any cause dear to him became nationally known. When in 1934 Sir Edwin Lutyens received an Honorary degree at Oxford, the students sang a song, to the tune of Good King Wenceslas, which ended:

   > *At Delhi in the mystic East Sir Edwin's star is rising,*
   > *And Jumna's plain is fair again with forms of his devising.*
   > *So don't be nervous, little Lut, and do not stand so shyly;*
   > *A gorgeous figure you will cut, when advertised by Reilly.*

   Christopher Hussey in *The Life of Sir Edwin Lutyens* (Country Life Ltd London 1950) 543, says this took place at Oxford; it is far more likely that it happened in Liverpool when Lutyens received an honorary degree in 1928.

67   C. H. Reilly, *op. cit.*, 249.

68   Lionel Budden (ed), *The Book of the Liverpool School of Architecture* (Liverpool University Press and Hodder & Stoughton, London, 1932).

69   From Mrs Sheila Morgan, the lady in question.

70   Professor Sir Charles Reilly and N. J. Aslan, *Outline Plan for the County Borough of Birkenhead* (County Borough of Birkenhead, 1947).

71   As stated earlier, most rich men who give money for academic purposes are very conventional in their choice. As the architect Frank Lloyd Wright wrote: 'There's nothing so timid as a million dollars.'

72   Letter from Lord Leverhulme to the Vice-Chancellor, May 1915 (*Univ. Archives*).

4

THE FIRST PROFESSOR

Stanley Adshead: 1868 - 1946

Stanley Davenport Adshead was appointed head of the new
Department of Civic Design in March 1909,[1] was called Associate
Professor in his Inaugural lecture in the autumn, and became the
first Lever professor - in full title as it were - in 1912.

In his prospectus for the new department's first academic year,
1909-10,[2] Adshead claimed that it was the first organization of its
kind - a claim that has never been disputed. It 'owed its inception to
the very evident demand which exists for a system of training in the
broader aspects of Architecture and Engineering'. This was the
subject matter of civic design, and indeed of town planning as
Adshead and Reilly then saw it. Reilly never changed his views, (see
letter to Holford in 1935 on hearing that Holford was to be the third
Lever professor. pp. 171-2) and perhaps Adshead always thought that
the central content of his subject was, or ought to be, the layout and
grouping of rather grand buildings. But he soon came to realize that
the profession of town planning required some knowledge of
demography, geography, economics, landscape on the regional
scale and, of course, town planning law and administration. He
learnt about these things quickly.[3]

Adshead, as first Lever professor, is central to this story but he
cannot be coaxed into being the dominant character, despite his
great talents as a draughtsman, considerable talents as an architect
and being an industrious student of a new subject. He was at
Liverpool for only five years, and full Lever professor only from 1912
to 1914. His short period at Liverpool and the novelty of town
planning as a subject of study meant that he had never more than
ten students. Yet he started it all, and he was followed to University
College London, where he was Professor of Town Planning till 1935,
by the second and third Lever professors, and so began a sequence of
events that ensured that most of the senior men in British and
Commonwealth town planning from 1940 to 1965 (the great
planning period) were Lever professors, or their former students or
close colleagues. To these results of the founding of the Lever Chair
we shall return more than once. They are, after all, the justification
for this book.

It seems fair to call Adshead unlucky. He was an impressive figure
- about 6 feet 4 inches in height and well built - and under a
benevolent manner could show firmness of mind on suitable
occasions. He has been called charming, a man of simplicity, and a
little shy,[4] and less is known about him than about Lever, Reilly,
Abercrombie and Holford. The first two of these were famous for

reasons other than town planning (though both in different ways were town planners) and the last two became internationally and widely known as town planners when it was too late for Adshead. Shyness and simplicity are not the qualities that come to mind in thinking of any of the other four, nor do they help much to ensure publicity and a generous share of the biggest jobs.[5] Moreover, it is often a decisive advantage for a professional man (or any man who achieves greatness) to be born at the right time. Real, widely publicized planning and plans – supported by vast public interest – only began in Britain as the bombs fell in 1940–1. Adshead was then seventy-three, Abercrombie sixty-two, and Holford a mere thirty-five. Adshead, filled with visions of cities beautiful in 1909, had had to plough through twenty-five years of 'advisory' planning, trying to make some use of ineffective, infinitely boring legislation; and he produced helpful reports ... then it was too late.

He was unlucky, but an impressive and lovable person to those who knew him well, and admired by his students. He was a worthy first professor.

Early Life

Adshead was born at Bowden in Cheshire in 1868.[6] His mother was born Eliza Davies of Bramhall and his father was Joseph Adshead, an artist and a member of the Manchester Academy. Joseph Adshead had been left about £500 a year by his father, a land surveyor and estate agent, who was responsible for, among other works, the layout of Victoria Park in Manchester. Such 'independent means' meant in the 1870s reasonable comfort for a family if prudently managed; and prudence came to be needed, as Stanley Adshead was the second child and eldest son of eight children – four sons and four daughters. Until Adshead was sixteen, the family lived in Buxton, where he attended the local grammar school. The family then moved to Manchester, where he attended the Manchester, School of Art for a year and then was articled to an architect with a dull office mainly concerned with churches.[7] He then moved to Salomon and Levi, also a Manchester firm of architects, where he learnt much from Salomon, an accomplished watercolour artist and a friend of Lord Leighton.

In 1890, aged twenty-two, Adshead moved to London and worked in several offices, among them those of John Belcher, Ernest George, Guy Dawber and William Flockhart. Other firms are mentioned now and then (Sherrin, Ince and Gibson). It is probable that Adshead was only a genuine assistant to a few of these, and that his work for the others was in preparing perspective drawings of intended buildings. He began this kind of work – presumably in his spare time – as soon as he arrived in London, and quickly built up a great reputation. As his father was an artist, Adshead was probably encouraged to sketch and paint at a very early age, and talent as a painter clearly runs in the family.[8] Adshead concentrated his talents in his twenties on portraying buildings and groups of buildings, and his only rival as a draughtsman at that time was E. A. Rickards, a busy partner in the firm of Lanchester and Rickards.[9]

A special feature of Adshead's drawings was that he did not first set up his perspectives mechanically (or have this done for him) as has been the custom of nearly all his many successors. He made freehand sketches from the architects' drawings and worked these up with minimum aid from instruments, until he felt ready for the final pen and ink or colour. Whether this method enabled him to work more quickly is open to argument, but remarkable powers of visual imagination must have been necessary to build up from plans and sections what the architect hoped or intended his building would look like when completed.

Adshead's reputation grew so quickly that he (as well as Reilly) states that he prepared perspectives for five out of six competitors for the new Central Criminal Courts (the Old Bailey) in 1896; and that twenty of his drawings were on exhibition at one Royal Academy Summer Exhibition. If these were all drawings of buildings, and the Architecture Room was then as small as it is now, Adshead's drawings must have dominated several walls. His reputation at the turn of the century was very high, as it continued to be until the first world war. In the competition in 1912 for the Victoria Memorial in front of Buckingham Palace, Adshead is credited with up to fifteen sketches for different architects.) Reilly writes:

> Adshead's views of other people's buildings were
> not just literal statements of planes ... but had an
> atmosphere and life of their own comparable at
> their best with the work of the great Dutch
> draughtsmen.[10]

In 1895[11] Adshead won the competition for a new town hall at Taunton, his first competition, but the scheme did not go forward. The next year according to one account he set up in practice for himself in Bedford Row, no doubt supported largely by his perpective drawings. He also won further competitions, including two at Ramsgate which led to his being asked to design the Ramsgate Pavilion (1903–04). In 1902 he moved his office to 46 Great Russell Street, and occupied the same rooms for almost forty years.

According to Kineton Parkes, writing about Adshead (probably after an interview with him) in the *Architects Journal* in 1927,[12] Adshead's independent practice began in 1900 and this seems more probable than 1896, as Adshead said that of his four years with Flockhart three were spent superintending the building of Rosenaugh, a tremendous mansion about ten miles from Inverness. This work may not have been full-time and these three years may have been 1896–99, so leaving Adshead six years for his experience as an assistant with the six other firms mentioned.

The mansion near Inverness had rooms decorated and furnished in different styles, and Adshead's job included going round London

sale-rooms to buy suitable period furniture. 'Adshead bought all the
accessories regardless of cost from dealers in London and this
increased his knowledge of interior decoration.'[13] In his cottage at
Rosenaugh, quiet periods would have allowed him to finish off
perspective drawings which he had brought up with him from
London.

His time near Inverness was however not wholly occupied with
work. Annie Blackie, a Scottish farmer's daughter, worked as a
school teacher on the Black Isle near Rosenaugh. They met, and
Adshead and she eventually decided to marry; by 1902 they had
moved into a small flat above the office in Great Russell Street,
where their daughter and only child Mary was born in 1904.

The period from 1902 to 1909 is not well documented professionally. Adshead went in for several competitions, obtained a first
prize for a Carnegie Library at Hawick, a second prize for
Pontypridd town hall, and his success at Ramsgate led to additional
work there. The preparation of perspective drawings for other
architects doubtless continued.[14]

Reilly first saw Adshead when the latter came to Belcher's office
about a perspective drawing. Reilly and Adshead also met socially:

> ... little Rickards arrived with a tall, gaunt young
> man, well over six feet, who said very little, but
> when he did reduced even Rickard's volubility to
> silence. He, who never listened to anyone, always
> listened to Adshead. His was the deciding word,
> the penetrating judgement.[15]

Some of Adshead's drawings were for the Liverpool Cathedral
Competition of 1901–03 for which he prepared perspectives for Reilly
and probably for others, as there were 102 competitors in the
first round. No doubt the drawings of Reilly's entry, which was
commended, strengthened the Reilly-Adshead acquaintance into
friendship and ensured that Adshead would be a possible candidate
for the Lever Chair when Reilly suggested it to Lever and received his
approval.

In 1904 Adshead enlisted as a studio instructor in the evenings at
the architectural school at King's College in the Strand, but his own
practice compelled him to resign after a year. In 1910 his fame was
such that he travelled to America to prepare some perspectives for an
architect in New York. He also visited relatives in Canada.

Adshead at Liverpool

The next big event in Adshead's life, and of course the greatest for
this story, was his appointment as head of the Department of Civic
Design at Liverpool University and eventually as the first Lever
professor. As described in the previous chapter, Reilly said he was
seized with the idea when he read the Rt Hon. John Burns's speech in
introducing a Housing and Town Planning Bill in May 1908. Burns
had not mentioned architecture at all.

Reilly, and indeed Adshead, must have known that the new
subject of study and source of probable jobs for the land-using
professions – first called 'town planning' in 1906 – was being as
much discussed as energy saving and law and order are now, and
that architects, surveyors and engineers (civil and municipal) all
hoped to obtain a share of the coming work. They may also have felt
that architects were dilatory in staking a claim. The great men of the
RIBA were then either building country houses or concerned with
the largest public and commercial buildings. They may well have
thought that town planning was either a matter for cranks in the
Garden Cities movement or a slightly low-class municipal matter. In
any case, they thought there was little money in it; and in this at
least they have been proved entirely correct, save for a few of the
very biggest offices in the boom period of 1960-75.

We do not know all that Reilly did in the autumn of 1908 to find the
man who, in his view, would be the right professor for the new
subject. But it is quite probable that he thought of no one save
Adshead, for the reasons given in the previous chapter (see p.58).
Reilly seems to have gone to London in the autumn of 1908 to
persuade Adshead to apply for the post of head of a Department of
Civic Design at Liverpool, if Reilly could persuade his Faculty to
establish one.

Adshead wrote to Reilly on 11 January 1909[16] and agreed with him
about the close connection between town planning and architecture.
He had become enthusiastic about the project:

> In the first place I may say that I regard a School
> of Town Planning as one in which its curriculum
> would embrace rather than be a branch of a
> School of Architecture. It is impossible to consider
> Town Planning without reference to Architecture
> but Architecture does not necessarily cognate
> Town Planning.
>
> ... Whoever may be entrusted with the organizing
> and carrying on of this new departure should be in
> the first place be an architect in the best sense of the
> word.
> His outlook must be a broad one, he must have order
> and system in his methods of design. His work must
> not be an expression of fads and fancies. It must be
> scholarly and academic ... not [of] a pedant ... not
> live entirely in the past. He must be abreast of the
> times and alive to the possibilities of the future.

Adshead goes on to say that the school should draw its students from
fully qualified architects:

> ... if well conducted it should draw from all over
> the country and the colonies ... a session at a
> school of Town Planning may in the near future

> *come to be considered a necessary completion to*
> *the education of any architect.*[17]

He then turns to the studies that should be the concern of the new department and discloses his principal interests and enthusiasms up to that time; and their limitations. The first three studies he suggested should be: architectural composition, architectural character, and colour. These were explained as 'the massing of buildings, the skyline, vistas, regularity and irregularity, and the choice of suitable, preferably local, materials'. Whether or not Reilly liked the idea of town planning embracing architecture, most of Adshead's suggestions were incorporated in the curriculum.

Things moved quickly. On 22 February 1909 the Faculty of Arts recommended[18] that a Department of Civic Design should be established with both day and evening courses in the first two terms of each session (i.e. October to the end of March). There were to be lectures and studio work concentrated on two main fields: engineering surveying and layout; and the architectural treatment of sites and areas. The co-operation of the City Engineer of Liverpool, the formidable J. A. Brodie would, it was said, be invaluable.

The professor was to be appointed for three years (no doubt this was a precaution in case the new department failed, but it may well have been agreeable to Adshead) at £400 a year and one third of students' fees, and he was to be resident for half the year. The professor was (as always) to conduct and direct research into problems of the design and development of towns and to publish the results of the research. There was £100 provided for a lectureship, £150 for a research fellowship for travel and research. £100 was to be kept in reserve for publication.

These proposals were approved and in March[19] Adshead submitted an application for the new chair, a *curriculum vitae*, and letters of support from Reginald Blomfield, Ernest George and H. V. Lanchester. None of these busy practitioners had time for that careful balancing of experience and virtues, and at the end, a few cautiously indicated defects, which are expected of and almost invariably supplied by the modern referee for an academic post. Ernest George and Lanchester each sent fifty to seventy-five words of testimonial, which were probably quite as influential as the modern references. Blomfield, MA, ARA, Professor of Architecture at the Royal Academy and on his way to becoming the fierce Sir Reginald of the 1930s, sent a short typewritten letter. This shows signs of hurry and a decided dislike of landscape architects, with some of whom he was having a feud. The man appointed 'should be free of all taint of the landscape gardener ... what is wanted is monumental design in the grand manner which is quite another affair'.[20] [21]

The spelling mistakes in Blomfield's letter may be safely attributed to the person then called a 'typewriter' and to Blomfield's careless reading, but one may also imagine that some of the selection committee raised their eyebrows at the three references and expressed the hope (perhaps in Reilly's absence) that this latest Reilly notion and candidate would not lead the university into real trouble. Reilly himself, of course, writes that all went well:

> Adshead came down, and Mackay and everyone
> liked the frank, honest way in which he expressed
> his views and enjoyed his sense of fun and
> humour. Lord Leverhulme liked him and was glad
> to find he came originally from Lancashire. It was
> decided that he and I should divide the world
> between us at his lordship's expense. Adshead was
> to travel through Europe collecting information as
> to what was being done in town planning in
> Germany, Austria and elsewhere and I was to go
> to the Eastern States of America and do the
> same.[22]

Adshead was certainly a man whose great height and simple dignity were impressive.[23]

In recommending the appointment of Adshead as head of the new department, the Committee stated that they had wished in seeking a suitable candidate to confine their enquiries to British candidates, because of the necessity for the chosen man to have intimate knowledge of the social and economic conditions in Britain. This is an interesting statement, and one wonders why it was put in. Perhaps some member of the Committee had suggested appointing a German, as the Germans had had various types of town planning in operation since 1875; or an American, where the City Beautiful movement was in full swing and landscaping was taking place on a far greater scale than in Britain. Adshead however only had 'intimate knowledge' of British social and economic conditions in that he had grown up here, whereas Patrick Geddes had been studying these subjects, among all else that can influence towns and regions since at least 1892,[24] although Committee members might not have known this. Whatever the reason behind the paragraph, one suspects that Reilly had a hand in its insertion.

The local paper gave Adshead a good start:

> Mr Adshead is a young man full of energy and
> enthusiasm, an architect of experience and an
> artist of great executive ability. I confidently
> anticipate that under him the Department will
> obtain a great reputation, and that Liverpool will
> become the centre of these studies in this
> country'.[25]

According to Reilly, he and Adshead did tour the USA and Europe in the spring and summer of 1909, as stated in the passage by Reilly just quoted. One notes, however, that in February 1909 the Faculty had set aside £500 for such a purpose, the details to be decided when the new professor was appointed.

Reilly did travel to the United States in the Easter vacation of 1909. The curious thing about Adshead's corresponding trip to Europe is that there is no record of it or of the use of the £500. There is however strong evidence that he did go, and probably did so by joining the National Housing Reform Council's first study tour of housing and planning powers and achievements on the Continent. This took place in 1909.[26] Joining the tour would have got over difficulties of language and introductions, and enabled him to meet Patrick Geddes and various other people of experience in what was to be his new field of study. According to his daughter, it was on this tour also that he first met Sir Walter Peacock, then in charge of the Duchy of Cornwall estates, and this led in time to Adshead's best known commission in civic design and architecture. As regards a report on his journey, Adshead must have been a very busy man in the summer of 1909, too busy to put his notes and sketches in order; and as a new boy, he may not have known that it was customary to submit a short report to the Faculty as Reilly did.

In June 1909 another important event occurred. It was agreed that Patrick Abercrombie, then aged thirty, should give most of his time to the Research Fellowship in Civic Design, which in practice was to mean editing the *Town Planning Review*, as well as collecting or writing much of its contents, and to give ten lectures each session. He too was going to be very busy; and one may say that the professional education of the greatest town and regional planner of the twentieth century began in June 1909.

The prospectus of the new department was ready by the autumn of 1909.[2] On page 1, Adshead states, as already mentioned, that the department 'owed its inception to the very evident demand which exists for a system of training in the broader aspects of Architecture and Engineering ... (and that) Town Planning is a distinct and separate subject in its own right'. The prospectus then gives Adshead's views about the desirable contents of the course and states that students should have already obtained some proficiency either as architects or engineers. There was to be both a Certificate and a Diploma 'and considering that in the near future some thousands of town plans will be required ... positions will undoubtedly be created, and should fall by preference to those holding ... the Certificate or Diploma'. The lecture courses included the outlines of town planning, civic engineering and hygiene, civic architecture and decoration, civic law, and landscape design. Studio work was to be guided by Adshead and Abercrombie, and was to take place from 9.30 to 4.30 and again from 6.00 to 9.30 pm. The work included instruction on draughtsmanship and (as one would expect from one of the best architectural draughtsmen of his age) in drawing perspective views of buildings and groups of buildings, 'draughtsmanship in its higher branches', preparation of layouts for suburban areas and the reconstruction of existing areas that needed improvement.[2] If large numbers of students had been attracted at once the labours of Adshead and Abercrombie would have been hard indeed. Fortunately, numbers grew slowly from six in the first year to nine in 1912.[27]

The three part-time lecturers whom Adshead recruited from associated professions outside the university were all men of distinction. Indeed, with the exception of J. J. Clarke in later years, it is doubtful if any outside lecturers in the department have known their business better. They all probably regarded it as their duty to help a worthy venture in its early years, even at some inconvenience to themselves. And since they were the first, and were all of regional or national reputation, each deserves a brief note.

The Part-time Lecturers: H. Chaloner Dowdall: 1868-1955

H. Chaloner Dowdall, a barrister who lectured in the new department on civic law, was Lord Mayor of Liverpool in the year of Civic Design's foundation[28] and so occupied one of the four or five greatest positions in local government at that time. He was a friend of Augustus John and commissioned him to paint the mayoral portrait. According to John, he stayed with the Dowdalls in Sefton Park and drove each morning to the Town Hall in a coach and pair, and there the sittings were held with the Lord Mayor and his attendant in full regalia. After the sittings John used to slink off, and return often very late and by devious routes to the mayoral mansion. Despite the fact that 'the *Rani* [Mrs Dowdall] was the most engaging character in Liverpool', his host's efforts to get Augustus John to return earlier and by more respectable routes did not work.[29]

The completed picture caused much uproar in the press and among more conservative councillors. Dowdall rather liked it and paid John an extra fee. The portrait travelled away from Liverpool and, despite later attempts to retrieve it, is now in the Melbourne Art Gallery.[30] Lord Mayor Dowdall's wife was a daughter of Lord Borthwick and found the great ladies of Liverpool rather stuffy. She liked to give them small shocks such as riding on the steps of a caravan down Bold Street (the local street of high fashion) without shoes or stockings followed by Augustus John and her husband on horseback. It must have been a picturesque little group, as Augustus John was then a splendid bearded man prone to fisherman's jerseys and gold earrings, and Dowdall was tall enough. Later Mrs Dowdall published a book – awaited with small shivers among the mansions of Mossley Hill – called *The Book of Martha*, which went through two impressions in three months.[31] To the relief of the dowagers of Liverpool it turned out to contain essays on cooks, housemaids, doctors and relations-in-law.

John Brodie: 1858-1934

The second recruit was John A. Brodie, City Engineer of Liverpool from 1898 to 1926, and as a photograph of him suggests, he ruled his considerable portion of Liverpool's mechanism without allowing any nonsense. Even the Faculty of Arts, in recommending the establishment of the Department of Civic Design, had noted that close co-operation with the City Engineer was essential.

Brodie made several proposals for improving Liverpool's roads, and was the author of the scheme for Queen's Drive, a peripheral road now completed. He was a member of the committee which went out to India to advise the Government of India about the new capital at Delhi.[32] A fellow member was Edwin Lutyens, to whose sometimes sharp wit Brodie fell victim. Lutyens described Brodie, in a letter,[33] as 'a great apple-shaped man, full of drains'. Brodie went on to become President of the Civil Engineers and the Municipal and County Engineers. In 1910 he was fifty-two, and an Honorary Professor in the university. Together with two Civil engineering colleagues, he lectured on road design, traffic, sanitation, city hygiene and distribution of population and housing.

Thomas Mawson: 1861-1933

The third external lecturer in the new department, and the most distinguished, was Thomas H. Mawson, then forty-nine and near the peak of his career as a landscape architect of international reputation.

Mawson's achievements have some resemblance to those of Joseph Paxton sixty years before him. He had had a hard youth as apprentice to firms of nurserymen – among the many that sprang up in the nineteenth century to supply the huge demand for plant material of all kinds from the newly rich, the old rich and indeed from nearly all who had acquired a garden, a greenhouse and £500 a year or more. Mawson was blessed with inexhaustible energy, and he self-improved in a way that excelled Samuel Smiles and equalled Lever. He says in his autobiography[34] that he was always determined to be a landscape architect and from his headquarters at Lancaster he built up a great practice, further helped by a book[35] that was confined to his own works. Seventy years later it is just a little difficult to account for Mawson's great reputation. His was the biggest practice in landscape architecture and he might be said to have had 'a monopoly', in the American sense of having a very large share of the market. The achievements of Edwin Lutyens and Gertrude Jekyll were then little known. Mawson's landscape practice, supported by his energy and his great knowledge of plant material, must have been the main attraction for his rich clients. He was not distinguished in appearance and his style of writing resembles now and then that in a nursery gardener's catalogue. His landscape designs as illustrated in his books were (like Reginald Blomfield's) formal, rigid and unimaginative. He detested the informal landscapes and gardens that had become customary in Britain in the eighteenth and earlier nineteenth centuries. He was a great man for terraces, balustrades, flights of steps, axial lines, squares and avenues. His somewhat 'romantic' layouts of winding paths and bridges on Highland estates give the impression that he disliked this side of his work, although some of the photographs in his book had been taken too soon after completion of the work, a common error in illustrations of landscape design schemes. Ten years later, appearances would probably have been much improved.

Mawson must, one feels, have had – like Lloyd George – an ability to charm that has vanished with him. At any rate, he suited his clients, who were many and distinguished and included the Prime Minister of Canada, the King of Greece and, of course, Lever. He had introduced himself to Lever in 1905 by asking for a contribution towards the completion of some panels in a Nonconformist church. Lever made a contribution and asked Mawson to come to Thornton Manor to help with the design of the gardens there – as related earlier. Mawson describes his arrival thus:

> *My client had already initiated alterations*
> *reminiscent of the best work of the past. All this I*
> *took in at a sweep as I passed through the house*
> *to meet Mr Lever, who was among his pictures in*
> *his palatial music room. I was received with a*
> *smile and a hearty handshake which put me at*
> *my ease at once.*[36]

Mawson says he was consulted about the establishment of the Department of Civic Design, but he had had to confine himself to lectures. Secretly, Mawson certainly thought that town planning should be subordinate to landscape design in the broadest sense. He had been much impressed with the powerful position of landscape architects in the United States, where town planning was almost unknown, and he himself produced plans for Regina and Coal Harbour (Vancouver) and eventually Athens. His big ambition was to found a great school of landscape design at Oxford or Cambridge. He writes of town planning and civic design:

> *The latter differs somewhat from the former in*
> *that it gives freer play to the imagination and the*
> *aesthetic perception, but it is not by any means*
> *divorced from its practical partner. Civic design*
> *would encourage the solution of idealism in the*
> *configuration and the planning of towns. Much as*
> *the Paris Beaux-Arts encourages ideal*
> *monumental architecture, yet by no means*
> *ignoring the practical part.*[37]

Mawson lectured on alternate Fridays, doubtless coming down from his Lancaster headquarters. His course:

> *will treat of the arrangement, construction and*
> *planning of parks, parkways, boulevards and open*
> *spaces with special reference to the kind of trees,*
> *shrubs and plants best suited to particular*
> *localities. It will discuss their culture and the art*
> *of pleaching, pollarding and plashing.*[2]

Mawson's energy, or power of attracting and organizing assistant authors, seems to have been immense. No sooner had he settled into his civic design lectures than he published *Civic Art*.[38] This may have been based partly on his lectures at Liverpool and have been a kind of counter-attack for his failing to incorporate civic design into his great school of landscape design. At any rate, the book was dedicated to the Rt Hon. John Burns, the politician in charge of what town planning then existed, and stated that 'Civic Art must embrace town planning ... and all factors ... that bear upon it'.[39] Both Mawson's sons studied for a period at the *École des Beaux-Arts*, so his admiration for the formal and monumental received no known challenge from the next generation in the family firm.

Mawson's clients must have been very tolerant men, as he travelled so widely in those pre-air-travel days, that he can have given little of his own time to his schemes for his many wealthy clients in Britain. In the end – as has been stated – Lever sacked him for inattention to the work that Mawson was supposed to be doing for him. Mawson says this gave him a great shock.[40] Fair-minded readers of his *Life* could see this coming to him some chapters earlier. In the end he was forgiven and taken back. Lever had, as stated before, the virtue of being able to forgive and forget after a fairly short period of time. By 1920 Mawson had hopes of an Honorary Degree from Liverpool, to which he had strong claims both as an internationally known landscape architect and for long service to the university. Nothing seems to have happened. Perhaps the new Vice-Chancellor cautiously left all such things to a Senate committee who favoured scholars rather than landscape architects.[41]

Adshead or, more probably, Adshead and Reilly, with a hint or two from Lever, thus deserve praise for recruiting as the Department of Civic Design's first external lecturers three famous Lancashire men, two of whom had a national, and one an international, reputation. One hopes that architectural students swelled the numbers that attended their lectures. If Mawson laid aside plans of Athens for the King of Greece to travel from Lancaster to Liverpool – even on a Friday evening – to lecture to six students, he must have been a most conscientious man.

Adshead's Views on Architecture and Planning

Until 1909 Adshead's training and practice had been as an architect and perspective artist. He now had to teach a new subject with vague boundaries, and of course he approached his new work primarily as an architect and his views on architecture up to 1909 are summarised in a paper he read in December 1908.[42] He defined architectural style 'as character which by repeated usage has developed into set form. Character ... denotes something more personal and fleeting ... style is character systematised by consistent and persistent effort.' He goes on to state that original

architecture interests us most. All great architecture is distinguished by originality 'but as a development and not an affectation
of something else'.

Adshead held that the huge amount of information that had
become available to architects in the previous half century by cheap
travel, and especially by drawings and photographs in journals, had
resulted in a maze of styles, and he hoped that by more consistent
teaching architects would move towards something approaching
agreement on style. He himself admired the Greek revivalists, and
poured scorn on the decadent adaptations of Jacobean, Elizabethan
and Dutch styles, and correctly forecast that Gothic would in future
be confined to ecclesiastical buildings. He then seems to have
remembered that some of his best clients, in his role of perspective
artist, had worked in the decadent styles, and handed out praise to
several of them. He also praised the rustic architecture 'although
derived from decadent styles' of Lutyens, Lorimer, Baillie Scott and
Newton, showing that the young rebels of the 1890s were beginning
to achieve recognition.

He talked a lot in the lecture about recent American work which he
praised, and conveys the strong impression that he had already been
there, although the testimony of his daughter and other evidence
point to 1910 as the time of his visit to the United States and Canada.
If he had already been before March 1909 it would explain why it was
Reilly who went to the USA during the Easter vacation while
Adshead went to Europe. Yet if Adshead had already been to
America, it is odd indeed that he did not mention this in his
application to become head of the Department of Civic Design. The
matter remains a minor mystery. Men and women are often
thoughtless towards those who in later years may wish to know why
and when they did certain things.

Adshead like all the rest of town planning's first teachers and
practitioners, had to learn the job as he went along. He set himself
first to learn what the Act of 1909 actually meant. There is a
suggestion of his trying to keep his spirits up in his note in the *Town
Planning Review* on clauses of the Act:

> *At first glance they appear to be complicated, but
> after careful study they reveal a sequence of
> procedure which, although complex, is very clearly
> set out, and by no means so involved as at first
> sight appears, having regard to the difficulties
> that must necessarily be met in dealing with so
> difficult a problem as that of town planning.*[43]

He greatly changed his views on planning between his Inaugural
Lecture in October 1909[44] and his book *Town Planning and Town
Development*.[45]

In his Inaugural Lecture, Adshead wasted no time on the pioneers
in the previous century, and paid no compliments to Liverpool for

being the first city to introduce medical officers of health, district nurses and local authority housing. Even more surprisingly, there is no mention of Port Sunlight, Bournville or Letchworth. He plunged straight into his subject. The establishment of civic design was of special significance because 'it marks a step in the progress of democratic organization where the necessity for unanimity of purpose in matters pertaining to Civic Development and control receives recognition'.

He then takes a grand architectural approach to the subject. The city was, as he saw it, the most comprehensive of man's works. When planned systematically cities show a strong administration, built unit by unit they present individualism:

> *In the well-organized city individual expression is*
> *subordinate to the civic expression of the city as a*
> *whole ... people are the reflection of the city in*
> *whose environment they have lived and ... so*
> *great a responsibility as that of city building*
> *ought not to be left entirely to individual control.*
> *And is not appreciation of this ... the very* raison
> d'être of Civic Design?

Adshead goes on to state that wherever cities were deliberately planned *de novo*, they were laid out on regular lines, but usually only parts of the greatest cities were carefully planned, other districts being irregular in layout (a word which Adshead sometimes regards as a synonym for picturesque). Washington DC and Hausmann's Paris offered great vistas, unknown to Rome or Athens.

A city might have its site chosen for one or more of many reasons. Whether it was regularly laid out depended on the power of the administration that controlled its plan and early stages of growth. Smaller classical cities were often the best laid out. Mediaeval cities might be harmonious in general expression and materials but lacked symmetrical arrangement. Adshead regarded Louis XIV and his architects as setting the pattern for later grand works in civic design, while Hausmann's Paris was the most comprehensive city reconstruction and remodelling that the world had seen up to 1909.

It was a grand affirmation of faith with a strong architectural bias. The sociological aspects of planning, that have now permeated the whole process in a way that has halted constructive action in far too many places, do receive a mention, mainly one feels as a tribute to Patrick Geddes, who since 1892 had been repeating *Folk, Work, Place* as the three key studies from which planning should start. The lecture then turns to 'moral force' - a phrase which would puzzle most planners today. Adshead knew exactly what it meant: its offspring were the law, the churches, local government and all undertakings which needed good communal supervision and organization - railways, fire services, schools. He asked also for comparative museums which apparently were to combine the work now done by the Council of Industrial Design, the various Building

Centres and perhaps the magazine *Which?*

He naturally stressed the need for a good city plan, as in his view most of the urban development between 1850 and 1900 already needed pulling down and rebuilding with broad tree-lined streets and proper grouping of buildings. He also prophesied the coming of smokeless zones, and removal of bad smells, but was too optimistic about the banishing of excessive noise and forgot about motor car exhaust fumes.

As a great architectural draughtsman and colourist, he expressed at the end his personal view of a city, perhaps an ideal city:

> *Mellowed in harmonious colour and reflecting the*
> *soft blue of the sky, the effect of its sunlit walls is*
> *such that the most brilliant stage display can but*
> *poorly suggest. And yet it is but the background of*
> *the citizen who traverses its ways ... The modern*
> *city calls not only for more highly organized*
> *building but for entirely new types ... Here, where*
> *complexity of existence and rapidity of movement*
> *are ever increasing, greatness of conception must*
> *have stringent control ... Relaxation and riot-*
> *running must happen but on rare occasions ...*
> *Mediaeval art is too free ... in an age permeated*
> *with an unhealthy craze for self-advertisement (it)*
> *would result in a too pyrotechnic display ... What*
> *we need is the controlling influence of the Greek ...*
> *the work based on the Greek, of earlier men who,*
> *studying the problems of the hour, had placed*
> *these first ... and then found ... the garments with*
> *which they could be suitably clothed. Such men*
> *were Adam, Chambers, Soane, Cockerel and*
> *Elmes.*
> *All great cities are either white or grey. That*
> *which is a golden red harmonising with the rich*
> *green verdure of the surrounding land will ever*
> *suggest ease of existence, simplicity and primitive*
> *life. Such a harmony can never suggest solidity of*
> *existence as does grey, nor vivacity as does white*
> *or cream.*
> *The characteristics of a city expressed in its*
> *colour, its texture, and its form, reflect on the*
> *citizen himself.*

Reilly had claimed, as previously described (p. 56),that it was the omission of all mention of architecture from John Burns's speech introducing a Town Planning Bill in 1908 which inspired him with the idea of a Department of Civic Design. He must have felt on hearing Adshead's first lecture that he had recruited just the right man to be the first professor. Adshead was essentially a blend of artist specializing in architectural and landscape scenes, and of an architect who favoured as much neo-classical or Regency detail as his clients would accept, or could pay for. He had to school himself in the rest of the new subject, and he was fortunate that he did not know that for thirty years he and a few others would have to try to contrive some constructive town planning out of legislation that was feeble, complex and very largely ineffective. And up to 1931 – if they were asked to plan at all – planners would have to try to suit the varying needs of 62 counties, 82 county boroughs (the large cities), 827 urban districts and 779 rural districts in England and Wales alone. By 1940 there were a few less. It was excusable for one exasperated research worker in the late 1950s to describe all inter-war published plans as 'Pious hopes, set in Baskerville with wide margins, and riddled with woodcuts'.[46] But in 1909 the future of planning seemed assured, and full of promise for good plans carried out by resolute city councils.

As has been mentioned, Adshead soon moderated his pro-architect bias. At a conference at West Bromwich in 1911 he said:

> The papers read before the Town Planning
> Conference in London, which was inaugurated by
> the Royal Institute of British Architects ..., when
> compared with those read here by the Engineers
> show a very striking difference in the attitude of
> the two professions towards town planning, and
> moreover prove conclusively that both architects
> and engineers have each their part to play.
> Neither are competent solely and entirely to take
> upon themselves the whole of the responsibilities
> affecting so vital a matter as that of town
> planning ...
> The town planner of today may emerge from
> almost any profession engaged in one way or
> another in the construction of towns and in the
> development of suburbs. All that is required in
> order that he may be justified in calling himself a
> town planner is that in addition to such primary
> qualification he must possess sufficient knowledge
> of the technicalities of other professions to be able
> to co-ordinate these with his own.[47]

In 1909 Adshead, as part of the School of Architecture, had moved into the old Bluecoat School, where a plan published in 1910 shows how he and Reilly looked at one another across the courtyard.

During Adshead's few years in Liverpool, or rather half years, between 1909 and 1914, he made a number of contributions to the *Town Planning Review*, mainly about improvements in garden cities, administration of the 1909 Act and the proper placing of fountains, statues, etc. in cities. He also wrote for other journals or gave papers that were reported in journals.

His main work however was to encourage his own students, and some architectural students, to prepare plans for the renewal of parts of Liverpool, such as Brownlow Hill and near the Pier Head - for which Lever offered prizes - and also to prepare plans for new suburban areas on Garden City lines. He also raised standards of draughtsmanship throughout the school, by preparing perspective drawings himself and encouraging students to do likewise.

The publication of his only substantial book, *Town Planning and Town Development*[45], did not take place until 1923, nine years after he had left Liverpool to return to London to become Professor of Town Planning at University College. In the early post-war years Adshead was very busy as an architect in private practice, as well as at University College, and cannot have had much time for writing. It may be that he felt that he ought to write a book because professional rivals - Raymond Unwin, Thomas Adams and Longstreth Thompson - had already done so.[48] At any rate, *Town Planning and Town Development* is a book of a jumbly kind. It was intended as a text book for students, and to be the first of a series dealing with the social, economic and administrative aspects of town planning. It was probably based on lectures given and notes made in the 1914–18 war, when Adshead had few students and was still teaching himself his subject. He had three students in 1916 and seven in 1917.

He acknowledges a great dept to Patrick Geddes, and one certainly notices how Adshead plunges *à la Geddes*, into sociology, anthropology, economics and other big subjects. He acknowledges help and comments from Chaloner Dowdall, J. J. Clarke, Raymond Unwin, and Sidney Webb's *The Story of the King's Highway*.

The book is pleasantly written with an enviable confidence that what he has to say about sociology and town planning is not likely to be challenged. There were few sociologists about in those days. *Town Planning and Town Development* is divided somewhat loosely into four groups of subjects: types of people, towns and regions; transport, traffic and roads; the various Housing Acts; and town planning in various private and local authority forms, including procedure under the Acts up to 1923. Large and small matters are dealt with as they come to mind, and there are some repetitions.

Adshead made a number of prophesies of coming changes in towns and most of these have proved correct: trams would give way to buses, the decline of dockside warehouses, development of holiday resorts, 'a long time will elapse before this (electrification) applies to mainline railways' (it was about half a century) and warning notices that should be placed on side roads at their junctions with major roads.[49]

Adshead was an enthusiastic motorist and also a very bad driver, with quite a record of collisions[4] including one where he hit a tram broadside on, and blamed the blameless driver.[50] It is therefore odd that, despite foreseeing a big growth in motor traffic, he thought 20 feet quite wide enough for trunk roads in the countryside although, possibly from personal experience, he favoured wide verges as escape zones (his term). He disliked divided carriageways, on the reasonable grounds that near big cities one carriageway would always be congested in the morning and the other in the evening. He did not foresee six and eight lane urban highways in which all lanes, save two, are switched twice daily to favour the major flow. He would certainly have been a dangerous user of them.

Adshead's views on town planning legislation up to 1923 are what one would expect. He condemned its rigidity and limitations but conceded that a local authority's power to control use and density of building without compensation could prevent some very unsuitable development. Here he was proved right.[51]

The book contains quite a lot about holiday resorts, on which Adshead was very well informed because of his work at Ramsgate, Worthing and Scarborough, and a majority of the photographs are of resorts or county towns.

The book may be summarized as containing what Adshead had taught himself and his students up to 1923 about the aspects of the subject of which he had known nothing when he became head of the Department of Civic Design. It treats most subjects rather loosely and broadly, although Adshead had made some more detailed study of growth, change and development in towns and parts of towns during the war, when he had few students and only limited architectural work of which the houses at Dormanstown for steelworkers are best known.[52]

He became a member of the Civic Arts Association, dedicated to encouraging cities and towns to employ artists and craftsmen, and, by 1918, to advise on war memorials. Adshead then wrote a booklet called *The Centres of Cities*[53] which contains twenty pages and the results of careful examination of the plans of towns, including traffic needs and the condition and uses of the various districts.

In his view, as democracies advanced they would appreciate the value of submitting development plans to communal control, and would produce extended compositions (plans in three dimensions for the rebuilding of extensive areas) which had hitherto been created only under autocratic influence. (He had Washington DC in mind, and the authorities there might have preferred the phrase 'under firm control by a fully democratic body'.) Civic grandeur called for self-denial by its citizens. In his view, if one removed half a dozen buildings and a few streets and squares from London, there would have been (in 1918) nothing worthy left. The pamphlet mentions types of towns, and compares Liverpool with London and describes the development of districts with specialized uses and many more types of specialized buildings.

Adshead as Architect and Architect/Planner

Before his appointment at Liverpool, Adshead's architectural practice had been based on successes in competitions, such as the

Carnegie Library at Ramsgate after which he was asked to design a concert hall for the same town. This appears to have led to some study of other holiday resorts and spas, and he was called in to redecorate the Old Assembly Rooms at Bath. Soon after he began work at Liverpool, he was entrusted with a survey of the Duchy of Cornwall's estates at Kennington in London and its subsequent partial rebuilding. This, to the architects and students of the inter-war period, was the work for which Adshead and his partner Stanley Ramsey were best known. It also led to some housing work for local authorities like that at Newburn, near Newcastle-upon-Tyne, which is quietly distinguished despite great economy in materials.

There are two stories of how Adshead came to be entrusted with work for the Duchy of Cornwall. His daughter, as mentioned already, thinks her father met Sir Walter Peacock, Secretary of the Duchy of Cornwall Estates, on a housing tour in Germany with Patrick Geddes and Henry Aldridge in 1909 and impressed Peacock as the right man to examine and report on the somewhat rundown Kennington Estate. Adshead's nephew and assistant thought that the two men met on the ship that brought Adshead back from America. The former seems more probable, since, as has been stated, it would solve the problem of Adshead's Continental studies and Sir Walter may well have been on the tour to pick up good ideas for the partial rebuilding of the Kennington Estate.

Adshead's report on the estate was submitted in 1911 or perhaps late in 1910.[54] There is no preface giving those useful details of when he was appointed, what he was asked to do or who, if any, were his assistants. He plunged straight into a description of the estate, its history, and condition almost house by house. The report is most thorough, dry and factual and must have entailed a great deal of work - probably in the summer of 1910 - and taught him all he needed to know about housing development and property management (mainly houses) in the days, which now seem so remote in history, when four-fifths to nine-tenths of the population lived in privately rented accommodation, and never contemplated anything else, or were quite unable to buy a house.

Most of the houses on the estate and the surrounding area had been built between 1780 and 1830 when the standard of architectural appearance was good, but the construction very shoddy. Adshead quotes Nash[55] on how bad the construction was in the early period of London's fast growth. He points out that trams and the underground railways had enabled the middle classes to move further out, and that the Kennington Estate was then just at the boundary point between land where only flats would be remunerative and land where better quality houses were still a paying proposition. There was some study of social composition based on Charles Booth's classic work,[56] but in the main it was the position of the various blocks in relation to transport and The Oval, and their condition, that received attention. There were also proposals for rebuilding substantial portions of the estate over an appreciable period. This was done in due course, though not normally in the forms Adshead had first proposed.

Those were great days for property developers and their estate planners, and architects and developers of the 1980s are likely to be astonished at one thing after another about conditions in 1911: the prices of land – £500 to £1,000 an acre, 1½ miles from the Houses of Parliament; building costs of 7½d a foot cube, or 52 middle-class flats for under £20,000; returns of 6 to 8½ per cent; and at what our grandfathers were prepared to accept – or were expected to accept – in their dwellings. A suggested block of five-storey middle-class flats had no lift, and in the two-storey cottages proposed for Central Square the only access to the one WC was from the back yards.

The external appearance of the proposed buildings was pleasant and vaguely Regency, as were the buildings actually built, mostly in the early 1920s. These have been well maintained. Reilly wrote:

> His architectural style may be described in general
> terms as an adaptation of classical modes to
> modern needs, with special attention to significant
> detail in windows, mouldings, cornices, and so
> forth.[9]

The report ended with tables of estimated costs and returns on the proposed reconstruction of most of the estate. The final table shows an average net return of £13,338 during 1905–10 on 831 properties of all kinds, including 84 shops and 13 banks, public houses and offices. An average annual return of £16 per property does suggest that radical improvements were overdue on a large estate near the centre of what still claimed to be one of the two or three richest cities in the world.

It is probable that the Duchy of Cornwall work and the rest of a growing architectural practice with Stanley Ramsey[57] decided Adshead to return to London and to accept an offer to set up a town planning course at University College, London. His disappointment at not being invited to join the New Delhi Planning Commission after his name had been suggested[58] may also have impressed on him that London was the place for important commissions. He had become a full Professor at Liverpool in 1912, after his first three years, and had been given at least two architectural commissions in Liverpool.

The first was the remodelling of the Star Theatre as the Liverpool Repertory Theatre as recorded in the previous chapter. For this considerable work he received no fee but generously accepted shares in the new theatre company instead. One doubts if he ever received a worthwhile dividend.[59]

He was also offered the job of being joint architect with Reilly of the new Students' Union. Such an offer always raises the question of who is going to do what, or, more bluntly, who is going to be the master and who the horse. Reilly always liked to play the leading part in anything he undertook and, as the Union was to be his first building work of any importance for the university after ten years as Professor of Architecture, it would be natural for him to feel that Adshead's part in the design should be small. He may indeed have resented the 'joint architect' proposal, and it is possible that some of those whom Reilly had offended in the past had suggested the arrangement because they thought Adshead would be a steadying influence on Reilly, Adshead, however, was too spry for them. He was, after all, a much more experienced architect than Reilly at that time, and he must have foreseen serious troubles if he and Reilly tried to design and build the Union jointly. He also felt, rightly, that he was under obligations to Reilly and that Reilly should be the architect.

He therefore wrote two adroit letters to the Vice-Chancellor[60] refusing to be joint architect, but offering his services as consultant architect (at a fee to be arranged with Reilly and paid by Reilly out of the normal fees). It may be that by March 1914 there were rumours in the university that Adshead was to leave Liverpool. At any rate he decided to end his second letter by scotching ideas that might have occurred to the Council:

> *It now appears to me that the Council might*
> *possibly interpret my refusal to accept the position*
> *of joint architect as indicating either a lack of*
> *interest or a feeling that co-operation [with Reilly]*
> *was impossible. Such a supposition would be*
> *entirely erroneous. I therefore make the suggestion*
> *[that he should act as consultant architect] (which*
> *I would be obliged if you would convey to the*
> *Council), feeling that it would satisfy the points*
> *raised in your letter and enable me in a real way*
> *to safeguard my interests in the School and*
> *contribute to the success of the building.*

We do not know what were the points raised by the Vice-Chancellor in his previous letter to Adshead, but it is probable that – as already suggested – the Council hoped that Adshead would have a restraining influence on Reilly. Adshead produced a coloured drawing of Reilly's design for the Union, as he had of his cathedral entry in 1902. We also do not know what consultation in fact took place between Reilly and Adshead over the first portion of the Students' Union, which was built between 1910 and 1913.

Adshead's last and somewhat florid statement on planning at Liverpool was contained in a book of tribute to J. M. MacKay, the forceful Professor of History when he retired in 1914.[61] Adshead writes of civic design:

> *He who excels in this art must have high ideals;*
> *ideals which, transcending the strata of*
> *convenience and comfort defy dependence on*
> *utilitarian motives and thought ...*

> *Already since Town Planning and Housing have*
> *captured the imagination of administrators,*
> *hundreds and thousands of wretched inhabitants*
> *of slums, crowded like vermin amidst the dust-*
> *heaps of an insensate industrialism, and now*
> *transported into healthy and attractive*
> *surroundings, have habituated themselves to an*
> *orderly existence; and like wild flowers planted in*
> *a garden, have unhesitatingly submitted*
> *themselves to culture, flourishing wonderfully in*
> *their new condition.*

Adshead's Later Career in London

It was probably F. M. Simpson, Professor of Architecture at University College London, who suggested to Adshead that he should return to London and set up a Department of Town Planning there, as he had done at Liverpool. This may be what happened, although, as has been suggested, there were other good reasons why Adshead might have wished to return to London. It will be recalled that Simpson had been Professor of Architecture at Liverpool for ten years before Reilly, had helped Reilly to succeed him (see Chapter 3), and had kept his eye on what happened in the Liverpool school since he had left. Indeed, this would almost have been forced upon him by Reilly's publication of *The Liverpool Sketch Books* and other devices for spreading knowledge of the Liverpool school and enhancing its reputation. Simpson would also have read the *Town Planning Review* and seen that Adshead's views on town planning agreed with his own, and that Patrick Abercrombie (then aged thirty-six) had proved himself, in five years, to be an able assistant, editor, writer and practitioner. If, therefore, Adshead moved to London there seemed to be a strong candidate trained and ready to take his place. At any rate, Adshead applied for the new professorship in London and was appointed in 1915.

Adshead actually left Liverpool in 1914, and the Town Planning Institute also held its first meetings in that year, and its first published list of thirty-five (full) members were headed, alphabetically but suitably, by Abercrombie and Adshead, and included two out of the three part-time lecturers in the Department of Civic Design – John Brodie and T. H. Mawson. Thomas Adams had visited Liverpool as early as 1910 to discuss the idea of a town planning institute.

The outbreak of war almost put an end to the practice of town planning in Britain for five years. This climacteric for Europe and the world was also seen by many as the end of 100 years of civilization and even of civilization itself. As 1914 also chanced to be an interlude between the departure of the first Lever professor and the appointment of the second, it would perhaps have been appropriate to summarize very briefly how far the new town planning movement had progressed by then in its aim of correcting some of the most grossly *uncivilized* developments of the previous century. But this task has already been done in the 812 pages and fully illustrated report of the RIBA Conference in 1910,[62] and the Liverpool Conference of 1914.[63]

Adshead thus began, as has been stated, the movement from Liverpool to London that was followed by both Abercrombie and Holford and formed one of what Lord Annan has called 'the dynasties' at University College. It was mentioned earlier that Adshead had few students between 1915 and 1918 – three to seven a year – building work generally came to a standstill, and, apart from his work with Abercrombie on the plan for Dormanstown and the building of 300 houses there, Adshead seems to have been able to do little professional work till the war ended. Perhaps he filled some empty weeks in preparing notes for his later book.

From 1919 at the age of fifty, Adshead entered the busiest period of his professional life. It is an appropriate date at which to try to sketch the man himself, apart from his professional life. He was, as stated, very tall – about 6 feet 4 inches – and had a long face rather like the late Jack Hulbert and he stroked his chin quite a lot in a reflective way. He gave the appearance of being shy, and was reserved at meetings with strangers. His body, as well as his legs, must have been long, since T. C. Coote recalls that he was fascinated, at a first interview, by the number of Adshead's waist-coat buttons. He thinks there were eleven, and is firm on ten, instead of the usual five or six. His partner for many years, Stanley Ramsey, wrote of him:

> For me Adshead's most distinguishing trait was a sense of greatness, a greatness of heart as well as of mind, and which I found in him to a greater extent than in any other man.

> In spite of his superb gifts, and he had many, there was an indefinable something which transcended all his work, something different from talent, something apart from genius, which I can only define by the word 'greatness'. He appeared to view all life and all creative effort as from a mountain top, and if at times he was careless of, or indifferent to, the minutiae of every-day existence this is only to say that ... he had the defects of his virtues.[64]

Apart from his terrifying habits as a motorist, Adshead was great fun on holidays with children. He took nephews and nieces and his daughter Mary to country cottages, the Norfolk Broads and once to France, and taught them to paint. He once wrote a play for them to perform for such nearby persons as could be corralled as an audience; and pushing a car up a hill, and being ready with a brick as a wheel-chock, were all part of the fun for twelve-year olds.[4]

Soon after the First World War, Adshead bought a cottage near New Milton in Hampshire in which he spent most holidays, and it was there that he eventually died. His London home for a number of years was right on the Thames at Mortlake, and there he and his wife welcomed visitors on Boat Race day and gave big children's parties. To these A. E. Richardson, later the vigorous and mildly eccentric Sir Albert, and his wife used to come in eighteenth-century dress. Abercrombie attended some of these parties.

When he was warmed up Adshead was a great conversationalist with people he knew well. His nephew remembers that when a guest was staying with them, it was not uncommon for them to talk till 11 pm, then make a cup of tea, talk on till 4 or 5 am, make another cup of tea, and then go to bed. Adshead, writes T. C. Coote, 'was quietly spoken and somewhat reticent except when meeting overseas planners in his office, when he shouted at them!'

Mrs Adshead was a strong character, good at organizing and fond of entertaining. She was very good to all nephews and nieces till they grew up, but then rather lost interest.[4]

Work Between the Wars

Adshead had introduced both a Certificate and a Diploma course in planning at University College, as there had been at Liverpool, and an annual average of forty students attended the courses from 1922 to 1925.

In addition to Dormanstown and Newburn, the main work of rebuilding a large section of the Duchy of Cornwall's Kennington Estate began soon after the war, and so did the commission for the Worthing Pavilion a few years later. The firm was never a large one and Stanley Ramsey, Adshead's partner, did not bring in much work though he was rated a first-rate architect by his assistants. He was, however, a good administrator and later became chairman of a building society.[4] For much of the time there was only one assistant, and even in the firm's most prosperous years there appear to have been only Carr (architecture), Coote (planning) and a junior. In comparison with many of the more famous architectural and planning offices of 1950–75, the office at 46 Great Russell Street seems extremely small. But its work was highly regarded in the profession, and most offices were small in the 1920s. Adshead may simply have preferred a small office, and certainly had not the qualities needed to run a big one. Calm, affable and impressive, he was also dreamy and absent-minded, and had been known to fail to turn up for quite important meetings as well as lectures. His secretary, Miss Young, expended much nervous energy in trying to keep him punctual. Despite his painstaking studies of Patrick Geddes and the current planning legislation, one does not doubt that Adshead remained convinced that the really important part of planning was, or ought to be, enlarged architecture – groups of grand buildings and broad streets, with obelisks, fountains, flowers and trees beautifully placed in squares, parks and boulevards. If he had been chosen as the planner of New Delhi he would certainly have prepared splendid proposals, but one has doubts about their acceptability.

His second chance at designing a capital city – Lusaka – did at least result in study of the actual site and the preparation of plans, some of which were carried out. But Lusaka was not in the new Delhi class. In 1930 it was little more than a small collection of East Indian stores and a few bungalows serving a small farming population.[65] In 1935, the decision was taken, partly no doubt as a result of Adshead's report, to make it the capital of northern Rhodesia. There was, however, no reckless haste: it did not become the capital in a full sense until about 1955.[66]

Adshead also enjoyed making the small sketches of landscape and village scenes for his planning reports. He always carried the materials with him in an old music case, and sometimes made lightning sketches from railway carriage windows as he trundled through the area about which he was being consulted.[4]

One had the impression that the period from 1920 to 1925 or 1927 was the best as well as the busiest for Adshead's architectural practice; and perhaps the only profitable period. After the completion of Worthing Pavilion there were no major architectural works, and Adshead's planning work was small in volume for a man of his reputation and never seemed to pay for itself.

To obtain planning work it was important to know county surveyors and to persuade them that their local authorities should make use of the feeble 1925 Act, with its string of model clauses, copied from plan to plan. It was a slow business. Even by 1930 the entire professional planning staff in the Ministry of Health (then the Ministry in charge of town and country planning) comprised George Pepler and two assistants.

Pepler, the subject of the next chapter, was an indefatigable propagandist for planning and knew most local authority surveyors and engineers. There were also few planners with a full-time private practice: Raymond Unwin (adviser to the Greater London Regional Planning Committee 1929–33), W. R. Davidge, W. Harding Thompson and the dominant firm Adams, Thompson and Fry were almost all of those in London. There were half a dozen firms outside London. Longstreth Thompson of Adams, Thompson and Fry was George Pepler's half-brother, and it was impossible for less successful competitors not to suspect that this firm's success in obtaining the bigger jobs was partly due to this relationship. And this may well have been so, without any reflection on Pepler's integrity, which no one who worked with him would doubt.[67] After all if one looks at the matter squarely, most local authorities did not really want to get involved in this complex, and in their view unnecessary, town planning business at all; and if the Ministry was pushing them to do so, who better to employ than the firm headed by Thomas Adams, who was internationally famous, and whose British expert was a half-brother of the Chief Planning Officer at the Ministry? It was a very reasonable kind of insurance policy.

Adshead tried very hard to obtain work and took on a special planning assistant, T. C. Coote, in 1929 and prepared reports for West and South Essex, East and West Molesey and part of the Oxfordshire plan (jointly with Abercrombie and Lord Mayo).[4]

The South Essex scheme[68] was typical of his work. It contained the surveys customary in that period: topography, transport, housing and industrialization, sewerage (or the lack of it), character and archaeology. The eighteen local authorities involved included some of the poorest in the country. Parts of the area were covered with hundreds of shanty-type dwellings on unmade roads without any services save water and occupied by poor families who appeared to have built the dwellings or additional rooms without the help of skilled craftsmen.[69] The Ministry of Health had seemingly taken no action to stop the local authorities allowing this type of dwelling, which brought in some additions to the rates (local taxes). Adshead naturally had to exercise great tact in trying to coax better development into existence. The report is illustrated by eleven maps and seventeen of Adshead's small pen and ink sketches. Among his recommendations was one that there was an excellent site at East Hordon[70] for a new town. This was the site chosen for Basildon New Town some twenty years later.

The fees then offered to planning consultants were small, and Adshead had a tendency to offer to do too much for too little (a failing fully shared by the third Lever professor), with the result that the fees sometimes fell well short of the net cost to the firm.[71] The great slump of 1929–33 brought his practice to such a low level that the staff was reduced to one. There was some improvement after 1933, but in 1935 Adshead, at sixty-seven, retired as Professor of Town Planning at University College and an income from which he had probably subsidized his planning work was reduced to a pension. By 1938 the available work was so small that the one remaining assistant left to enter local government.

Adshead's last book was published in the midst of bombs and war damage and was small and short.[72] As one would expect from an author aged seventy-three, it contains a lot of retrospection. There are twelve chapters, of which four concern London where Adshead spent most of his life, but no great significance attaches to the chapter headings, as Adshead as author always wandered agreeably from subject to subject as they came to mind. The book repeats a number of the views (both good and bad, as we now see them) contained in his earlier book, but this also was to be expected.

Quite a number of Adshead's 1941 expectations have been fulfilled: for example, that 'everyone' would have a car, that railways would be amalgamated, cut down in number and electrified, the need for new towns, a rising demand for second homes, the desirable routes for Motorways 1, 6 and (very nearly) 4 and 5, the need for Butlin-type holiday camps, for the reservation for agriculture of large areas of the country, for National Parks and preservation of the coastline. He also, like others later on, toyed with the idea of prohibiting the entry of motor vehicles to the City and other large districts of London, save of course for those owned by residents and tradesman's vehicles. He was too innocent to foresee the black market in permits, and the leap in sales of second-hand vans, that would at once occur if such schemes had been adopted. It took twenty-five years before somewhat similar ideas began to be applied to single streets or small groups of streets. Adshead also foresaw the needs for flexible planning and provision for the review of plans and, like many before and after, asked for the statutory registration of the ownership of all land.

On other matters his views were naturally influenced, probably unconsciously, by thirty years of planning practice under the feeble pre-1947 legislation. A review of *A New England* stated:

> *Professor Adshead does not approve of joint*
> *planning schemes, but says that all towns of over*
> *10,000 population should, together with the area of*
> *that land which might reasonably be expected to*
> *be absorbed in the near future by their suburbs, be*
> *the subject of separate schemes. Not many*
> *planners are likely to agree with this view.*[73]

He could not believe that very large areas would come to be preserved from building development without payment of any compensation, or that urban roads would be built that provided no access for adjoining buildings. It is odd that a man of his great imaginative powers could correctly foresee a huge growth of building around towns and of motor traffic without appreciating the new solutions that would be needed for them. If publication of his book had been delayed for three years he would have realized that this time the public meant to have real planning powers entrusted to the most powerful local authorities.

A New England received a few polite reviews, but planning and reconstruction were at last being taken seriously by committees and teams guided by Mr Arthur Greenwood and Sir John Reith. The Interim Uthwatt Committee report on compensation and better-ment appeared at the same time as *A New England*, and was followed by the Final Report, the Scott Report, the John Dower Report and the Abercrombie Reports on the planning of the London County Council area, and then of Greater London. The Ministry of Town and Country Planning was set up in 1943 and gathered its own experts. Adshead was not consulted. It is not surprising. There were plenty of experts on the twenty inter-war years of non-planning, half-plans and jigsaw alliances between local authorities – all trying to avoid claims for compensation if they really tried to guide development, and each of course trying to enlarge or safeguard its own area. Such were the parochial, nationwide machinations among which Adshead had been forced to try to plan. What was wanted from 1941 onwards were practicable suggestions for real, forceful planning and for better development and re-development. There was a passionate public determination to build a better Britain with a good, powerful physical planning apparatus as its main instrument. In the 1980s it is difficult to believe that this widespread determination existed and lasted for seven years or more. But it was so.

The real obstacle to Adshead's participation in the new deal for planning was that which comes in time to all men: he was thought too old. He was seventy-three in 1941 and – as stated earlier – Abercrombie was sixty-two and much better known, Thomas Sharp was forty and Holford only thirty-five. The first Lever professor's day was over. He died in 1946 and the obituaries stressed the qualities attributed to him by his partner and assistants and quoted in this chapter: calmness, a certain shyness and quite a lot of greatness.

NOTES AND REFERENCES

1   Faculty of Arts Minutes 1908-10 (March 1909) 97 (*Univ. Archives*). The committee recommended Adshead as Associate Professor of Civic Design for three years, at a salary of £400 for about six months' work each year.

2   *School of Architecture; Department of Civic Design. Prospectus for the Session 1909-10* (Liverpool University Press, 1909).

3   For example, see his book published in 1923 (see note 45) and earlier articles in the *Town Planning Review*.

4   Information from his nephew, Frank H. Carr, and Thomas C. Coote both of whom were Adshead's assistants for some years. The information was derived from interviews with and letters from Messrs Carr and Coote in 1978.

5   S. C. Ramsey, Adshead's later partner, quotes Adshead's daughter as saying

> *that one of the outstanding characteristics of her father's career was that he always did all his own perspectives, illustrated his own reports, drew or superintended his plans himself, continued to paint landscapes in watercolour to the end of his life and was interested in all painting.*

Stanley Ramsey, *Journal of Royal Institute of British Architects* Vol. III (May 1946) 309.

6   Information from his daughter Mary Adshead (Mrs Stephen Bone), the artist. Letter June 1978. *Who was Who 1941-50* gives his place of birth as London.

7   An anonymous obituarist wrote of Adshead: 'he was articled to a Manchester architect, most of whose practice was building churches for men who had made fortunes in cotton. The plans arrived mysteriously from London and it was Adshead's job to trace them' - presumably to enable his employer to claim them as his own. (This intriguing story is unknown to Adshead's daughter and to his nephew, an architect and town planner. Perhaps Adshead told it as a joke.) *Town Planning Institute Journal* Vol. XXXII (1946) 157.

8   For instance, the work of his artist daughter, Mary, is well known.

9   According to Reilly, Adshead met Rickards in his first London office and they became lifelong friends. Emeritus Professor Charles H. Reilly (later Sir Charles Reilly), 'Eminent Living Architects and Their Work' *Building* Vol. 4 (1929) 249.

10 C. Reilly, *Scaffolding in the Sky* (George Routledge, London, 1938) 51.

11 Writing to Reilly in 1909 Adshead says 1885, but this is clearly a slip of the pen. Letter from Adshead to Reilly 17 March 1909, (*Univ. Archives*.)

12   Kineton Parkes, 'Draughtsmen of Today' *Architects' Journal* Vol. 66 (Aug 1927) 175-77. This article contains an excellent description of Adshead's drawings.

13   *The Times* (13 April 1946).

14   The author's father possessed a perspective drawing by Adshead of a large proposed public house in Northumberland which almost certainly belonged to the 1905-10 period.

15   C. H. Reilly, *op. cit.*[9], 251.

16   Letter from Adshead to Reilly 11 January 1909, (*Univ. Archives*).

17   This proved to be a true prophecy. For half a century the majority of civic design students were architects by original training, and a total of 203 students came from 52 different countries.

18   Liverpool University Senate Papers Vol. 3 23, (*Univ. Archives*).

19   On 24 March 1909 W. Dixon Scott, a journalist of some repute, wrote to Mrs Reilly: 'You'll be horrid lonely tomorrow, and you'll hate the name of Lever and you'll wish his Town planning scheme (the propsed Chair?) had never been born.' Mary McCrossan, *The Letters of W. Dixon Scott* (Herbert Joseph, London, 1932) 74.

20   Senate Papers, *op. cit.*, 31.

21   A great Battle of the Styles was going on in garden and landscape design from the 1890s to 1914. The principal champions of the formal, architectural approach of axial lines, terraces, flights of steps and symmetry were, in Britain, T. H. Mawson and Reginald Blomfield, author of *The Formal Garden* (Macmillan, London 1892), and later architect of the new Regent Street. Formal landscaping gave the rich man more for his money, and it was a lot of money. On the other side, influenced by the English tradition of informal landscapes made famous by Capability Brown and Humphrey Repton, were William Robinson, editor of *The Gardener*, and, as a practitioner, Gertrude Jekyll who worked with Edwin Lutyens on nearly all of his garden and landscape work. The informal garden could and can involve as much skill and effort as anyone could manage to devote to it, and resulted under Miss Jekyll's guidance in seasonal scenes of great beauty in different parts of even quite a small garden. But full appreciation of it required some knowledge of flowers, shrubs and trees and even of horticultural possibilities. A large formal garden impressed the observer at once with its obvious high cost, and perhaps this accounted for its popularity with a certain kind of client - and with his landscape architect. Eventually the whole argument (in which Blomfield, a choleric man, took a big part), died away: good, small gardens being informal and large gardens a careful blend of formality and informality. After 1918 fewer and fewer people could afford to pay for large new formal gardens or their up-keep. (Based on Betty Massingham's *Miss Jekyll* Country Life, London 1966). Christopher Hussey wrote in *The Life of Sir Edwin Lutyens* (Country Life Ltd,

London, 1950) 175 that when each main combatant got a country home of his own he was influenced by the needs of the place, rather than his conclusions.

22   C. H. Reilly, *op. cit.*, 127.

23   The author of this book only met Adshead once, though he had seen him at meetings. He was applying for a job in the very difficult days of 1930-31. Adshead, then sixty-two, was kind and took an interest in what, to him, must have been awful drawings, and seemed genuinely sorry that he could not take on another assistant. We know now that he - like many other architects and planners - was then finding it extremely difficult to keep his office open.

24   The Outlook Tower in Edinburgh was set up in 1892. (see Philip Boardman, *Patrick Geddes, Maker of the Future*, University of North Carolina Press, 1944, 167).

25   *Liverpool Daily Post and Mercury* (30 March 1909).

26   For a report on the tour see *The Builder* Vol. XCVI (May 1909) 511.

27   In 1913-14 there were eight students (five taking the diploma and (three taking the certificate).

28   Michael Holroyd, *Augustus John* Vol. I (Heinemann, London, 1974) 303. Dowdall was Lord Mayor in 1908-9.

29   Augustus John, *Autobiography* (Jonathan Cape, London, 1975) 173-74.

30   M. Holroyd, *op. cit.*, 309.

31   The Hon. Mrs Dowdall *The Book of Martha* (Duckworth & Co., London, 1913).

32   Adshead had been proposed as a member, and received congratulations from Lever, but was not in the end invited. Perhaps two Liverpool men were thought too many. Much more probably Lutyens did not want another architect. He managed later to drop Blomfield as well, but in the end accepted Herbert Baker.
And this wasn't the only in-fighting over a juicy commission:

> ... during the previous winter, Lanchester had approached the Viceroy in Calcutta, when Lord Hardinge had asked him whether he would serve on a Planning Committee with S. D. Adshead and Brodie. To the Viceroy's surprise and without his knowledge Lanchester reported to Lord Crewe (Secretary of State for India) that Lord Hardinge had asked him to serve on the Committee. In order to avoid unpleasantness, he had therefore been invited to spend a month on the site and make a proposal. C. Hussey, *op. cit.*, 260.

33   C. Hussey, *op. cit.*, 246.

34   Thomas H. Mawson, *The Life and Work of an English Landscape Architect* (The Richards Press, 1927).

35   Thomas H. Mawson, *The Art and Craft of Garden Making* (1912), 5th Edition (Batsford, London, 1926).

36   T. H. Mawson, *op. cit.*,[34] 115.

      Mawson, however, was very observant of the eccentricities of other people, and tells some stories well, including that of Andrew Prentice and C.F.A. Voysey. Prentice had written the standard work on Spanish Renaissance architecture and Voysey was then the leader of those who believed that an architect should rely on his own imagination, skill, and experience in matters of design, and should never copy from books. Prentice at the end of an introduction to Voysey by Mawson asked Voysey if he had ever designed anything after the manner of the Spanish Renaissance. To this Voysey replied: 'Sir, I have only one book in my office and that is *Bradshaw's Railway Guide* which I have to use much oftener than I like.' (T. H. Mawson, *op. cit.*, 79).

37   T. H. Mawson, *op. cit.*,[34] 176.

38   Thomas H. Mawson, *Civic Art: Studies in Town Building, Parks, Boulevards and Open Spaces* (Batsford, London, 1911).

39   T. H. Mawson, *op. cit.*,[38] preface.

40   T. H. Mawson, *op. cit.*[34] 190.

41   Two further notes from Mawson's autobiography are of general interest. In July 1914 at the National Liberal Club he met John Burns, who told him that a war with Germany would last three years, cost £7,000 million and Britain would lose a million men. Mawson regarded this as an extreme exaggeration. (Mawson was also a founder member of the Royal Fine Arts Commission in 1924, and was the only landscape architect to be a member.) T. H. Mawson, *op. cit.*,[34] 242, 348.

42   Stanley D. Adshead, 'Style in Architecture' *RIBA Journal* Vol. XVI 3rd Series (March 1909) 304-8.

43   Professor Stanley Adshead, 'The Procedure Regulations of the Town Planning Act' *Town Planning Review* Vol. I (1910) 132.

44   Professor Stanley D. Adshead, *Civic Design*, An Inaugural Lecture delivered at the University of Liverpool, 8 October 1909 (Liverpool University Press Price 1/-).

45   Professor Stanley D. Adshead, *Town Planning and Town Development* (Butler and Tanner Ltd, London, 1923).

46   D. H. Crompton while Lever research fellow at Liverpool.

47   Professor Stanley D. Adshead, 'The Town Planning Conference at

West Bromwich' *Town Planning Review* Vol. II (1911-12) 175.

48   Raymond Unwin, *Town Planning in Practice* (Fisher Unwin, London, 1909). Francis Longstreth Thompson, *Site Planning in Practice* (Hodder & Stoughton, London, 1923). Thomas Adams, *The Garden City and Agriculture* (Simpkin, Marshall, Hamilton, Kent & Co., London, 1905). Thomas Adams, *Guide to the Garden City* (of Letchworth), (London, 1906).

49   S. D. Adshead, *op. cit.*, [45] 28, 60, 62, 63.

50   Maxwell Fry writes:

> *Adshead turned out to be disarmingly unconventional. He drove an old car from which he had removed most of the dashboard instruments as being superfluous for a man of simple tastes, and for convenience he carried the door handle in his pocket. He would have suited me, but he had no work to offer.*

Maxwell Fry, *Autobiographical Sketches* (Elek London 1975) 120.

51   Under this somewhat doubtful device many local authorities ... have attempted to do something towards that preservation (of agriculture and the countryside) and at the same time dodge ... compensation by zoning the greater part of the rural land in their areas at ... densities of 1, 3, 5, 10 or even 50 *acres per house* ... so that by 1937 ... the amount of land zoned for housing was large enough to accommodate ... 300,000,000 people, additional to our present population of 41,000,000. *The Scott Report* (HMSO, Cmd 6378, 1942).

52   *Architects' Journal* Vol. 49 (May 1919) 370-71.

53   Professor Stanley Adshead *The Centre of Cities* The Civic Arts Association of Gawthorpe Hall, Burnley, Lancashire, 1918. The association's executive committee contained twenty-four names among them, besides Adshead, people like Clutton Brock, Beresford Pite, E. S. Prior, Sir John Lavery, W. R. Lethaby, A. E. Richardson, William Rothenstein and St Loe Strachey. The association published at least ten pamphlets including *The Amenities of our Streets* by Halsey Ricardo, *Towns to Live in* by W. R. Lethaby and *A Sketch of Town Planning* by Beresford Pite.

54   *The Duchy of Cornwall Estate in London.* Report on the present condition with suggestions for improvement and reconstruction. (London, HMSO, 1911).

55   John Nash, 1752-1835, best known for the buildings around Regent's Park and nineteenth-century Regent Street.

56   Charles Booth, *Life and Labour of the People in London 1890-1900* (Macmillan & Co. Ltd, London, 1902).

57   His partner 1911-31. They continued to share offices and collaborate on some work till 1944. S. Ramsey, *op. cit.*

58   Letter from Lever to Reilly, 7 March 1912 (*Univ. Archives*).

59   Grace Wyndham Goldie, *The Liverpool Repertory Theatre* (Liverpool University Press & Hodder and Stoughton, London, 1935) 57.

60   Letters from Adshead to Vice-Chancellor (Sir Alfred Dale) 12 and 18 March 1914 (*Univ. Archives*).

61   Professor S. D. Adshead, 'The Ideals of Civic Design' *A Miscellany* presented to Professor J. M. MacKay July 1914 (University Press Liverpool and Constable & Co., London, 1914) 14–15.

62   *Royal Institute of British Architects Town Planning Conference 1910 Transactions* (RIBA, London, 1911).

63   Professor Stanley Adshead and Patrick Abercrombie (eds), *Liverpool Town Planning and Housing Exhibition 1914 Transactions of Conference* (University Press of Liverpool, 1914).

64   S. C. Ramsey, *op. cit.*

65   Charles Allen, *Tales from the Dark Continent* (Andre Deutsch, London, 1979).

66   Sir Geoffrey Jellicoe was called in as a planning advisor for Lusaka in 1949–50. In an article in *The Twentieth Century* in 1951 he wrote:

> *Lusaka lies 313 miles north of Livingstone, 1,100 miles south of the equator and at a level of over 4,000 feet, and has a climate characteristic of the central African plateau. The temperature ranges from an average minimum of 50 degrees in June to an average maximum of 88 degrees in October, when the heat can be disagreeable and even demoralizing.*
> *Professor Adshead laid out the new capital, on classical lines, on an east-west spur of low hills, beginning about amile north of the existing village of Lusaka. Great care and foresight were taken in the planning of buildings, the layout of roads, and perhaps most of all in the planting of trees. Nearly all the dignity and graciousness that Lusaka contains dates from this period of the early 'thirties, for since that time there has been an almost unbroken record of development by expediency. The most precious single physical feature, for example, is unquestionably the tree, and nowhere better than from the air can be seen how the initiative for tree planting not only stopped suddenly, but actually gave way at times to the destruction of what was already there. The town itself did not develop according to the original intention, and today there are two towns: the high-class residential area on the Ridgeway, mainly occupied by civil servants; and the commercial centre that developed round the old village street and railway station. Messrs. Bowling and Floyd, town planning consultants of Johannesburg, reported in 1947 that 'it would be difficult to find a comparable state of affairs anywhere in the world where the only shops available to a new and rising town are situated two to three miles away.'*

> *This ungainly city is set in a region of quiet but considerable*
> *landscape beauty. It is impossible to stand on the high ground to*
> *the north and not to feel moved by the bowl in which the town is*
> *set, with the hills of far-off Chilanga bounding the view across the*
> *flat oolite plain.'*

Geoffrey A. Jellicoe, *The Twentieth Century* Vol. 149 (1951) 109–16.
When the author visited Lusaka in 1964 it had one fine tree-lined main
street and several other broad and tree-lined roads which were
probably part of Adshead's plan. But the roads and building
development still petered out rather quickly into African shanties and
rondavels and then into the vast empty distances of Africa.

67   The author worked in the Ministry of Town and Country Planning,
      and sometimes with Sir George Pepler, for three years.

68   Professor Stanley D. Adshead, *The South Essex Regional Planning*
      Scheme (J. Alexander & Co., London, 1931).

69   The author passed by many of these dwellings on a bicycle trip in June
      1945, when they had of course suffered six years of wartime lack of
      repair. He was so horrified and fascinated by their existence and
      appearance that he much annoyed his companion by the time he
      wanted to spend examining what she called 'those beastly little
      shacks'. It seemed incredible that any inter-war local authority could
      have allowed them to be built, or that the Ministry of Health should
      have failed to take stern action against the Councillors and officers
      concerned.

70   S. D. Adshead, *op. cit.*[66] 81.

71   In a letter to the author in February 1978 T. C. Coote quotes a case in
      which Adshead was believed to have offered to prepare a plan for Ham,
      near Richmond, for £5.

72   Professor Stanley Adshead, *A New England* (Frederick Muller Ltd,
      London, 1941).

73   *Town Planning Institute Journal* Vol. XXVIII (July-August, 1942) 226.

5

THE MAN WHO PREPARED THE WAY

Sir George Pepler: 1882-1959

In the previous chapter it was stated that there was little real planning between the two world wars - in the sense that local authorities had not the will and the power to guide redevelopment, new building development, conservation of landscape and amenity, and related matters.

For thirty-two years after the Department of Civic Design was founded there was, as we now see it, a scandalous, and only slowly diminishing neglect of slums and of badly sited and badly designed buildings. Five of these years were of course occupied by the 1914-18 war and immediate post-war problems. After that, there seems now to have been little excuse for the continuing apathy over planning. An Act of 1919 was passed which made town planning compulsory for a proportion of local authorities of over 20,000 population, and that power was, thereafter, ignored by practically everyone including the relevant local authorities.

From 1919, for four or five years, most of the older influential people tried to forget lost sons and to pretend that the war had not happened - and some of them made quite a good job of it as the novels and biographies of the period show.[1] The younger generation - the survivors of the carnage - spent their gratuities, joined parties of 'Bright Young Things' or similar goings-on led by the Prince of Wales. More commonly, they finished university or professional training or, for the mass of ex-Servicemen and women, got jobs where they could, and after the immediate post-war boom these became scarce. The war was not discussed, and the nearest things to gloom were Emil Jannings' films even though they included Marlene Dietrich. More usual thrills of the 1920s were Rudolf Valentino, the tango and, believe it or not, the Black Bottom.

The boom, however, did take place for a few years. Clough Williams-Ellis, who had returned from the Welsh Guards to his practice as an architect, wrote of the years 1919-22:

> *The world, or at all events the English world, had*
> *decided after some hopeful hesitation to go on as*
> *near as might be, as before the War.*
> *These were the boom years, and the great money*
> *flood of the war was still swirling impressively,*
> *and even surprisingly eddying around in strange*
> *new pockets where had formerly been the financial*
> *shoals and shallows.*
> *Building prices, like the hopes of the rich, were*
> *high, if uncertain, and though it was exceedingly*

difficult to get a job carried through satisfactorily
with regard to materials, workmanship, time or
cost, there was plenty doing, and on the
percentage basis, one was well enough paid for
one's extra trouble.[2]

The end of the short replacement boom and renewed flows of imported food also meant the end of high farm prices and thus the ability of agriculture to defend itself; and owners and farmers, trying to survive, were ready to sell land for building at £100 or (in bulk) at around £44 an acre.[3]

The price of the actual land for houses at six or twelve to the acre therefore meant little to 'the speculative builder' as he was soon called. This became a term of abuse more deserved than some of the things said about 'property developers' or 'property tycoons' in the 1970s, for the buildings of the latter have usually been structurally sound. It was only the cost of roads, drains, water supply, building materials and labour that really concerned the builder in the 1920s: especially roads, where the local authorities (with an eye to future maintenance costs falling on the rates) nearly always and rightly insisted on a high standard of construction. Hence 'ribbon development', the stringing of houses along either side of existing roads, since access to a building plot adjoining a public road could rarely be prohibited until the Act of 1935.[4] Many, probably three-quarters, of the cheaper dwellings soon became dreadful in appearance and even construction.[5] They were certainly cheap. The author clearly remembers semi-detached houses near London advertised for about £500 freehold and the Dudley Report quotes houses priced at £335.

The dwellings put up by local authorities (Lloyd George's *Homes Fit for Heroes*) were usually a little better, in two respects. They were more soundly built, as the local authority itself would have to maintain them, and they were not so obtrusive on the public view. Usually built in groups of 25, 100 or more, the majority were necessarily placed at some distance from the public road, so that only a proportion of them were visible to passers-by. With few exceptions local authority estates – 'Council housing' – varied, in appearance, from the dreary to the outrageously bad.

Public opinion was slow to protest against what was happening. Most people were too concerned with precarious jobs and mounting unemployment, and local authorities wrestled with a huge housing need, and were worried by changes in Government subsidies which soon demanded that the local authorities should make a greater contribution to the cost of local authority houses than the product of a penny rate. The small contribution by the local authority was fixed immediately after the war so as to encourage maximum production of dwellings. This it did but, of course, prices rose rapidly.

It was with this non-planning world that George Pepler started to grapple in 1919, as Planning Inspector to the Ministry of Health (which had been saddled with town planning as a tiny part of responsibilities that included supervision of local government administration and finance, housing and health). One feels, looking back, that Pepler and the country were immensely lucky. He proved to be exactly the right man in the right place at the most suitable time for the exercise of his great assembly of unobtrusive talents: patience, good humour, and determination to create in time an effective planning system, a profession to operate it and a reputable institution to look after the profession and raise standards. He had also a great ability to make friends with many influential people who could help the good cause.

For nearly forty years he coaxed, persuaded and influenced, and when the bombs began to fall in 1940–41, the outlines of a system existed and all the faults[6] of the inter-war years were known and some had been remedied. Also the way had been cleared for the contributions of the two greatest Lever professors (Abercrombie and Holford) and their ex-students and close colleagues. They built, on the Pepler foundation, and in collaboration with a few most able administrative civil servants, an effective British and indeed Commonwealth planning system; and twenty-six New Towns as well.

Pepler's was an extraordinary achievement against great obstacles: the ineffective 1919 Act, an apathetic public, an uninterested Ministry, and, of course, the contempt in which the non-specialist administrative class civil servant has always held his scientific or professional colleagues. One wonders what Pepler really thought of his superiors in the civil service and the ministers whom he eventually influenced so greatly. So far as is known, he never wrote this down.

To anyone else the planning outlook in Britain in 1919, as has been said, was grim. Not to Pepler. His widow and he himself have put his view in words that cannot be bettered:

> *This is the story not of a great Town Planner but of a great Compulsion. 'It is wonderful,' George used to say, 'that even if I didn't have to earn my living, this is what I would choose to do.' Lacking the spur of vanity or pride, or even, for himself, ambition, he was nevertheless compelled forward, seizing every opportunity that offered to spread the good news, despising no contact however uninformed, however important and experienced, that would assist the crusade. No frustrations, no set-backs, no prejudices, no petty political squabbles, could quench that inner light, which burned steadily, acceptingly, even humorously, within him. And he hoped, perhaps a little secretly, that he might be permitted to pass on something of this compulsive urge.*

Favourable descriptions of a man's work, outlook and virtues written by his widow are usually and properly subject to some discount by readers. To those who read in their youth of Pepler's various doings or watched his methods at the Ministry of Town and Country Planning, or the Town Planning Summer School later on, Lady Pepler depicts the man as he was. Immense patience, immense perseverance and a humorous acceptance of all human frailties in superiors and local authorities were indispensible qualities for one who achieved what he did. Pepler may have been no more lucky than Adshead in having to endure the general apathy towards town planning in the inter-war years, but he simply made his own good luck and progress from, at first, trifling opportunities.

Pepler's Early Life

George Lionel Pepler was born in 1882, son of a brewer, with Quaker associations. He was educated at Bootham School at York and the Leys School Cambridge. He became a chartered surveyor and strengthened his Quaker associations by his marriage to a Quaker, Edith Amy Bobbett, in 1903. He went into practice in 1905 as Pepler and Allen and won a number of medals in housing competitions. When Thomas Adams, the first British town planner to become internationally known, went to the Local Government Board (later the Ministry of Health), Pepler took over Adams's planning practice; and it was perhaps natural that when Adams went to Canada in 1914, Pepler should take his place at the Board.[8]

In 1919 at the age of thirty-seven his real life's work began. Before then he had been one of those who laboured to create a profession of town planning, and was a founder member of the Town Planning Institute, of which he was Hon. Secretary and Hon. Treasurer for an almost incredible forty-six years from 1913. One must, therefore, repeat that he had, throughout his long working life, two complementary and interlocked spheres of work: to bring local authorities to recognize the importance of planning and to begin the town planning process within their boundaries; and to create a profession and a professional institution to help local authorities to undertake that planning work.

Having surveyed the absurd patchwork of local authorities in England and Wales in 1919 (82 county boroughs – that is, large cities – and 62 counties presiding over 1600 urban and rural districts), Pepler at once began to think of planning 'regions' which would conform at least approximately to the realities of geography, population, economics and transport. In this he had been influenced by Patrick Geddes's studies and teaching since 1892. In 1920 Pepler arranged that Abercrombie and Johnston should prepare the Doncaster Regional Plan, that became a pattern for those that followed.[9] It marked the start of all the Joint Town Planning Schemes that were to come, within which groups of local authorities – with enthusiasm or apathy, jostling for position and/or pleading poverty – were coaxed by Pepler to pay some attention to major planning and development problems.

Examination of a list of all the schemes in 1930, which increased in number year by year, gives the impression, first of all, of a massive wasted effort; and secondly, after reflection, that they represented a necessary, countrywide and valuable educational and propaganda effort which the reader, if a town planner, is thankful to have missed. It is not so much that most of the proposals came to nothing, for that has always been the fate of town planning proposals. But the coaxing, the ineffective legislation and the use of dubious legal devices to make any progress, must have imposed a great burden on those concerned. By 1930-34 schemes had been approved, 928 begun and 33 regional schemes published.[10]

Pepler's work called for a nice sense of balance. He and his few staff had first to help to prepare, and then to judge, planning schemes. Nervous senior civil servants or disgruntled local authorities could therefore hold that Pepler and company were trying both to lay down the rules and then to judge their own cause. And Pepler's constant work for the Town Planning Institute could also be thought to be unsuitable for a civil servant. But Pepler, in 1921, was quite firm about the need for continued support of the Institute.[11]

Pepler was untiring in getting to know the officers of local authorities and in coaxing them to undertake some planning responsibilities, and he also kept watch for and encouraged voluntary bodies which in one way or another might help public opinion to favour an effective planning system. He was also quick to note and cultivate influential people who became interested in some aspect of planning. For example he exchanged many letters with Lord Milner - the great African authority and former member of the War Cabinet - over the development of the Kent Coalfield in 1920-25. He was a great believer that whom you know is as important as what you know.

In 1926 the Council for the Preservation of Rural England was formed, with the Earl of Crawford and Balcarres as Chairman and Patrick Abercrombie - then the second Lever professor - as Hon. Secretary. The society's aims were soon sent to newspapers:

> to organize concerned action to secure the
> protection of rural scenery and of the amenities of
> country towns and villages from disfigurement
> and injury
> to act, either directly or through its members, as a
> centre for furnishing or procuring advice and
> information upon any matters affecting the
> protection of these amenities
> to arouse, form and educate public opinion to
> promote the objects of the Council.[12]

The CPRE campaigned vigorously against ribbon development and disfiguring advertisements in rural areas, and probably persuaded many county councillors and rural landowners to try to prevent widely scattered houses that spoilt views, and other countryside disfigurements.

Pepler wrote in favour of more open spaces, mainly for recreation, in 1923[13] and took an interest in the National Playing Fields Association from its establishment in 1925. He may also have started the National Parks movement in 1929 with a report on a Lake District park.

Local authorities had no experience of planning in 1920 and were somewhat reluctant to use the 1919 Act powers, so Pepler began to encourage the employment of consultants who could coax authorities to begin planning, and in particular to join together in groups as Joint Planning Committees, and so consider the development and conservation problems of sizable areas, often called 'regions'. Between 1920 and 1937 published reports had been prepared by, among others: Patrick Abercrombie (six), Thomas Adams and Longstreth Thompson who were later joined by Maxwell Fry (fourteen), W. R. Davidge (seven), and Adshead, Mawson and J. H. Forshaw also each prepared one or two. A greater number of reports were published in the sense of being available in printed form on application to various authorities. Some thirty of these printed reports were listed by 1931 but it is not clear who were the authors of a number of them.[10]

The 1932 Town and Country Planning Act was much reduced in effectiveness from the Labour Government's first intentions in 1930. The first draft Bill allowed local authorities to collect the whole of the betterment (added value of land) resulting from their planning, road building and other development activities. But the Great Slump of 1930–33, the formation of a National Government, and its obsession with economics and unemployment, absorbed most public attention and the Bill fell victim to determined opponents of planning.[14]

By then books were appearing that were very rude indeed about the results of feeble or unused planning powers. Clough Williams-Ellis's *England and the Octopus* appeared in 1928.[15] This attacked every form of bad development and the absence of all real powers to protect the beautiful parts of Britain. The book had great influence and was reprinted the next year. Other books of influence were *Britain and the Beast* (1937)[16] and Abercrombie's two little books *The Preservation of Rural England* (1926),[17] and *Town and Country Planning* (1933).[18] Thomas Sharp's *Town and Countryside* (1932)[19] and his *English Panorama* (1936)[20] are specially noteworthy. His *Town and Countryside* was a fine and thoughtful survey of landscape, countryside, villages and eventually towns and traffic problems. Only towards the end does he chastise the wrongdoers and incompetents in the way which in later years he used too much. *English Panorama* was largely a condensed *Town and Countryside*, with equal condemnation of ineffective 'Town and Country Planning' but it also contained some admiration for the best of the modern buildings that were then beginning to appear.

The writing and travelling for *Town and Countryside* when he was a junior planning official in Liverpool must have entailed considerable financial and other strains for Sharp, and these perhaps were the first cause of later polemics. Pepler must have admired Sharp but – infinitely patient and tolerant himself – he probably had serious and justified doubts whether he could recommend him to take to consultancy in those days of feeble and self-satisfied Joint Planning Committees. And yet later, the fourth Lever professor wrote of the time when he shared a room with Thomas Sharp in Reith's Ministry for a year: 'I greatly admired Tommy Sharp and we never had a cross word.'[21]

By the early 1930s so many professional and preservation bodies had joined in the outcry against despoliation of the countryside that the passing of the Restriction of Ribbon Development Act in 1935 became inevitable; though of course by then the horse had bolted. The approaches to a majority of towns, large and small, are still sadly damaged by pre-1935 roadside development.

The progress towards effective town planning was sadly slow, but one feels sure, now, that durable foundations were being laid down and that Pepler, from his central position, was doing all that – at that time – one man could do. His membership of associated societies and committees must have helped a great deal. Apart from being the guide of the Town Planning Institute for forty-six years, he was a member of the Council of the Town and Country Planning Association for forty, and eventually an Hon. Member of the Royal Institute of British Architects and the Institution of Municipal Engineers; and also Chairman of the International Federation for Housing and Town Planning during the three sad years of refugees and drift to war, 1935–38. He was also vice-chairman of the committee on airfields that was set up in 1934.

As the Second World War came near, Pepler must have been conscious that the country was becoming ready for real planning and that a lot of the preparation had been his. He had been an examiner for the Town Planning Institute for ten years up to 1930, and for twenty-eight more was chairman of the Joint Town Planning Examination Board. Of the 1,026[22] members of the TPI in 1939, all who had been students of the three Lever professors had, in a sense, also been Pepler's students. He had been external examiner both for Abercrombie at Liverpool and Adshead in London. His obituary notices stress his kindness to and help for all young planners.

He was supposed by the late 1930s to have known almost all town and county clerks (and according to his secretary had played golf with most of them) and also many of the city and county engineers and surveyors who were in charge of local authority planning; but it was probably the best practitioners and preferably practitioner-propagandists that received most of his attention. There were not so many of these. Abercrombie (second Lever professor) probably ranked highest in his estimation by being a near-contemporary, for his devotion to 'regional' planning through joint committees, his ability to work well with often prickly local officials, and of course for his knowledge of planning and planners, at home and abroad, equal but complementary to that of Pepler. Sir Raymond Unwin, who had guided the first Greater London Regional Planning Committee, was seventy-two by 1935, and Adshead at sixty-six as recorded in the last chapter – was not a good organizer, and found that little work came his way after retirement from the chair at University College London.

On the other hand, the third Lever professor, William Holford, received his first important commission as a consultant in 1937 by being appointed as planner for the Team Valley Estate near Newcastle-upon-Tyne. This was one of the two government-sponsored industrial estates (the other being in South Wales) that were intended to counter the drift of lighter and more profitable industries to the Home Counties in the south-east of England around London. The drift also made them and Britain more vulnerable to the air attacks for which Nazi Germany was obviously and quickly preparing. Shadow factories – for the manufacture of armaments and other goods needed for war – were also sited in suitably dispersed positions and in some cases had actually been built.

The War Years

The feckless, frightened drift towards the Second World War was marked, though in no way slowed down, by the appointment in July 1937 of a Royal Commission on the Distribution of the Industrial Population. The report – the Barlow Report – was published in January 1940, four months before the bombs began to fall on Britain in quantities.[23] To thumb through this well-remembered report forty years afterwards brings back vividly the sensations of rage and hopelessness, and (two years later) respect with which it was read. In 1937, nearly everyone knew that unless Hitler was shot another war was inevitable – everyone, that is, except, seemingly, Ministers and all spokesmen for the Labour Party. And in 1937 everyone also knew that the expanding industries were tending to gather around London or in the south Midlands and that in the north and west the old industrial areas had too many contracting industries, where managers and workers struggled on with out-of-date equipment, bad housing, unemployment and, too often, poor physique. There was plainly no time to do anything about these things before another war came.

In January 1940 – in the Phoney War period – when the Barlow Report was published, it seemed impossible that recommendations for a central planning authority would ever be carried out, whether in the war or peacetime. Still the Report was treated seriously. *The Times* noted that the Reservations to the Majority Report and the Minority Report itself carried a 'sense of urgency and a note of conviction', which were not found in the Majority Report. It felt that the new Ministry which had been recommended in the Minority Report would not fit into the political system at that time 'but a

Board, with large executive powers and informed by the spirit of the reservations and the Minority Report could do great things for industry and for Britain'.[24] Patrick Abercrombie, second Lever professor and member of the Commission, signed a dissentient memorandum with Herbert Elvin and Mrs Hichens, and wrote another entirely by himself which is referred to in Chapter 6.

George Pepler prepared Appendix IV - a short description of planning in other countries - which showed that seven European countries, and the United States, were well ahead of Britain in the scale of their planning and reconstruction works, or in detailed control of development or in freedom from liability to pay compensation for planning decisions - and sometimes ahead in all three respects. It is also probable that Pepler provided the information about garden cities, satellite towns and trading estates.

To the younger readers in 1940 (including the author) it seemed that the Barlow Report would be put aside for at least five years if not for ever. But they proved to be wrong. Within two years Barlow had become the main guide for those concerned with physical reconstruction and post-war town and country planning, in the sense that it listed all the important problems that must be solved.

When the bombs began to fall in large quantities and, in the main, on London, the Government first had to survey damage and make arrangements for patching up all buildings where this was practicable. They then turned their attention to wider problems of reconstruction. Pepler's activities during the new war are not known in detail. He remained with the Ministry of Health at the time when, during 1941-43, much of the action concerning planning and physical construction passed to Lord Reith's Reconstruction Group at Lambeth Bridge House - since Reith was a powerful character, and as Minister of Works and Building took over preparations for physical reconstruction for eighteen high-pressure months. It was at Lambeth Bridge House that, in 1941-42, Reith recruited Holford (third Lever professor), John Dower, Thomas Sharp and later Gordon Stephenson (fourth Lever professor); these events are described in Chapter 8. It was also Reith who appointed Abercrombie and Forshaw to prepare the County of London Plan in 1941. Only Reith and Lewis Silkin had the driving force to start, and to carry through, preparations for realistic town planning.

Pepler must have felt some concern at the recruitment of so powerful a team to tackle, in another Ministry, problems he had been studying for thirty years, and on which he was supposed to be the Government's chief adviser: probably not for personal reasons, as he never showed himself ambitious for personal power, but because it was obviously absurd that the great experience of the planning section of the Ministry of Health should not be used when real town and country planning was being prepared for, at last, Pepler was consulted by Reith's team, but the extent of this is not known. The muddle was at length sorted out. In 1943 a Ministry of Town and Country Planning was set up which brought together all physical planning problems and planners from the Ministry of Health and from (what had become under Reith) Works and Planning. Pepler was appointed Chief Technical Adviser to the new Ministry, although most of the new ideas were to emerge from the Research Division whose head, for planning matters, was William Holford, then aged thirty-six. One of Pepler's duties, for which he was supremely suited, was to advise bombed cities on how best to plan for the future. He visited Liverpool for this purpose in 1942 or early 1943.[25]

Pepler and Holford always appeared to be most friendly collaborators, and one may assume that while Holford's group produced new ideas, Pepler contributed his immense experience of what had worked or failed in the past, and in particular would advise on how best to secure the co-operation of local authorities. He certainly would have given advice during the preparation of the 1944 Act and the all-important 1947 Act, which provided the British planning framework for the post-war years.[26] He headed 'the Pepler group' which considered the legislation and administrative basis for the New Towns[27] and gave evidence to the Uthwatt and Scott committees. The Dower Report on National Parks was written entirely by John Dower himself but he would have been foolish not to draw on Pepler's great knowledge of the countryside, both cultivated and more wild, and his knowledge of the CPRE's activities since its formation in 1926. The author remembers John Dower talking of discussions with Pepler though he cannot remember what was their subject.

Pepler's retirement in 1946 seems to us now to have been perfectly timed. The Second World War was over and the 1947 Act about to be passed. He had prepared the way for real planning when few were interested and often in the face of hostility from senior officials and local authorities. He had done more than anyone else to make the Town Planning Institute a respected professional body; he had encouraged the first consultant town planners and all the younger men he had met, so that by 1946 there were 1,850[28] members of the Town Planning Institute, and by 1944 – according to Professor Gordon Cherry – 1,021 local authorities out of a diminished total of 1,441 were doing some kind of planning as members of 179 Joint Planning Committees.[29] By 1946 the new team – headed by William Holford as chief technical adviser – was in full working order and Patrick Abercrombie had finished, at the age of sixty-seven, his greatest works, the plans for the County of London and for Greater London.

Pepler's preparation of the way, his role as a John the Baptist for British and Commonwealth planning, therefore ended in 1946, and that date is a fitting time to end his part in this story of the Lever professors and their influence. He himself did not stop work, far from it. He married for the second time in 1947 and worked steadily for a further twelve years. He was appointed with P. W. MacFarlane to prepare a plan for the north-east of England in 1946. He was also interested in the New Towns and suggested some members for the corporations and helped to recruit good planners for them. At one time there was a suggestion that he might join the Corby New Town Corporation, for which the third and fifth Lever professors acted as consultants,[30] but nothing came of this.

Pepler was knighted most deservedly in 1948, became President of the International Federation for Housing and Town Planning, President (for the second time) of the Town Planning Institute, and in 1953 was presented with the Institute's first Gold Medal. He was planning consultant to Singapore, continued as President of the Town Planning Summer School and did much else. He died full of years, and with the respect of planners throughout the world, in 1959.

In 1949 Pepler wrote for the *Town Planning Review* a kind of swan song called 'Forty years of Statutory Town Planning' in which he concluded that despite the importance of social, industrial and economic problems, town planners 'are bent on ... the provision of gracious opportunities for their fellow men to live a good life of their own choosing'.[31]

NOTES AND REFERENCES

1   Relief at 'returning to normal' and renewed availability of low-paid domestic servants is seen in the dissimilar works of John Galsworthy, Evelyn Waugh, Michael Arlen, Dornford Yates, and Roy Harrod's *The Prof* and elsewhere.

2   Clough Williams-Ellis, *Architect Errant* (Constable, London, 1971) 136.

3   The *Estates Gazette* (Vol. III, 1928) says that between 1919 and 1924, the taxable income of farmers fell by 60 per cent.

4   Certain local authorities had private Acts which empowered them to control access to roads.

5   The design and construction of dwellings for private ownership could be grossly defective. When the author was unemployed in 1933–34 he made long evening walks around Newcastle-upon-Tyne and inspected houses in course of construction. Much of the construction was so bad that it could only be explained by corrupt or grossly negligent building inspectors. In the 1930s a deplorable system called 'collateral security' came into existence by which the building societies and builders could usually escape liability for building defects at the expense of the unfortunate house purchaser (see *Architects Journal*, Vol. 88, 1938, 749).

6   'The Minister of Health's Town and Country Planning Advisory Committee had reported in 1938 that there had in the past 20 years been two outstanding sins – the misplacing of building generally and the poor design and character of individual buildings.' From *George Pepler – Knight of the Planners* (MS p. 91) an unpublished study of Sir George based on his papers at the University of Strathclyde and other sources by the late Helen McCrae. The author is indebted to this careful study for a number of references to Pepler's interests and achievements, published in a variety of journals.

7   From Lady Pepler's introduction to H. McCrae, *op. cit.*

8   H. McCrae, *op. cit.*, MS 13.

9   Professor Gerald Dix, 'Little Plans and Noble Diagrams', *Town Planning Review* Vol. 49 (July, 1978) 334–36.

10   George L. Pepler, 'Twenty One Years of Town Planning in England and Wales', *Journal of Town Planning Institute* Vol. XVII (January 1931) 49–67.

11   H. MacCrae, *op. cit.*, MS p. 15.

12   From a current brochure of the CPRE now called the Council for the Protection of Rural England.

13   George L. Pepler, 'Open Spaces', *Town Planning Review* Vol X (January 1923) 11–24.

14   H. McCrae, *op. cit.*, MS p. 78.

15   Clough Williams-Ellis, *England and the Octopus* (Geoffrey Bles, London, 1928). New edition with foreword by Lewis Mumford (Portmeirion, 1975).

16   Clough Williams-Ellis (ed), *Britain and the Beast* (J. M. Dent & Sons Ltd, London, 1937).

17   Patrick Abercrombie, *The Preservation of Rural England* (Liverpool University Press and Hodder & Stoughton, London, 1926). Also printed in *Town Planning Review* Vol. XII (1926–27) 1–56.

18   Patrick Abercrombie, *Town and Country Planning*, (Thornton Butterworth Ltd, London, 1933).

19   Thomas Sharp, *Town and Countryside* (Oxford University Press, 1932).

20   Thomas Sharp, *English Panorama* (J. M. Dent & Sons, London, 1936).

21   Letter to author from Emeritus Professor Gordon Stephenson, August, 1979.

22   *Journal of Town Planning Institute* Vo. XXV (1938–39) 301.

23   *Royal Commission on the Distribution of the Industrial Population. The Barlow Report* (Cmd 6153, January, 1940).

24   *The Times* (1 February 1940) 4, 9.

25   Frederick J. Osborn (advisory editor), *Planning and Reconstruction Year Book 1943* (Todd Publishing Co., London) 292.

26   'His last major work before leaving (the Ministry of Town and Country Planning), was the policy and machinery embodied in the planning sections of the 1947 Act, which established comprehensive and obligatory town and country planning as a normal function of local and central government.' *The Times* (15 April 1959) 15, quoted by Helen McCrae.

27   H. McCrae, *op. cit.*, abbreviated *curriculum vitae* in the introductory pages.

28   *Journal of Town Planning Institute* Vol. XXXII (1945–46) 179.

29   Gordon Cherry, *The Evolution of British Town Planning* (Leonard Hill Books, 1974) 125.

30   H. McCrae, *op. cit.*, MS p. 131.

31   George L. Pepler, 'Forty Years of Statutory Town Planning', *Town Planning Review* Vol. XX (1949) 108.

6

THE FIRST GIANT

Sir Patrick Abercrombie: 1879-1957

When Adshead left for London in 1914 the Lever Chair became vacant after only two years' existence as a full professorial appointment. (Adshead had been Senior Lecturer and Associate Professor from 1909 to 1912.) The university did not have to look far for a suitable successor. The thirty-six-year-old Patrick Abercrombie had been Adshead's assistant for five years, editor and part author of the *Town Planning Review* since it began in 1910, had travelled widely on the Continent and written much about its great cities. Smallish, dark, brimming with vitality, talking and lecturing at - so it seemed - over 150 words a minute, Abercrombie saw with his one eye more than others saw with two. In any gathering he would have been picked out as a most interesting person as any photographs of him show.

Lever had backed Abercrombie to succeed Adshead in 1914,[1] but he was not appointed till June 1915. In the meantime the Department of Civic Design had been struggling to stay in existence, since, as described elsewhere a 'tiny new department' without a professor was a most tempting sacrifice to wartime economies.

Abercrombie's application for the chair was supported by written testimonials from Thomas Adams (the first consultant in town planning to achieve international fame and later author of the New York Regional Plan), Patrick Geddes and Raymond Unwin (both later knighted) and H. V. Lanchester, a prominent architect who was interested in civic design and a founder member of the Town Planning Institute.[2] He was also strongly supported by Adshead. Quotations from his supporters appear in the notes for this chapter.[3]

Not surprisingly, Abercrombie with such support and his excellent record was chosen as second Lever professor. Rival applicants included men of standing. One was Barry Parker, Unwin's partner in the planning of Letchworth, the first garden city in Britain, and on many other works. Unwin must have had a high opinion of Abercrombie to support him as well as his own partner, but his letter of support is not quoted in the committee's papers. Another candidate was C. R. Ashbee, an architect who had founded the Guild of Handicraft, notable for its fine printing. He later became Secretary and adviser to the pro-Jerusalem Society, and did much for the cleaning and preservation of the city's buildings and the revival of Arab handicrafts.[4] He had really been a handicraft man since the age of twenty-five, and imagination shrinks from trying to visualize what would have happened to the department had he been appointed as second Lever professor. Institutions share with the humanity that runs them a tendency to have very narrow escapes.

In the end, it was almost certainly Abercrombie's known merits -
on his home ground - as teacher, practitioner, writer and
tremendous worker that secured him the chair. In a letter to Reilly,
Lever remarked: 'I did not think it was probable that a more
experienced man would be found available.'[5] So in the midst of a
dreadful war, in which he was exempt from active service because of
his monocular vision, Abercrombie began his twenty years as Lever
professor. He also continued the professional self-education that
was to make him the greatest planner to hold the Lever Chair, and
the most famous of all British town planners.

If one calls the years up to 1909, when he was thirty, the years of
preliminary education for Abercrombie, his working life covered the
whole period from the beginnings of official town planning in
Britain to its firm establishment as a permanent system, based on
counties and county boroughs, by the 1947 Act, and the hard practice
and distinguished achievements of the following decade. He also
lived to see the beginning of the falling-off in the employment of
consultants like himself.

Abercrombie resembled his successor in being small, dark,
vivacious, witty, with a wide range of interests, and a tremendous
worker. He was interested in draughtsmanship and art generally,
in music, furniture and literature and spoke French well and
German pretty well. The late Cecil Beaton held that 'people who
have succeeded in one aspect of life would have done equally well if
their innate talent had been used in other directions'[6]: and Cecil
Beaton had known a multitude of famous people on easy terms.
Abercrombie would almost certainly have succeeded in other
careers; but fortunately for him and for Britain he had the gifts and
tenacity to be able to work out the most rewarding approaches to,
and the essentials of, town and regional planning and rural and
urban conservation during the twenty inter-war years of little
achievement anywhere. He never lost his enthusiasm for all
planning and even for loosely associated subjects.[7] And he was still
young enough when real planning began in 1941 to be entrusted
with both of the London plans and many others.

Town and regional plans are rarely carried out as the planner first
recommends. He is indeed a lucky man who can point to anything on
the ground that has been done exactly as he suggested; and
Abercrombie had his moments of disillusion. Towards the end he
said to a friend that nothing he had done had ever come off.[8] But he
could hardly have meant this in any broad sense. He was the
greatest teacher, guide and practitioner in British and Commonwealth planning, and as a Gold Medallist of the Town Planning
Institute in 1955 he could have looked around and seen almost
nothing being done which he had not influenced in some way.

His Youth and Early Career

Leslie Patrick Abercrombie was born on the 6 June 1879 at the

Manor House, Ashton-on-Mersey, and was the seventh of nine children. His father, William Abercrombie, came originally from Fife, but worked as a stockbroker in Manchester; and his mother, Sarah Ann Heron, came from Yorkshire. William Abercrombie is said to have had wide interests in both literature and art. At least two of his children, Patrick and Lascelles, shared these interests, which were perhaps, for the father, too engrossing for success as a stockbroker, at which he at length failed; and around the turn of the century William and his wife and at least the same two sons moved to a small house in Oxton, part of Birkenhead. Both sons then had to earn their own living and Lascelles started training as a quantity surveyor. He hated this, and like many others of his time, trained himself in what did interest him, which was literature and poetry. He became a lecturer in poetry at Liverpool while his brother held the Lever Chair, and later became Professor of English Literature at Leeds, and helped Patrick with his study of Stratford-on-Avon in 1923.

The two brothers were very different. Dixon Scott, a journalist and letter-writer of some note in the north-west of England, once remarked that Lascelles 'says things that you can remember. With Pat – well its Pat himself you remember.'[9] Patrick Abercrombie was educated at Lockers Park Preparatory School, Hemel Hempstead, and at Uppingham, where he first began to appreciate the beauties of the English countryside. He also spent one year at the Realschule in Lucerne, studying French and German. His knowledge of these languages was to be a great help to him in later years, when he became prominent at international gatherings of architects, housing experts and town planners.[10] This fairly liberal education, which cost money even in those days, was ended before his father's failure as a stockbroker, as also were his four years as articled pupil to the Manchester architect Charles Heathcote.[11]

On moving to Birkenhead, just across the Mersey from Liverpool, Abercrombie entered the office of Sir Arnold Thornely for three years.[12] He also entered for design competitions run by the Liverpool School of Architecture, and won some prizes; he was not, however, a student at the school. Abercrombie, despite his early loss of an eye,[13] was a highly skilled draughtsman, especially in sketching and drawing maps and diagrams. His unmistakable style and method of presentation of maps suggests that nearly all of the illustrations in his reports up to 1939 were drawn by himself. It is probable that it was in his last year in Thornely's office (1904), that he met and impressed Reilly, the new Professor of Architecture at Liverpool University, and only five years older than himself.

From Liverpool Abercrombie moved to Chester, sixteen miles away, in the hope of becoming a partner in a local firm of architects. In this he was disappointed, but it was probably in Chester, where the growth and form of the town can be traced with considerable accuracy from Roman times, that he first became interested in town structure and development. He saw in Chester and successive maps of it the effects of trying to check the silting-up of the river, of the coming of the canal and railways, and Chester's long history as an administrative centre and garrison town.[14] He was almost certainly influenced by the writings and lectures of Patrick Geddes about civic surveys in the previous decade. Geddes's *City Development* was published in 1904. In 1907 Abercrombie was very pleased to be offered by Reilly a post in the School of Architecture as Assistant Lecturer and Drawing Instructor at the then normal salary of £150 per annum and £20 for the drawing.[15]

His Appointment to Civic Design

Two years later came the big change. In November 1909 the Minutes of Council and Senate at Liverpool University recorded, as a follow-up of Adshead's appointment as Associate Professor of Civic Design six months earlier, that:

> The Town Planning Bill submitted to both Houses of the Legislature during the autumn, has directed attention to the evils that arise from the lax and casual way in which our cities are allowed to develop, and to some extent has prepared the public mind to pay regard to beauty as well as to comfort and health. But civic design, in the large sense, has not as yet been studied as a system by our architects or our engineers; and if any effectual progress is to be made, principles and methods must become the subject of regular instruction.

In June of the same year Abercrombie had been appointed Research Fellow in Town Planning and Civic Design, at a salary of £120 plus £30 for travel,[16] although he continued to draw a small income from work in the School of Architecture. In the following year he became editor of the new and eventually famous *Town Planning Review*. He continued to lecture in the School of Architecture on building construction and Gothic architecture until 1911, when his work in civic design became so great – comprising evening as well as day courses – that he could not continue to help in architecture.[17]

As has been stated, the specialized professional educational life of Britain's greatest town and regional planner may be said to have started in earnest in 1909. It was a rigorous, almost masochistic education. He wrote at least 16 articles totalling 163 pages in the first two volumes of the *Town Planning Review* and, one suspects, a number of the anonymous notes.

All these in two years. One reads of such labours with awe in present times, when a lecturer who performs his teaching duties and produces one tolerably good article every two years is considered to be doing well enough for his career and his department's record.[18] Admittedly most students in the first years of civic design were evening students.

It is therefore pleasing to find that just before the great year of
1909 he made time to marry Emily Maud Gordon, and that his
courtship showed that the industrious apprentice had quite
another side to his character. Crossing as he did twice daily on the
Birkenhead–Liverpool Ferry, it was Abercrombie's habit (as it was
of many passengers) to walk round and round the deck, seeing the
liners and relishing the sea-breezes. In 1906 or thereabouts he
spotted Emily Maud, a strikingly pretty girl of fifteen or sixteen who
also travelled on the ferry, and was probably a very junior office girl
in Liverpool. She was the daughter of a family 'in humble
circumstances' as the phrase then ran. After observing her quite a
number of times, Abercrombie found out her name, approached her
father, declared honourable intentions and Emily Maud was sent for
about two years to a school of some social and perhaps academic
pretensions. For this, it is almost certain, Abercrombie paid, though
what he paid with is not so clear. Perhaps family finances had
improved since the move to Oxton, or Abercrombie had some
earnings other than his university salary.[19] They were married
when Emily Maud was probably seventeen or eighteen.[20] It was a
happy marriage. Thomas Sharp said that when he first saw
Abercrombie in 1924, walking with many mayors at a conference at
Canterbury, Abercrombie linked his arm affectionately with his
wife's, an action that was rare in those more formal times. The
Abercrombies had a son and a daughter.[21]

Patrick Abercrombie is today rarely thought of as an architect, and
it is true that he never designed any major architectural work, and
that his planning so dwarfed the buildings he did design that
most obituaries never mentioned them. Yet he was wholly an
architect till 1909, an architectural draughtsman of skill – though
not so good as he was with maps – and he intermingled architectural
and planning work whenever opportunity and time allowed. For
instance, he became a partner in the Chester architectural firm of
Lockwood, Abercrombie & Saxon in 1920,[22] and consultant architect
to the Department of Health for Scotland in 1936. He became an
Associate of the Royal Institute of British Architects in 1915, a Fellow
in 1925, Vice-President in 1937, and Royal Gold Medallist in 1946;
this last being a rare honour for a man who had designed hardly any
buildings.

Abercrombie did not see town planning as merely enlarged
architecture as Reilly always did, and as Adshead had in his first
planning years. He saw both of these as different but almost
interchangeable aspects of one great subject, which embraced
architecture, civic design, landscape design (large and small),
housing, regional planning, and the conservation and amenity
aspects of towns, villages and countryside. Probably he saw them all
as different facets of how to use land well, and keep it and buildings
in good heart. He was to work on, or at least to write of, all these
things and (as Holford wrote) 'countered the statistical and

ideological with a certain eighteenth-century elegance'. He felt, no doubt because he was an architect, that architecture was a sound base from which to start. In this he inspired others, or set a fashion from which the University of Liverpool has seen no reason to depart. All holders of the Lever Chair, to this day, took their first degree in architecture.

According to Professor Gerald Dix - the foremost authority on Abercrombie's life and work - 'One essential ability his architectural work gave him was that of considering concurrently and then mastering a range of functional and aesthetic requirements'[23] and 'few had his capacity to learn from their experience as well as to use it for teaching purposes, and he was apparently indefatigable'.[24] He was always a teacher in the *atelier* manner, as well as practitioner, and inspired all students - once they had speeded up their mental processes to cope with his fast speech. Every lecture was different, and illustrated by the latest examples and problems drawn from his professional practice.

Abercrombie plunged into teaching, travel and writing all the articles in the *Review* that have already been mentioned. Derek Plumstead, his pupil and assistant on several planning schemes, wrote of him: 'He was a tremendous inspiring force. The whole atmosphere of a room would become electrified by his enlivening spirit.'[25]

> *He had a breadth of culture and depth of knowledge which is almost unknown today in our specialist-ridden world ... words came racing out of his mouth with the spluttering rapidity of machine-gun fire. He had a loud resonant voice which went echoing round the lecture hall or committee room: it was irresistible to imitate him ... to the end of his days there was a sparkle about him and his voice retained its youthful urgency.*[26]

T. C. Coote, who worked with him on several plans repeats that Abercrombie 'had the delightful facility of making one feel inspired when with him'.[27]

Abercrombie's great energy[28] was coupled with another quality, which was also shared with his successor William Holford. He too could relax, and could do so 'with startling completeness whenever he was free'.[29] He was interested in calligraphy as well as the furniture and literature previously mentioned. His other great love was music particularly that of Schumann. Sir George Pepler, in his appreciation of Abercrombie in 1957,[30] was reminded of the time when he was external examiner for the Department of Civic Design and was staying with the Abercrombies in Birkenhead. When Pepler came down for breakfast he found his host in the Chinese-style drawing room playing Schumann with great gusto on a grand piano. It seems natural, therefore, that Abercrombie should be a member of the Sandon Studios Society - then the meeting place for artists of all kinds

Above: Holford at the age of
22-23 years. *Below:* One of the
'cowshed' studios of the
Liverpool School of Architecture
in 1930. Reilly is standing in
the foreground. This is said to
be a photograph of the 5th
(final) year but neither Holford
nor Gordon Stephenson, the
best known of that year in later
life, can be identified.

Holford in Italy.
Above: The main
entrance of Holford
design for a Museu
of Fine Arts which
won him the Rome
Scholarship in 193(
Middle: The tomb c
the baker Eurisace
Rome of which
Holford made his
first measured
drawing (*see below*

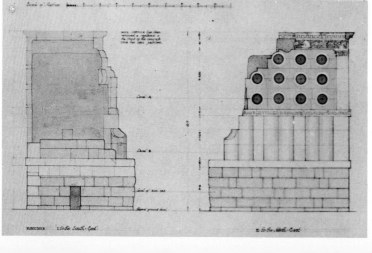

Above: Holford's watercolour drawing of the Piazza del Populo. *Below:* Marjorie Brooks, who was studying in Rome at the same time as Holford was a Rome Scholar in Mural Painting. Blond and good-looking she 'had a great deal of trouble with Italian men'. She and Holford married in 1933.

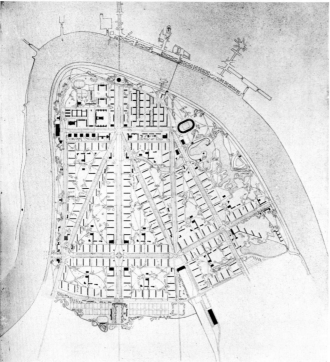

Above: Oil painting by Holford which may have been prepared as part of the design for housing on reclaimed land near Antwerp in 1933. *Middle:* Layout plan for the Antwerp scheme, prepared by Holford, Gordon Stephenson and others. It did not win a prize, and there were doubts whether the main parcel of their large drawings had ever been opened by the competition's promoters. *Below:* Garden front of a pair of houses at Icklesham in East Sussex. These were the only buildings designed by Holford himself in the Modernist or Functional style of the 1930s.

Above: Bedford Street and Abercrombie Square in Liverpool. The house with the gable roof was Holford's home and office from 1933–65. The new building, with the milk float in front, is the Department of Civic Design. *Below:* The Team Valley industrial estate near Newcastle-upon-Tyne in 1939. Holford designed the administration building in the foreground.

Above: One of the lounges in the 20 hostels intended for munition workers, designed and built by the Holford team in 1941–43. *Below:* A dining hall which could also be used as a theatre or cinema.

Above: Drawing by Gordon Cullen of the Holden and Holford proposal for a pedestrian way leading from St Paul's to the Thames. This formed part of their general proposals prepared in 1946–47 for the rebuilding of the City of London.

Below: Aerial view of central Cambridge drawn by Holford to show the location of the main proposals in the Holford-Wright plan of 1950.

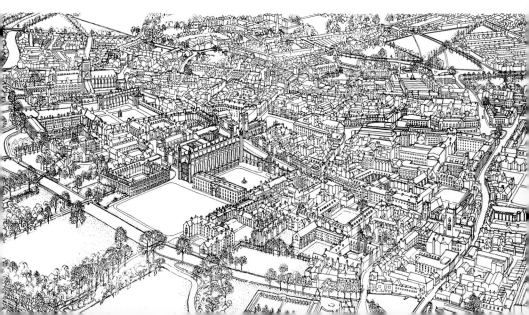

Above: Holford's house, nearest to the camera, in Cambridge Terrace, Regent's Park, London where they lived from 1952-64. *Below:* The Holford's corner house on Marine Parade, Brighton. They later bought the adjoining house on the right. For the house of a famous architect it had peculiarly no rear access, which proved very inconvenient.

Above: Photograph of the model of Holford's proposals for the west end of St Paul's Cathedral by which two new pedestrian squares would have been formed. *Below:* One of the many drawings which Holford prepared when studying possible new layouts around St. Paul's.

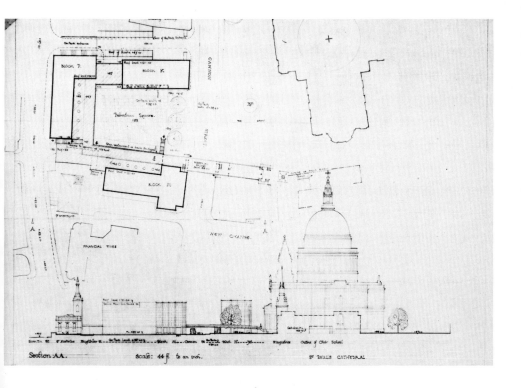

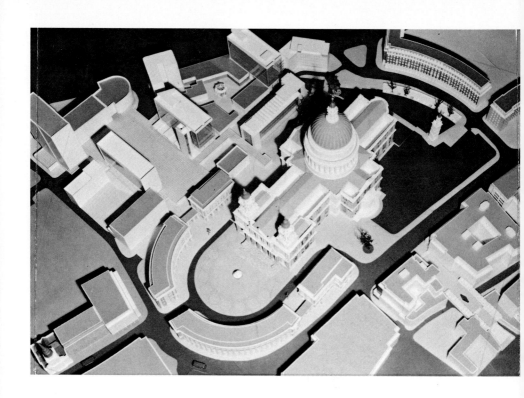

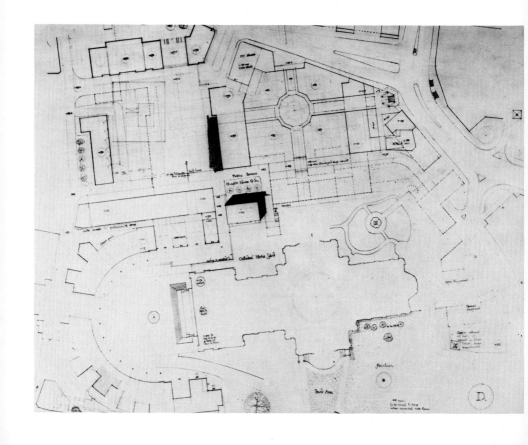

Opposite page above: Model of an earlier Holford proposal for the layout around St. Paul's. *Opposite page below:* Another Holford drawing for St. Paul's.
Above: Holford in later life. He remained youthful in appearance and movement until just before his death. *Below:* Holford's drawings for Barclays Bank, Maidstone (see overleaf).

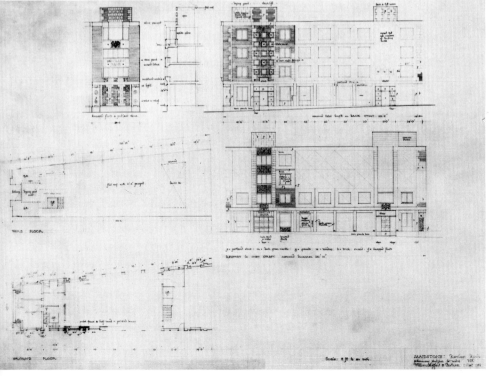

Above: Barclays Bank at Maidstone, designed by Holford. To his colleague he seemed often to be trying to express in a modern way all the recesses, surface detail and shadows which he had admired in Italian Renaissance buildings. *Below:* The tower at Exeter University designed by Holford. Tower fascinated him and he proposed 'to break the height barrier' with a very tall building near St Paul's - this came to nothing.

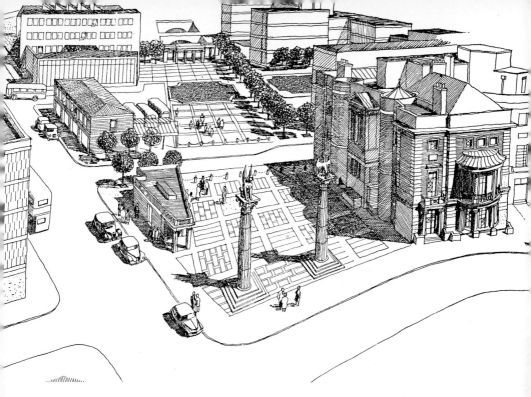

Above: Proposals for new buildings at Liverpool University in 1952. A drawing by Howard Mason. *Below:* Layout for the centre at Corby New Town 1951-52. The first stages of building the town centre closely followed this design.

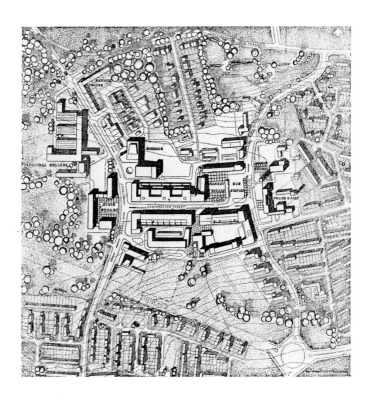

Above and opposite page: Photographs of Holford's 1962 model for a new layout for Piccadilly in which the Eros fountain was placed on a pedestrian platform raised above the level of the roadways. *Below:* The new library for Tonbridge School, one of the last buildings in which Holford took a close personal interest.

The Department of Civic Design at Liverpool University celebrated its Jubilee in 1959, a date at which it is suitable to end this record of the achievements of the four men who made the Department famous and of their students and colleagues. Thereafter things could not be the same; by 1979 120 institutions in Great Britain offered courses in planning and associated subjects. Things were not the same for Liverpool either. Chambré Hardman's winter photograph of the 1950s, taken from the steps of the Museums at Liverpool, perhaps typifies 50 years of decline since the great days of pre-1914.

in Liverpool. Along with Adshead and Reilly, he was on the first provisional committee elected in December 1909 to draft the rules and regulations for the new society[31] and in 1930 he became the chairman. 1909 was indeed the springboard year in Abercrombie's life.

After becoming editor of the *Town Planning Review* in 1910, Abercrombie added to his interests and knowledge by attending conferences in Vienna and London and won the first prize for the layout of a housing estate at Prestatyn.[32] He wrote, as has been stated, 16 articles under his own name in the *Town Planning Review* for 1910-11 and 1911-12 and also probably some of the anonymous reviews - like that of the Birley Griffin plan for Canberra - and notes on the proposed New City at Delhi. As he also wrote three articles on the planning of Brussels, and others on Ghent and Berlin, he plainly made full use of the modest sum available for travel. He probably helped students in architecture as well as his own students with the proposals for replanning parts of Liverpool and for new housing at Port Sunlight, for which Lever offered prizes. He won a third prize in the Bradford housing competition, was assessor for one at Doncaster and in 1914 helped Adshead edit the report of the Liverpool Town Planning Conference held in that year.

Evening as well as day courses were held for the nine to twelve students in the department, and one wonders at what time of night Abercrombie usually managed to take the ferry back to Birkenhead. Such constant work and travel and membership of international bodies may explain why he instinctively chose a wife who probably had no intellectual pretensions. Professor Dix suspects that home life was rather incidental to Abercrombie, and that his vitality may have absorbed some of that of his wife and children. The advantages of being the wife or child of a great man are perhaps written up a little too much: there are also distinct drawbacks.

In 1914 Patrick Geddes had organized one of his famous Civics Exhibitions in Dublin,[33] and this led Lord Aberdeen, the Lord Lieutenant, to offer a prize of £500 for an international competition for plans for the future development of Dublin. The assessors were Patrick Geddes, Charles McCarthy of Dublin and John Nolen of Massachusetts, a well-known American planner and author of planning books. Abercrombie decided to enter the competition and submitted his scheme in partnership with Sydney and Arthur Kelly. The outbreak of the 1914-18 war delayed assessment of the schemes, and Abercrombie and the Kellys were finally placed first in the autumn of 1916. It has been repeatedly stated that Abercrombie won the Dublin competition in 1913, even by careful men like Pepler and Holford. But it was not so. The conditions for the competition were in fact published in the *Town Planning Review* for July 1914 and the announcement of the result was in the *Builder* Vol. CXI for 1 September 1916.

In 1914 the Town Planning Institute had been founded and Abercrombie was a founder member. His absence from the Provisional Committee set up in July 1913 is no doubt explained by

Adshead being a member.[34]

In 1914 the war began which for quarter of a century was just called The Great War, and a multitude of books assure us that things were never the same again. A million British dead should have made it certain – as the politicians often promised – that in the post-war world life for the poorer three-quarters of the population would be greatly improved. What seems to us now the utterly disgraceful pre-1914 contrasts between the lives of the rich and the poor were slowly diminished – the more slowly because of economic crises and heavy unemployment. These problems, and the building of 4½ million houses between the wars, meant that town planning received small attention and, as is described in the next chapter, only small progress was made. In Britain between 1914 and 1941 it was Abercrombie who achieved most of the progress with plans which, if they had been carried out, would have been great forward steps; though George Pepler prepared the opportunities from his position in central government.

As Adshead had departed to London in 1914, Lever wrote to Abercrombie about civic design for the first time, so far as is known.[35] Lever had helped the School of Tropical Medicine as well as the Department of Civic Design and when the former received a substantial legacy Lever deducted £400 a year from the sum he paid to Tropical Medicine and raised the Department of Civic Design's annual payment from £800 to £1,200. This upset the university greatly, and Vice-Chancellor Dale and Hugh Rathbone, then Treasurer of the university, tried hard to persuade Lever to change his mind. They used what seem (to judge from Lever's letters) not very convincing arguments. One feels Lever quite enjoyed writing one or two of his replies. For example:

> ... I am unable to be of any relief in this matter. I
> cannot in any way at present increase my
> contributions to the Liverpool University. My
> proposal was made with every desire to help the
> School of Town Planning and Civic Design, but of
> course I need hardly point out that the decision on
> the matter rests with the Council of the Liverpool
> University and not with myself. In my opinion I
> am doing far more for Liverpool University than
> the Liverpool University has claims upon me.
> Liverpool is a wealthy city and has the great
> privilege of counting amongst her sons some of the
> wealthiest as well as the most warm-hearted and
> generous citizens that any town or city could
> possess, and I am confident you will have no
> difficulty in any appeal you make to them.
> With all good wishes ...[36]

The Bolton man who had given a lot to Liverpool enjoyed poking mild fun at Liverpool men, and the suggestion of a threat was not lost on the university, but perhaps some of those in authority still grudged money spent on the Department of Civic Design. At any rate, early in 1915, there were rumours that the department was to be closed down. That was indeed an obvious wartime economy: its professor had gone, and its Diploma students numbered three in 1914-15 and fell, at one time, to one. Yet if closure had occurred, the history of British and Commonwealth town and regional planning would have been quite different, and Britain during the great planning period of 1941-65 would have been grievously short of talented men.

In February 1915, the Vice-Chancellor told Lever that the university intended to appoint a new professor of civic design. Despite that, rumours continued that the Department was threatened. Both Reilly and Abercrombie, however, were on the alert, and in May Lever wrote to his solicitor George Harley asking him to seek 'for an assurance ... that there is no intention to cripple or hamper or close the Liverpool School of Civic Design'.[37] After that salvo the plotters gave up, and Abercrombie was appointed as second Lever professor from October 1915. Perhaps the salary of £400 a year without share of fees showed some continuing displeasure, because by 1914 Reilly was being paid over £800 by the university.

The extent of Lever's help to civic design, as seen by Abercrombie, is summed up in a letter he wrote to the second Lord Leverhulme in 1931:

> ... my Department of Civic Design has always
> been quite self-contained as regards its money and
> like so many other creations we have never had
> any grant out of general University funds either
> for stationery, library, secretarial or what not.
> Your father's money has paid for everything, and
> the only thing one can say is that after the quarrel
> over the School of Tropical Medicine, he no longer
> agreed to us occupying the Old Bluecoat Chambers
> and we have been in rooms found by the
> University, but through your own kindness in
> carrying on your father's wishes when we get the
> new School of Architecture we shall then again
> not even be quartered in buildings found out of the
> general University fund'.[38]

The Second Professor

Abercrombie did not deliver an Inaugural Lecture at Liverpool, doubtless because of wartime dispersal of staff and students. In the following year he and the two Kellys were announced as winners of the Dublin competition, as stated earlier. This was Abercrombie's first major plan and despite the war - or perhaps because the plan was about something peaceful - it brought him wide recognition.

He published the plan as *Dublin of the Future: The New Town Plan* in 1922,[39] just after a civil war had greatly extended the damage of 1916. The frontispiece of the report, sponsored by the Civics Institute of Ireland, is a haunting cartoon by Harry Clarke of Death or Disease pointing to the dreadful Dublin slums with one hand, and with the other to flames engulfing (as they had) famous Dublin buildings.

Abercrombie stated in the introduction that the main drawings were of the 1914 scheme, as it would have been unfair to other entrants in the competition to incorporate all the improvements the authors had thought of since 1914. Such punctilious behaviour is uncommon, and might reasonably have irritated Dubliners who wanted the best available ideas for their city, and did not care a fig about Abercrombie's feelings towards ex-competitors. In fact, the proposed amendments are explained in the report.

The most conspicuous proposal was to double the number of bridges at the centre of Dublin and to create a huge square or traffic circus, nearly half a mile long, into which all approach roads - all fifteen of them - would discharge. This no doubt was the feature to which Abercrombie referred in writing: 'The *spectacular* is impossible to avoid when competing against others: it is necessary to arrest the eye with features whose boldness are (*sic*) perhaps more evident than their practicability.' Nothing came of the great square.

The remaining proposals are familiar to one who has worked on the same problems[40]: parks or park walks on Bull Island and along the Tolka and the Dodder, improvements to the docks and the two canals, and to the various main roads. The only really dated proposal is that for *Parkways*: that is, main roads flanked by trees and providing routes for trams, road vehicles and pedestrians. The trees would certainly help to reduce the traffic noise that reached nearby buildings, but it is a mystery why the designers of parkways in the United States and Britain between 1895 and 1930 thought that pedestrians, no doubt with children and dogs, would like to take their walks in a 'Central Promenade' with trams rattling past on one side and on the other motor vehicles, some with solid tyres.

Dublin dwellings were decaying in 1916 faster than they could be repaired or replaced. Even this had changed little up to 1966, by which time the powerlessness of landlords to enforce repairs was putting at risk the mass of unique Georgian Dublin. Very little of the plan was carried out, though houses have been built on some of the sites recommended. In 1940-41 Abercrombie was again called in for advice on the planning of Dublin.

For the remainder of the 1914-18 war Abercrombie did what he could. He took part in the preparation of a civic survey for South Lancashire, and joined Adshead on the planning of Dormanstown, the housing estate for steel workers outside Redcar in Yorkshire on which 300 dwellings were built during the war. They were among the first to have steel frames and reinforced concrete walls.[41] In 1917, the Department of Civic Design collaborated with University College London in a Replanning of Belgium Exhibition, and Abercrombie gave two lectures about Brussels. He also edited the one volume of the *Town Planning Review* for 1917–18. In 1919 Abercrombie ran a six-week course in civic design to bring ex-Service architects and surveyors up to date with planning developments since 1914. In this course he continued to have the help of H. Chaloner Dowdall and T. H. Mawson.

Regional Planning

Abercrombie's first introduction to regional planning was when he served on the South Wales Regional Planning Committee in 1919 and 1920 [42,43] but his first big chance came in 1920 when he was invited, through the agency of George Pepler, to prepare with T. H. Johnson a plan for the Doncaster coalfield which covered 169 square miles and had a population of about 140,000. This plan's main contents have been summarized by Professor Dix.[44] Doncaster was then regarded as a growth area, and the authors paid great attention to topography, recommendations for roads, and suitable sites for housing and industry. In later years Abercrombie told Clough Williams-Ellis that of all his plans he took most pride in that for Doncaster.

Abercrombie may be regarded as the planner with the greatest feeling for topography whom Britain has produced: particularly for that of country or mixed town and countryside areas. He had a passion for maps, and by examining Ordnance Survey maps and re-drawing them in whole or part, he seemed to be able to create in his mind a relief map of an area and of all its principal topographical features.

He was a talented draughtsman as an architect, as a sketcher of village scenes and in designing layouts for villages, but it was in cartography that his distinctive skill and style were most apparent. One cannot mistake an Abercrombie drawing, whether wholly drawn by him, or worked up by him over an Ordnance Survey map as base. When he wanted to prepare a diagram he could reduce his material to the barest essentials – as in the proposed road system for Dublin – but his skill and enthusiasm were at their greatest when mapping part of a county or a small town. Then enthusiasm would bubble over, as it did when he was drawing a map of Sandwich in the East Kent report; he added the Borough's Coat of Arms in a convenient vacant space, in great detail and with gentle fun: for waves are rising from the green fields and breaking in foam against the Arms just to call attention to Sandwich's former role as one of the Cinque Ports. He also obviously enjoyed his reconstruction of the plan of Thanet when it was still divided from the rest of Kent.

If one looks through the published Abercrombie reports one feels sure that – up to the Second World War – he drew nearly all the maps himself, as well as the sketches of street scenes. As there were fourteen or fifteen published pre-war reports, as well as others unpublished, the sheer labour involved must have been prodigious. Towards the end of his life in a note to George Pepler[45] Abercrombie excused himself from attending a dinner on the grounds of indigestion caused, so his doctor said, by a lifetime bent over a drawing board. On the other hand, even his greatest admirers will admit that Abercrombie could sometimes lapse into stilted mannerisms, such as dividing the East Kent report into PART THE FIRST, THE SECOND and so on in big Roman capitals.

Abercrombie attached much importance to private practice, both for extending his own knowledge and enabling him to provide for his students current examples of planning problems and solutions. He wrote: 'without these external contacts and experience, teaching (in planning and architecture) would gradually be etiolated into a pallid enunciation of theory based on second-hand information.'[46] Professor Gordon Stephenson confirms that Abercrombie brought current examples from his practice into every lecture.

Abercrombie never had his own office save one he shared in Suffolk Street, London, with Clifford Holliday for two or three years before 1939; and only for a few post-1945 years did he have one constant assistant, Derek Plumstead. Abercrombie, like Holford, was very much an individualist: an artist with all his ideas in his own head or in documents that could be contained in one room. His method of work on his bigger schemes was to seek a collaborator in the locality concerned. This was often an officer of the principal local authority. Abercrombie thus obtained general local knowledge, and speedy access to local specialist knowledge, of most valuable kinds; and usually local office space and some junior assistance. The men concerned were proud to be joint authors of a published report which would be read by many influential people, beginning with the Councillors who employed them. Being human, they became the more proud as Abercrombie became more eminent.

Abercrombie possessed great charm and simplicity, and must have been able to talk to everyone about things of mutual interest without any condescension. In those days, principal local authority engineers and surveyors had usually come up the hard way, and could sometimes be gruff in manner, but there is no record of quarrels between Abercrombie and a collaborator.[47] Whether Abercrombie rewrote the contributions from others in his earlier reports is not known. Later on – on the two London plans for example -he certainly did not as is explained on p.144.

In the Doncaster plan, begun in 1920, Abercrombie was lucky in that he had already assessed a competition there, and had previously known his collaborator T. H. Johnson with whom he was to work again at Sheffield in 1930. The Doncaster plan, as has been said, became the pattern for many more – both by Abercrombie and others. It was not too long, ninety-three far-from-crowded pages, and was divided into a few chapters that may be called 'Survey', 'Appropriate Developments', 'Communications' and 'Effect of Proposals'. There were in all sixteen maps or diagrams, all by Abercrombie or prepared under his guidance. The coloured map of suggested future growth (coloured maps were at that time very rare in published planning reports) shows a number of satellite towns or settlements near collieries, and proposals for satellite towns thereafter became common in planning reports.

One of the Doncaster maps showed land that should not be built on because of the dangers of subsidence or flooding or both. Sir George Peopler wrote later that despite this warning a local authority decided to build on some of this land, and invited Dr Addison, then Minister of Health and therefore in charge of planning and housing, to lay the foundation stone of the first house. On the appointed day the site was found to be under five feet of water.[48] In 1925 Abercrombie and Johnson prepared plans for one of the proposed Doncaster satellite communities. This was Kirk Sandall, near Messrs Pilkington's Doncaster works.

From 1920 on, the consultant work that was offered to Abercrombie quickly increased, and it was as well that, after the 1919–21 peak, student numbers fell off to an average of eight for four years, and usually they were evening students. Thomas Sharp wrote of him at his death:

> *Britain has lost its first and probably its last great town and country planner. He was fortunate in his time, as the time was fortunate in him. The first forty years of deliberate planning, the years of opportunity for the new profession of planning consultant, coincided almost exactly with all but the last years of his working life. And since he had qualities that were far superior to those of his contemporaries, he dominated the planning field for the whole of that time.*[49]

In 1923 Abercrombie undertook a study of Deeside with two collaborators, and in the same year produced the report on Stratford-on-Avon on which he was helped by his brother Lascelles. Perhaps he felt that in studying and writing about the town so closely associated with Shakespeare a specially high standard of writing was called for, with suitable literary allusions, and that it would be helpful to have the Professor of Literature at Leeds at his elbow.

Between 1920 and 1924 Abercrombie carried out (with R. H. Mattocks) the work published as *Sheffield: A Civic Survey and Suggestions towards a Development Plan.*[50] In this study he paid tribute to his old mentor Patrick Geddes by very full studies of population, industry, housing and topography, and so acknowledged Geddes's constant (and it must be admitted, rather boring) insistence that what mattered for full understanding of a town and its needs were *Folk, Work, Place.*

Sheffield contained a thorough examination of thirty aspects of the city: from contours, geology, wind and smoke to back-to-back houses, accessible moorlands and licensed premises. The proposals were hardly less thorough: thirty-three items under eleven main headings, and there were forty-nine illustrations including many maps, several in colour. The Sheffield survey also became something of a model for planners, and Geddes himself was understandably very pleased with it.

Abercrombie's chief fame lies in his studies of 'regions' - or, as they could be more accurately described - parts of mainly rural counties from 100 square miles up to, in the case of East Kent, about 400 and more than 500 in the Bristol and Bath region. 'There [in regional planning] he was both pioneer and indisputable master' with his 'highly developed sense of large-scale design'.[51] It was Abercrombie who first converted Geddes's regional planning principles into a practical plan which could be copied by all local authorities and by central government. Regional planning was an attempt to break down the jealous independence of the multitude of local authorities, many very small. Abercrombie wrote that regional planning

> aims indeed at setting before the community a
> scheme for its growth upon rational lines, having
> in view its industrial prosperity and the health of
> its inhabitants, and above all it attempts to
> eliminate that parochialism which is inevitably set
> up by the artificial boundaries between local
> authorities, which are so necessary for the detailed
> carrying out of their services but which without a
> regional committee, tend to produce isolated
> communities resentful of any interference with
> their own existence to meet the needs of their
> neighbours.[52]

It was Abercrombie's analyses and arguments for regional planning - combining industrial, agricultural, economic, social, technical and architectural factors - that inspired other planners to follow his example.

It may, therefore, be forgotten that he prepared reports on a number of urban areas besides Sheffield, Dublin and Stratford. These included Warrington, Bath, Haifa, Plymouth, Warwick and Edinburgh. Yet Thomas Sharp wrote:

> ... it has to be admitted that some of the later town
> plans with which his name is associated are below
> his best work. But because of his manner of
> working, it is difficult to estimate the full measure
> of Abercrombie's direction or participation in
> these.[53]

The County of London and Greater London plans, referred to later, are exceptions. The list of smaller urban studies, housing estates, etc. runs to more than twenty.[53]

On looking through the long list of Abercrombie's work, and after reading one example of his writing on each new field of interest that attracted him, one has the impression that he came to his full powers

in the 1920s (aged forty-one to fifty-one); that in the 1930s he applied
his great knowledge and experience rather than added to them; that
his experience of the broadest planning matters was summarized in
his minority report to the Barlow Commission (1939); and his final
flowering came in the two London plans, published when he was
sixty-four and sixty-six. He continued to do valuable work later on,
but by then he had become an elder statesman, guiding younger
men, and he no longer did the groundwork himself. For example, in
the Clyde Valley regional plan he had the support of Robert
Matthew and Robert Grieve (both of whom were later knighted for
distinguished services to architecture and planning).

It is difficult to credit that in the early 1920s Abercrombie
accomplished so much and maintained so high a standard. Besides
his Doncaster, Deeside, revised Dublin, Stratford-on-Avon and
Sheffield reports and the beginnings of East Kent – all of which have
been mentioned already – he undertook a Teeside Survey and
Scheme with Adshead, and became a Fellow of the Royal Institute of
British Architects and President of the Town Planning Institute.
His inaugural address as president was on the theme of 'The
Extension of the Town Planning Spirit'.[54] Abercrombie defined this
phrase as 'A programme of requirements upon which is based an
organic plan leading to a process of harmonious development...' He
held that the extension of the town planning spirit was shown in the
number of town plans that had been submitted voluntarily to the
Ministry, but foresaw possibilities for further expansion into
industrial planning. He also emphasized the need for harmony
when designing streets, and the danger to the countryside of
uncontrolled urban expansion. Civic survey was the home of this
town planning spirit and Abercrombie concluded: 'It is not a
dissipation of energy that I am advocating but a radiation of
influence.'

These labours should have been enough for any man, and one
hopes that Abercrombie found a little time to relax and see his family
in the holiday homes he had, successively, at Cilcain in North Wales
from about 1915 to 1925, and from 1925 to his death in houses near
Holyhead. Nevertheless, Abercrombie soon took on another responsibility. He was one of the few hundred people, of all who loved the
countryside, who had become appalled by 1925 at the dreadful
ribbon developments that were occurring on the outskirts of many
towns and villages or scattered in the countryside, and were
determined to do something about it. The poverty of design, cheap
materials alien to the locality and shoddy construction were
especially painful to Abercrombie, whose deep affection for
traditional methods of building (above all in the Cotswolds and
Wales) had grown since his student days.

He made time to write of his fears and proposed solutions in 'The
Preservation of Rural England,'[55] an article published in the *Town
Planning Review* in 1926. This is a penetrating and succinct account
of the problems of the land – all the land – in 1925–26. Abercrombie

wrote that the preservation of a few historical monuments was very worthy but it was the good use and conservation of all the land, cultivated and wild, with streams, rivers, lakes and hills, that really mattered. When first published in the *Town Planning Review* the essay ran to fifty-six pages, and covered almost all aspects of the use of land which were assisted or brought under protection in the following fifty years: national parks, footpaths, village surveys, afforestation, layout, building materials and the rest. It is at once a prophetic list of what ought to be done and a call for action. In it he wrote:

> *This rural England of ours is at this moment*
> *menaced with a more sudden and thorough*
> *change than ever before: it is not safe to leave*
> *these changes to adjust themselves, hoping that*
> *somehow a general harmony will result from*
> *individualistic satisfactions: it should be possible*
> *for a just balance to be struck between*
> *conservation and development: certain parts must*
> *be preserved intact and inviolate but others can,*
> *after suffering a change, bring forth something*
> *new but beautiful, provided a conscious effort is*
> *made.*[56]

The short book that followed[57] led almost immediately to the foundation of the Council for the Preservation of Rural England with Lord Crawford as Chairman and Abercrombie as Hon. Secretary, as has been related in the previous chapter. It was followed closely by a similar Council for Rural Wales sponsored by Abercrombie and his friend Clough Williams-Ellis, whose *England and the Octopus* appeared in 1928. Nine years later Clough Williams-Ellis edited *Britain and the Beast*[57] to which Abercrombie contributed a suitable chapter on country planning. *Britain and the Beast* was a less directly propagandist publication than *England and the Octopus*. The contributors included J. M. Keynes, G. M. Trevelyan, Lord Horder and Thomas Sharp (rather typically his chapter was called 'The North East: Hells and Hills'). All the authors dealt in one way or another with problems of the countryside and its conservation, and some with aspects of urban sprawl. But by 1937 most people of knowledge and goodwill – and this did not exclude all politicians – agreed with nearly all of the constructive suggestions in the book. The case was already proven; and directly the Second World War ended, action began which has done a great deal to safeguard the countryside and smaller towns, and even to recover a proportion of land damaged by industrial and mineral working. The great, painful and inexcusable exception has been the licence enjoyed by farmers to create or expand small packets of squalid buildings almost anywhere. In time no doubt even this last abuse of the countryside, by a prosperous section of the community, will be remedied.

Between 1927 and his departure to London in 1935, Abercrombie increased even further the number and range of his activities, or what would now be called his 'work-load'. Working usually with a colleague, he prepared plans or reports, not always published, for Bristol and Bath, the Wye Valley, Sheffield and district (no doubt in consequence of his admired Civic Survey), South Yorkshire, Oxfordshire (with Lord Mayo and Adshead), Cumbria, Gloucestershire, North Wales, East Suffolk and the Lincolnshire coast. In addition, he prepared reports on the urban estates or rural villages of various big-wigs, including Lords Astor, Salisbury and Stanford and several other titled people. It may be that the Duchy of Cornwall's example in consulting the first Lever professor suggested to some great landowners that they should consult the second, but more probably it was the result of a greater sense of duty to their tenants, coupled with Abercrombie's very high reputation. To these labours Abercrombie added those of being President of the Liverpool Architectural Society 1929–31 and, as already mentioned, Chairman of the Sandon Studios Society.[58]

In 1933 he published his small and very influential book *Town and Country Planning*.[14] This was a summary of his lectures, illustrated for the most part with his own diagrams. In his review of the book[59] T. F. Thomson praised the concise information and the completeness of Professor Abercrombie's treatment of his subject. The book is divided into three parts. The first deals with the background of the subject, 'An historical sketch on an International Basis'. The second part deals with 'The Practice of Town Planning', and the third with 'Country Planning and Preservation'. With its complete index and bibliography it was, and still is, an extremely valuable introductory statement of the bases of planning.

However true or untrue it may be that:

> *The heights by great men reached and kept*
> *Were not attained by sudden flight*
> *But they while their companions slept*
> *Were toiling upwards through the night,*[60]

Abercrombie and his successor were outstanding examples of men who seemed to believe in these lines, which were often quoted by Winston Churchill and his son.

As recorded in the previous chapter, there were a number of planning consultants in the 1930s who in a real sense followed Abercrombie's lead in preparing 'regional' planning reports. But it was Abercrombie who led. His closest rivals in the number and scale of his planning reports were Adams, Thompson and Fry, who prepared about a dozen reports which were published. Not all of these have been examined, but comparison of the contents of two or three, including *The North Middlesex Regional Planning Scheme*,[61] with Abercrombie's schemes leaves the advantage with him. The Middlesex report contains more about communications, but a less thorough survey of other aspects of the area, history, character of towns, villages and countryside, and not much about population and industry. There are also more photographs, but fewer of the maps that show how deeply Abercrombie himself studied the topography of the districts for which he was making proposals. The Adams, Thompson and Fry report does, however, include more on zoning and, surprisingly, more on amenities and conservation than is found, for example, in Abercrombie's East Kent report.

As time went on there was an increase of detail in Abercrombie's reports and also more evidence of outside help - including acknowledgement of specialized help - and chapters on how the financial and administrative aspects of the proposals may be tackled.

The Move to London

In 1935 Abercrombie decided to try to succeed Adshead as Professor of Town Planning at University College London. 'Try to' in this connection perhaps imputes unnecessary modesty to Abercrombie. His private practice had begun in the North of England and North Wales, but by 1935 had spread to Bath and across to the Thames Valley, East Kent and the Lincolnshire coast. He was known throughout the country, and also internationally. Raymond Unwin and Thomas Adams were perhaps still a little more widely known as both pioneers and leaders in town planning, but Unwin was then seventy-two, and Thomas Adams was sixty-four and was still much concerned with *The New York Regional Plan*, of which the main publications had appeared from 1928 to 1931, and with his British practice. Abercrombie, at fifty-six, could offer University College a great reputation and eleven years before reaching retirement.

In making professorial appointments universities are apt to hover in their choice between the fully established man who - even if he may not have much more to offer - will at least retire in ten years or less: and, on the other hand, the supposedly brilliant youth with whom - if the supposition proves wrong - they might be stuck for forty years. University College did not hesitate for long over choosing Abercrombie, though there must have been some doubts, or some administrative error, as Abercrombie was nominated as an external referee for what proved to be his own appointment. Of the five actual referees, Raymond Unwin and Albert Richardson are now the best remembered. Abercrombie had other influential sponsors, including Seebohm Rowntree.

The main difficulty proved to be salary. Adshead had been a part-time professor whose practice had, it was alleged, enabled him to accept a low salary. Abercrombie was, however, to be a full-time professor - one wonders if anyone at all believed this! - and had been receiving a salary of £1,000 at Liverpool. University College was prepared to offer £700 but not more. The gap was bridged by £100 a year from the Rowntree Trust and a similar sum from Sir John Stirling-Maxwell.[62]

So the Abercrombies moved to London and Abercrombie gave his Inaugural Lecture at University College in May 1936. He called it 'Planning in Town and Country – Difficulties and Possibilities.'[63] The lecture considered the levels of planning – national, regional and local – and dominant topographic and motive forces – slum clearance, industry and transport. In this lecture Abercrombie was one of the first to propose motorways. He asked for:

> *The creation of a system of completely new main*
> *roads for motor traffic only, on the model of the*
> *Italian and other Continental autostrada … these*
> *could be made much narrower-would require no foot-*
> *paths or cycle-tracks and would only have connection*
> *with the countryside at appropriate intervals, like*
> *stations on a railway.*

He deplored the scattering of houses over the face of the land which was directly encouraged by the planning Acts, and suggested satellite towns. To us in 1981 he seems to have been very self-controlled in saying only:

> *the balance must be struck between complacency*
> *at the number of acres which can be shown to*
> *have come under planning control, and impatience*
> *at the continuance or even flourishing state of*
> *ignorance and ignoble operations.*

In the same year Abercrombie became a member of the Royal Fine Art commission and so remained until 1949.

The students of planning at University College numbered from eighteen to twenty-six between 1936 and 1939 and were chiefly evening students. As lecturers there were F. H. Carr (Adshead's nephew) and T. C. Coote as well as J. D. M. Harvey (a very well-known perspective draughtsman in the 1930s) and specialist lecturers in law and engineering.[64] Abercrombie was of course relieved of the responsibility of being editor-in-chief of the *Town Planning Review*, even though most of the editorial work at Liverpool had been undertaken from 1930 to 1935 by Wesley Dougill. Although always a first-class and inspiring lecturer, it is probable that Abercrombie left a large share of the rest of the teaching at University College to his assistants, and felt free to undertake more committee work. In addition to the Royal Fine Art Commission, he was a member of the Minister of Health's Committee on the Town and Country Planning Act in 1935, consultant architect to the Department of Health for Scotland in 1936 and a Vice-President of the Royal Institute of British Architects from 1937 to 1939.

One of the few planning developments to which Abercrombie was not sympathetic, at least to begin with, was the founding by the Architectural Association of a School of Planning and Research for National Development, of which E. E. A. Rowse was Principal for some years. Abercrombie, in a letter to the Provost of University College in 1935, thought so ambitious a scheme should be attached to a university – presumably University College London, to which he was about to move. An appeal for further funds in *The Times* of 8 December 1937 had many distinguished signatories, but not Abercrombie. Perhaps the Architectural Association School's most valuable years were after 1945, when many ex-Servicemen benefited from its short and well-designed refresher course in planning.

The best known of Abercrombie's work on committees was that which he did for the Royal Commission on the Distribution of the Industrial Population (the Barlow Commission)[65] to which he was appointed in July 1937, although the report, delayed by the outbreak of the Second World War, was not published until 1940. The Commission was set up far too late for any action before the approaching war, although the gathering of new industries round London – the obvious first target for Hitler's bombers – was certainly an important reason for its establishment. The decline of the heavy industries in the North, and their out-of-date equipment and decayed physical surroundings, were well known at the beginning of the Great Slump of 1930–33. A rigorous enquiry then might have resulted in something of a New Deal (both in the general and American senses) for British planning and development, administratively and physically.[66] Though it must be admitted that, given the quality of the governments of the 1930s, the chances were not very great.

The commission took evidence on twenty-nine days and people and institutions concerned with town and country planning were well represented. There were in all four reports – a main one and three minority reports. All asked for a new authority to guide the location of industry and to try to ensure the rebuilding of rundown cities and a reasonable dispersal and balance of industry throughout the country. The difference between the majority report and the first minority report (Sir W. E. White, Professor J. H. Jones and G. W. Thomson) was chiefly that the latter demanded regional bodies and more urgent action. The second minority report (Abercrombie, H. H. Elvin and Mrs Hichens) distrusted any Board and wanted a brand new Ministry, not unlike the present Department of the Environment, and asked for a system of guiding the location of industry with similarities to that at length provided by Industrial Development Certificates. Indeed, in a number of ways this minority report outlined what was actually to happen after the Second World War.[67]

Abercrombie alone wrote the last report: 'A Dissentient Memorandum'. He maintained that existing planning powers could not effectively guide the location of industry nationally, or even regionally, and that no improvement was possible till the question of compensation and betterment was adequately resolved. He described the other defects of existing planning powers and procedures with all the authority of one who had battled against them for a quarter of a century. He emphasized that the new ministry for which he and two other members had asked was needed as a centre for co-ordination of conflicting needs between recreation and forestry, land drainage and water supply, trunk roads and agriculture and much else. Routine submission of a scheme from one department to another for comment was not enough. Nor should statutory undertakers (Gas, Electricity, etc.) and Crown lands be exempt from control. Professor Dix has written of this document:

> ... it represented the reasoned voice of massive
> experience. Abercrombie's argument was that as
> local authorities were not generally interested in
> commitments that involved individual sacrifice
> 'however enlightened and far-seeing a regional
> out-look can be, there must be some national
> guidance in the background'. A national outline of
> development was required, 'rather a policy than a
> plan, something flexible and continually evolving,
> based upon research, surveys and experience',
> prepared under the auspices of a ministry having
> the planning powers of the then Ministry of
> Transport.[68]

Abercrombie then listed other defects in existing planning, and mentioned prophetically that Greater London in particular needed an actual outline plan, since the work of an elected advisory body had broken down.

In January 1940, while Britain waited for the bombs to fall, the commission's work seemed rather useless, and the majority report in particular to be feeble in its recommendations. Yet within a year or two the report supplied the menu for all major preparatory work on post-war planning, including the Uthwatt, Scott and Dower reports, and indeed the establishment, in 1943, of the co-ordinating Ministry of Town and Country Planning.

In 1939 another war swept away most of Abercrombie's students. Numbers in the town planning course at University College dropped from twenty-six in 1938–39 to three in 1939–40. But even this was better, Abercrombie must have thought, than it had been in 1914, when he wrote to the Vice-Chancellor of Liverpool University that he was glad to report *one* Diploma student. He had not long to wait this time for war work exactly suited to his talents. In 1941 Lord Reith asked him and J. H. Forshaw (Architect to the London County Council) to prepare a post-war plan for the LCC area. Forshaw was a former Liverpool student, and Abercrombie also gathered in two other former students, Wesley Dougill and Arthur Ling. The *County of London Plan* was published – despite all wartime difficulties – in

1943.[69] It was a sad time for Abercrombie, as his devoted wife Emily Maud had died in 1942. Writing of the plan in 1957, Holford stated:

> The distinctive mark of the County of London Plan was its comprehensiveness. It is not surprising that in the absence of an economic forecast, and in the middle of a War, certain proposals had to be modified later. The inner ring road was abandoned, and the tunnels; and nothing has come of the precincts suggested for Westminster and Bloomsbury. The important point was, that over an urban area as complex as any to be found in the world, Abercrombie and Forshaw and their team designed a pattern that was unified and coherent. It was a magnificent effort. The Plan, in book form, found its way eventually into most corners of the globe. It was followed almost at once by preparations within the newly established Ministry of Town and Country Planning to enable Abercrombie to lead another team in a study of Greater London.[70]

One of the memorable diagrams in the County of London Plan was the 'eggs in the basket' drawing which showed how various districts in London had become centres for specialized activities, such as finance and commodity markets in the City, newspapers in Fleet Street and so on. The plan also reminded its inhabitants that London was really a pattern of coalesced villages, and it was one of the aims of the plan to distinguish these and enhance their individual characters.

The plan was produced in 1941–42 during the worst of the war for the people of London. The whole of the team had part-time duties in Home Defence, and two of them, Wesley Dougill and William Walcot, died as the plan was about to be published. According to J. H. Forshaw they were worn out by work and extra Civil Defence duties.[71]

Of Abercrombie's methods of working in later life, we have direct evidence from two of his assistants on the Greater London Plan. Professor Gordon Stephenson and T. C. Coote have recorded that Abercrombie outlined his ideas and divided up the work, and then rarely altered the contribution that was submitted to him. Professor Stephenson prepared Chapter 8 of the Greater London Plan, on community planning. T. C. Coote had worked for Abercrombie in 1930, and had written two chapters of the Oxfordshire Plan and Regional Report, and he writes[72] that it was Abercrombie's famous memory, especially for old students, that probably accounted for his recruitment to work on Greater London. (Coote was being unduly modest. He had been one of Abercrombie's lecturers at University College.) In all there were five former students who worked on the Greater London Plan, published in 1945.[73] Over this great document

Abercrombie exercised remote control. Harry Stewart, from the Standing Committee on London Regional Planning, was editor-in-chief, and Coote confirms the trust Abercrombie placed in his assistants:

> *Briefly, we worked as a team, and Pat (Abercrombie) turned up once in a while when he could. He stayed with us for several days at the beginning, and soon roughed out or sent us brief chapter heads. Then Stewart MacFarlane, Peter Shepheard and I sat down with him, and occasionally Gordon Stephenson popped in too. Pat suggested who should write the various chapters of the Report, told us which he would do himself, and got Peter to be responsible for the co-ordination of all map design work, as well as working out the special projects such as the Lea Valley Park and a New Town. A small nucleus of drawing office staff, including Bud Fleming (a former Liverpool student), prepared the necessary maps. The staff was first of all found a few rooms in Lambeth Bridge House, where the nucleus of the new Ministry was being assembled - Holford, Sharp and Vincent and Willatts were there then - and our staff was put on the Ministry's payroll. Pat himself got a fee. I have always understood that he disliked setting up offices himself, preferring to get others to do that for him. He used to come and see us from time to time when asked to by Harry Stewart, or when we badly needed his guidance. We used to write our own chapters and give them to him. He left us a very free hand indeed, never I think altering what we had written but suggesting new lines of thought or new sub-headings.*[72]

The preparation of the *Greater London Plan* was beset not only by three moves of offices but also by the Luftwaffe. The Ministry of Town and Country Planning occupied various buildings in St James's Square in London; and so did General Eisenhower (then with his staff in Norfolk House) preparing for D-Day in June 1944. This may have been known to the enemy, who made at least one determined attack on Norfolk House, or perhaps on Churchill's citadel a few hundred yards away, in early 1944, by fast fighter-bombers at night. They missed Norfolk House by about 100 yards, but severely damaged and caused fire in 19 St James's Square, then occupied by part of the Ministry of Town and Country Planning and the *Greater London Plan* team. The team had to redraw or repeat some drawings and drafts.

The *Greater London Plan* is the document for which Abercrombie will probably be remembered longest. George Pepler says that he 'developed a technique which came to full flower in his *Greater London Plan*'.[74] Later Holford wrote of it:

> *In this report ... Abercrombie and his assistants*
> *set the standards for post-war development all*
> *over the country – not only in regard to New*
> *Towns, but for the size and form of*
> *neighbourhoods and schools and shopping centres*
> *and arterial roads. From this he went on to apply*
> *its principles in other places, and with other*
> *collaborators.*[75]

The plan divided Greater London into four rings: Inner, Suburban, Green Belt and Outer Country, and pointed out how the area, like the county within it, was historically a collection of villages and small towns which needed to be defined, completed or reclaimed. There were fourteen chapters, and in Chapter 11 there were detailed studies of Ongar (as a New Town), Hatfield and West Ham – as being three very different but typical communities physically and socially within the 2,599 square miles of Greater London. The plan was particularly concerned with decentralization and the problems of over-spill from congested central London. It had, as Holford wrote, immense influence, perhaps specially because its publication came just at the end of a war that had destroyed hundreds of cities and urban regions which the surviving inhabitants had to rebuild, and wished to rebuild well. The *Greater London Plan* became for many their exemplar.

The plan dealt with the problem of overspill from the closely built urban areas into the surrounding more open districts, and devised a programme of decentralization which would place this overspill in new and independent satellite towns. It was this recommendation which led to the creation of the New Towns in Britain, and three of Abercrombie's suggested sites were adopted among the eight London New Towns. Yet Abercrombie was not invited to plan a New Town either in London or elsewhere. He regretted this and so did his admirers, but the ommission may have been wise. In 1946 when consultants and staff for the first group of New Towns were first appointed, Abercrombie was sixty-seven years old. It was thirty-four years since he had 'laid out Prestatyn' (as A. A. Milne had put it) and the planners of the New Towns were in the thirty-five to forty-five age group and full of the new ideas. Just as the Royal Academy plan for London – dominated by Lutyens – had, in 1942, caused many smiles among the visitors for being quite out of date, so it is possible that Abercrombie too might have shown that, in the detailed layout of buildings and small housing groups, the world had moved past him.

In 1943, in the midst of the war, Abercrombie had joined J. Paton Watson, the City Engineer of Plymouth, in producing a new plan for that much damaged city. It is not the most admired of Abercrombie's works, and it is difficult to see how he himself could have given much time to it.

Immediately the war ended Abercrombie laboured to reorganize, or to recreate, the International Union of Architects. It was felt appropriate that the Chairman should be a Frenchman, but at least several of the most promising candidates had been collaborators.[76] Eventually the elderly and revered Auguste Perret was chosen. Abercrombie was endlessly patient with the Russian delegate, who arrived three days late and wanted everything to be repeated.[77]

Abercrombie also plunged back into consultancy work, as well as arranging instruction for the increase in town planning students – mostly ex-Servicemen – at University College. He prepared a plan for Bath in 1945–47 and for Hull (with Sir Edwin Lutyens) also in 1945. In 1946 he reached the retiring age for his professorship at University College and ended an official teaching career that had lasted thirty-nine years. It was a memorable departure.

The Last Years

Abercrombie had been a witness of, and the most vigorous and famous participant as teacher and practitioner during, the whole development of British town planning, from the first legislative beginnings in 1909 up to the time when the great 1947 Act – which set the pattern for British and much Commonwealth post-war planning – was just about to be passed. Thus the second Lever professor, and the greatest town and regional planner, ended his teaching appointments, but not his work.

By 1949 he had completed three major schemes. In the *Clyde Valley Regional Plan*, published in 1949, he had had the assistance – as already mentioned – of two notable Scots, Robert Mathew and Robert Grieve. At Edinburgh he prepared a civic survey and plan in which he was assisted by Derek Plumstead; and in his plan for Warwick he was helped by Richard Nickson. Both of these were completed in 1949, as was the North Staffordshire plan in which his collaborator was Herbert Jackson. Between 1945 and 1955 he paid five or six visits to Palestine and did much work with A. C. Holliday. He also visited Ceylon.

If Abercrombie was disappointed, as Derek Plumstead has written,[78] that he was never entrusted with the planning of one of the fifteen British New Towns which were to some extent the result of his suggestions for Greater London, he had little time to mourn. He certainly had his share of disappointments, some of which are inescapable by all men, and certainly by all great men as they approach old age. But Thomas Sharp was perhaps describing his own experience almost more than Abercrombie's when he wrote:

> After 1947, Abercrombie, along with other
> consultants, was denied almost all work in
> connection with planning in Britain. While junior
> assistants in planning offices (the upper officials
> being too busy with committees) were designing
> the redevelopment plans for the cathedral cities,
> the County towns, the market towns which are one
> of the glories of England (to say nothing of the

> *industrial towns which are not) ... Abercrombie*
> *and his fellow-consultants were unemployed.*[79]

Clough Williams-Ellis perhaps put Abercrombie's disappointments in better perspective:

> *But even he, with more planning patients on his*
> *panel than any other practitioner, had his share of*
> *disappointments, though I never knew them get*
> *him down. Having put all he had into his reports*
> *and plans, if they were not acted on - well, there*
> *was nothing more he could do about it. But he*
> *would battle for ideas that he thought important,*
> *with pertinacity, yet with such friendly*
> *understanding of other points of view that he*
> *would generally win opponents over, or, if he*
> *failed, leave them at least well disposed and never*
> *hostile. He was a great believer in 'planning by*
> *persuasion'. I well remember his guilefully gaining*
> *the support of some wavering university dons at*
> *an Oxford conference with: 'You quadrangular*
> *gentlemen, naturally accustomed to square*
> *dealing', and so on: his really weighty arguments*
> *deftly made acceptable - as so often - by his light,*
> *his gay approach.*[80]

Abercrombie followed Auguste Perret as President of the International Union of Architects - a post he held till 1956. Other honours came tumbling in. He was knighted in 1945; he received the Royal Gold Medal for Architecture in 1946, the Gold Medal of the American Institute of Architects in 1949, the Town Planning Institute's Gold Medal in 1955 (this medal had been instituted in 1953) and, to his particular delight, the Légion d'Honneur in 1956. He also received several honorary degrees.

Supported in his home life at Aston Tirrold and near Holyhead by his daughter Mrs Farey, Abercrombie took his skills even further than to Palestine and Ceylon. He prepared a report for Hong Kong in 1947 and for Addis Ababa in 1954-56.[81] His resident assistant in Addis Ababa for eighteen months, Gerald Dix, was to become in time the sixth Lever professor.

At the time of his death in March 1957, at the age of seventy-seven, Abercrombie was working on his last plan, for a part of Winchester.[82] As the obituary notice in the journal *Town and Country Planning* stated: 'He never began to ossify mentally'.

History is likely to say of him that he was the greatest of British town and country planners, and that he invented and developed the techniques of survey, analysis and plan, as they could best be applied in practice - at various times - to towns and portions of counties. He was probably at his best in examining and prescribing for parts of rural counties - as in Kent, Suffolk and near Bath and

Bristol - where his understanding of, and love for, the English countryside and small towns could be used most fully. He was also probably the greatest of the personal planners who, like some great consultant physicians, carried nearly all his knowledge and experience in his head.

He died at Aston Tirrold not far from Oxford and was buried at Trearddur Bay near Holyhead in Anglesey, where with his wife, son and daughter he had spent many holidays. More fortunate than Holford, his successor at Liverpool and University College, London, he left two children and several grandchildren. His memorial service was held at St Martins-in-the-Fields, and the address was given by Clough Williams-Ellis, his oldest and one close friend, with whom he had fought the battles for the Councils for Preservation of Rural England and Rural Wales, thirty years before.

NOTES AND REFERENCES

1   Letter from Lever to Vice-Chancellor Dale, 12 August 1914 (*Univ. Archives*).

2   University of Liverpool Report Book, Vol. III, (11 May 1915) 216 (*Univ. Archives*).

3   Among the letters of support for Abercrombie's candidate as second Lever professor were the following:
Professor Adshead
'... there is no one as well qualified as Mr. Abercrombie'.
'Mr. Abercrombie is an interesting and able lecturer, he possesses the capacity for acquiring information and the ability for imparting it clearly. As Research Fellow I consider that his work always showed analytical ability and that power of human discernment which is essential to the successful town-planner. His writings were always apt, clear and to the point.'
'He is well known to everyone interested in Town-planning and it is reasonable to expect that he will have a brilliant future, and that in a short time he will be entrusted with many important Town-planning commissions.'
Letter from Thomas Adams to Patrick Abercrombie
'I regard as one of your chief qualifications for the position the wide experience you have had in conducting and directing research into civic problems and I have often been struck with the critical and painstaking way in which you have carried out work of this kind in the past.'
'Your knowledge has been supported by a critical insight and saneness of view which is so necessary to enable students to form correct ideas regarding the new science of town-planning.'
Professor Patrick Geddes
'His constructive imagination, applied to their (i.e. cities') extension and their improvement, is thus soundly based and wisely directed; and I look forward to his becoming of wider and wider civic service, and this throughout an ever extending area, as his exceptional combination of scholarly and practical preparation with original architectural powers, becomes fully recognised.'
'As a teacher he fulfils already that double duty of immediate instruction and of wider appeal, which lies before every important and responsible Professorship, but none more than that of Town-planning.'
(*Univ. Archives*).

4   *Dictionary of National Biography* (1941-50) 21. *Who Was Who* (1941-50) 35.

5   Letter from Lever to Reilly, 16 June 1915 (*Univ. Archives*).

Cecil Beaton, *1948-1955, The Strenuous Years* (Weidenfeld & Nicolson, London, 1973) 211.

7   ... he could, as in a flash, illumine the arid wastes of the legal page, bringing the subject into blazing life, and if he did not make the law entirely clear (for that was not his responsibility) he did what was more important – he made the whole thing appear so utterly worthwhile and so right. Desmond Heap, *The Times* (3 April 1957).

8   Letter from Austen Harrison to Lord Holford, 21 June 1968 (*Univ. Archives*).

9   Letter from Dixon Scott to Clifton Moore, 8 March 1907, quoted in Roderick F. Bisson, *The Sandon Studios Society and the Arts* (Parry Books Ltd, Liverpool, 1965) 66.

10   Amongst numerous other honours he was to become Officier de la Couronne of Belgium, President of the International Union of Architects and President of the Franco-British Union of Architects, and especially the *Legion d'Honneur* mentioned on p. 148.

11   Professor Gerald Dix, 'Little Plans and Noble Diagrams', *Town Planning Review* Vol. XLIX (July 1978) 330.

12   Obituary *Royal Institute of British Architects Journal* Vol. 64 No. 7 (May 1957) 292.

13   The loss of sight in his right eye occurred during a childhood disease, probably measles. This handicap may account for the absence of evidence that Abercrombie ever played games of physical activity or drove a car. Letter from Professor Dix to the author, 12 November 1979. Professor Dix has the custody of all the Abercrombie papers and is preparing a definitive biography.

14   Professor Patrick Abercrombie, *Town and Country Planning* (Home University Library and Thornton Butterworth, London, 1933) 23-4.

15   Minutes of Senate Meetings, 15 May 1907, 36 (*Univ. Archives*).

16   Faculty of Arts Minutes, June 1909, 104 (*Univ. Archives*).

17   'P. Abercrombie resigned his lectureship at the School of Architecture. It was agreed to recommend that the value of his research fellowship be increased from £120 to £200 p.a.: the additional £80 to be paid out of the sum of £100 reserved by Council for publication of the *Town Planning Review*.' Faculty of Arts Minutes, 14 December 1910, 236 (*Univ. Archives*).

18   Some lecturers of course labour hard in other fields. A few years ago the Vice-Chancellor of X University and his wife, motoring 60–70 miles from X, found they needed some eggs and stopped at a trim small farm. The wife obtained the eggs and complimented the burly young farmer about his farm. 'Oh', he said, 'this is only one of my jobs ... . I am a university lecturer'. 'Indeed ... where?' 'At X'. 'Oh, how interesting, I have heard about X from friends ... part-time I expect?' 'Oh no, full time!' And it was so. The young man went in for two days a week, had a bed in a colleague's house, gave two lectures and a seminar,

interviewed two or three students and was back at his farm by 9.0 pm on the second day. His academic department was not connected with agriculture. Not at all.

19   This story was told in the mid-1930s to Paul and Lenore Rathbone by Lionel Budden, (Reilly's successor as Professor of Architecture) as being of common knowledge and rather romantic. It was also told to the author by Lord Holford and by Mrs Maud Budden in Abercrombie's lifetime; and has been confirmed (all but the school fees) by Professor Gordon Stephenson in 1979 as a story well known to students at the School of Architecture in 1925–30.

20   According to a drawing by Abercrombie for his wife's funerary urn, Emily Maud was born in 1893 making her fifteen at the time of her marriage. Apart from a simple mistake at a time of grief Abercrombie's statement can easily be explained. Many a husband does not remember his wife's exact age, and all wise ones deduct a year or two from what they believe is probable.

21   One thinks of the middle classes in 1908 as being rather rigid and Victorian in behaviour, and no doubt many of them were. But at much the same time as Abercrombie was educating his bride-to-be, another young man, later to be well known as André Maurois, was doing the same; but *he* sent his Janine from Paris first to school at Brighton (surely not to Roedean?), and then to attend lectures at Oxford for a year. He excused his many visits to her by posing as her brother. One longs to know more. As her surname was Szymkiewicz and his Herzog, which did they use? And to whom were school bills and reports sent? Either Edwardian headmistresses and Oxford dons and their wives were very gullible, or real innocence of intention was, as always, a great protection. André Maurois, *Memoirs 1885–1964* (Bodley Head, London, 1970) 80.

22   Professor Sir William G. Holford, *Dictionary of National Biography* (1951–60) 1.

23   Professor Gerald Dix, 'Leslie Patrick Abercrombie: a centenary note', *Town Planning Review* Vol. 50 (1979) 257.

24   G. Dix, *op. cit.*[11] 343.

25   Derek Plumstead, *Journal of Town Planning Institute* Vol. XLIII (June 1957) 188.

26   Professor Robert Gardner-Medwin, 'Patrick Abercrombie: Pioneer in Regional Planning', *c.* 1957; publication untraced.

27   Letter from Thomas C. Coote to the author, 18 July 1979.

28   'It is said that genius is a prolonged adolescence – which appears to mean that a genius is one who keeps young energies and a fresh outlook on life long after the time when most men have grown cynical and discouraged.' Dugald Macfadyen, *Sir Ebenezer Howard and the Town Planning Movement* (Manchester University Press, 1933) 11.

29 Clough Williams-Ellis, *The Times* (28 March 1957) 15.

30 George Pepler, 'Patrick Abercrombie: An Appreciation,' *Journal of Town Planning Institute* Vol. XLIII (May 1957) 130.

31 R. F. Bisson, *op. cit.*, 56.

32 Reviewing *Who's Who* for 1919, A. A. Milne wrote that he liked his novels long, and was delighted to find by p. 3 that there were 2,725 more pages to come. 'I returned with a sigh of pleasure to page 4 where Leslie Patrick Abercrombie wins the prize "for laying out Prestatyn", some local wrestler, presumably, who had challenged the crowd at a country fair'. George Pepler, 'Presentation of the T.P.I. Gold Medal to Sir Patrick Abercrombie', *Journal of Town Planning Institute* Vol. XLI (1954–55) 229.

33 According to P. Kitchen, Abercrombie remembered an incident at the Civics Exhibition in Dublin:

> '... one Sunday afternoon the only person left in charge of it was Lady Aberdeen herself. An enormous flock of people from the Dublin slums came to visit the Show that Sunday afternoon. After they had had a look round and found only Lady Aberdeen in charge, they began one by one to remove the chairs and the tables and carry them off home. At the end of the afternoon the Exhibition was not quite empty, but a large number of exhibits and the whole of the furniture had disappeared. The late Lord Leverhulme was very delighted when he found out what had happened to the model of Port Sunlight, saying it was the greatest compliment that they could have ever paid him. Each thief would have a model of a little cottage on his mantelpiece and that would show him the sort of place he should be living in, instead of the slums. Geddes of course was delighted too.'

Paddy Kitchen, *A Most Unsettling Person* (Victor Gollancz Ltd, London, 1975) 250.

34 Along with, among others, Thomas Adams, H. V. Lanchester, Raymond Unwin, W. R. Davidge and George Pepler. Among the first thirty-five full members of the Town Planning Institute there were eighteen architects, including Lutyens and Aston Webb. Gordon Cherry, *The Evolution of British Town Planning* (Leonard Hill Books, 1974) 57–60.

35 Abercrombie seems to have been as skilful as Adshead in managing the often obstreperous Reilly. They were indeed on such friendly terms that Abercrombie became godfather to Reilly's son, the present Lord Reilly. Lord Reilly, interview 15 March 1978.

36 Letter from Lever to Vice-Chancellor Dale, 23 November 1914 (*Univ. Archives*).

37 Letter from Lever to George Harley, 11 May 1915 (*Univ. Archives*).

38 Letter from Abercrombie to the 2nd Lord Leverhulme, 11 March 1931 (*Univ. Archives*).

39   Professor Patrick Abercrombie, Sydney Kelly and Arthur Kelly, *Dublin of the Future. The New Town Plan* (Liverpool University Press and Hodder & Stoughton Ltd, London, 1922).

40   Fifty years after Abercrombie's plan, the author when fifth Lever professor, prepared another plan for the Dublin Region. Neither plan had more than modest influence on the future of Ireland's beautiful capital.

41   'The Industrial Village of Dormanstown, Redcar, Yorks', *Architects' Journal* Vol. 50, 31 December 1919) 812-14.

42   *Town Planning Review* Vol. VIII (1919-20) 125.

43   'The South Wales Report, then, was not really a Regional Survey (though so-called), and much less a Regional Plan, but a preliminary study and proof of the need of Regional Planning; and it is well worth reading as a textbook as to what Regional Planning means and what a Regional Plan should contain.' Professor Patrick Abercrombie, 'Regional Planning', *Town Planning Review* Vol. X (1923-24) 113.

44   G. Dix, *op. cit.*,[11] 333-36.

45   Letter from Abercrombie to G. Pepler, 2 March 1955.

46   Quoted by Professor Dix from Abercrombie's manuscript, *op. cit.*,[11] 331.

47   'It is ... a surprising thing that he became so influential without arousing in any quarter personal dislike or partisan bitterness. I [Frederic Osborn] think it is because, shining through his clear thinking and vigorous expression, there was always visible a sincere, essentially modest, deeply understanding, and kindly personality.' Frederic J. Osborn, *Town and Country Planning* Vol. XXV (1957) 191.

48   G. Pepler, *op. cit*,[32] 230.

49   T. Sharp, *Architectural Review* Vol. 122 (July 1957) 75. There is distortion here. No one knew better than Sharp that the inter-war years were not the years of opportunity for town planners, but years of frustration and sometimes bitterness. Sharp may have meant 'years of the first slender opportunities when planning consultants could learn and overcome the difficulties of a new trade'.

50   Professor Patrick Abercrombie and Robert H. Mattocks, *Sheffield: A Civic Survey and Suggestions towards a Development Plan* (University Press Liverpool and Hodder & Stoughton, London, 1924).

51   T. Sharp, *op. cit.*, 75.

52   Professor Patrick Abercrombie, *op. cit*,[44] 118.

53   Despite all this work Abercrombie was thought by Reilly to have deserted 'real' town planning, in that he did not prepare great designs for parts of cities and coax his clients to carry them out. Letter from Reilly to Holford, 23 December 1935; see Chapter 7 pp. 171-71.

54   Professor Patrick Abercrombie, 'The Extension of the Town Planning Spirit', *Journal of Town Planning Institute* Vol. XII (1925-26) 1-7.

55   Professor Patrick Abercrombie, *The Preservation of Rural England* (University Press, Liverpool and Hodder & Stoughton, London, 1926). Also published in the *Town Planning Review* Vol. XII (1926-27) 1.

56   Quoted by Clough Williams-Ellis in 'A Genial Wizard: An appreciation of Sir Patrick Abercrombie', *The Listener* Vol. 58 (8 August 1957) 199. The quotation came from the *Town Planning Review* Vol. XII (1926-27) 56.

57   He continued to write for the *Town Planning Review* and in 1930 summarized his views on town and country thus:

> The general conclusion of this study of the polarity between Town and Country may be stated as follows: that the sheer urbanity of the Town should be leavened by some natural tincture, increasing as the country is approached; that the country, except in some few wild spots, must necessarily be sophisticated by human treatment. But let Urbanism prevail and preponderate in the Town and let the Country remain rural. Keep the distinction clear.

Clough Williams-Ellis (ed), *Britain and the Beast* (J. Dent & Sons Ltd, London, 1937).

58   Professor Patrick Abercrombie, 'Planning in Town and Country: The contrast of civic and landscape design', *Town Planning Review* Vol. XIV (1930) 12.

59   Review by Thomas F. Thomson in *Town Planning Review* Vol. XV (1932-33) 295.

60   Kay Halle (ed), *Randolph Churchill: The Young Unpretender* (Heinemann, London, 1971) 256.

61   Adams, Thompson & Fry, *North Middlesex Regional Planning Scheme* (August 1928).

62   Letter from B. Seebohm Rowntree to Allen Mawer, Provost of University College London, 14 March 1935.
     Letter to Sir Edwin Deller, Principal of University College London, 18th March 1935 (*University College London. Records*).

63   Review in *Town Planning Review* Vol. XVII (1937-8) 305.

64   Professor Patrick Abercrombie, 'Notes on the Department of Town Planning University College, London 1935-39' *Journal of Town Planning Institute* Vol. XXV (1938-39) 130.

65   *Report of the Royal Commission on the Distribution of the Industrial Population* (Cmd 6153, 1940).

66   Sir Isaiah Berlin has said of those days: 'People say how awful things are now. But they are not as awful as the Thirties. Then there was

darkness everywhere for anyone with any kind of wish for liberty or equality. The only point of light was Roosevelt's New Deal, which showed that it was possible to do something without being either a Fascist or a Communist.' Quoted in *The Times*, 3 November 1980.

67 'Abercrombie was zealous for a great "renewal"; he was a reformer in the sense that he sought change by Reformation rather than by Revolution. His long pleading for landscape protection had perhaps become misunderstood, for latterly he had felt that some regarded his viewpoint as that of the mere preservationist. His convictions were firmly held and the independent attitude which he often maintained, as reflected in his Minority Report of the Royal Commission on the Location of Industry, was courageous and inspiring, John H. Forshaw *Journal of the Royal Institute of British Architects* Vol. 64 (May 1957) 293.

68 Professor Gerald B. Dix, 'Patrick Abercrombie: Pioneer of Planning', *Architectural Review* Vol. CLXVI No. 990 (August 1979) 132.

69 John H. Forshaw and Professor Patrick Abercrombie *County of London Plan 1943* (Macmillan & Co. Ltd, London 1943).

70 Professor Sir William Holford 'Leslie Patrick Abercrombie 1879-1957' *Town Planning Review* Vol. XXVIII (1957-58) 83.

71 John H. Forshaw, 'Presentation of the TPI Gold Medal to Sir Patrick Abercrombie', *Town Planning Institute Journal* Vol. XLI (1954-55) 232.

72 Letter from T. C. Coote, *op. cit.*

73 Professor Patrick Abercrombie, *Greater London Plan 1944* (HMSO, London, 1945).
The five students were J. H. Forshaw, P. W. Macfarlane, L. F. Richards, P. F. Shepheard and V. N. Prasad. T. C. Coote had been a pre-war assistant as well as evening lecturer.

74 G. Pepler, *Architects' Journal* Vol. 125 (28 March 1957) 454.

75 W. G. Holford, *op. cit.*[70] 83.

76 Professor Gordon Stephenson, interview August 1979. Stephenson had studied in Paris, had been in Le Corbusier's office and was the confidant of a number of French architects.

77 Ernö Goldfinger, *The Times* (4 April 1957) 14.

78 D. Plumstead, *op. cit.*

79 T. Sharp, *op. cit.*

80 C. Williams-Ellis, *op. cit.*[56] 200.

81 Gerald B. Dix, 'Addis Ababa: The Master Plan', *Town and Country*

Planning Vol. XXV (1957) 405. Abercrombie had previously been invited to Ethiopa in 1946 as adviser.

82   J. H. Forshaw, *op. cit.*[67]

7

THE VERY DIFFERENT EMINENCE

Preface

In February 1936 it was announced that William Graham Holford was to become the third Lever professor. He was then almost twenty-nine. He became the most famous of all holders of the Lever Chair. His fame rests to no great extent on his achievements as a town planner - for which, in range and variety of work and personal commitment, Abercrombie must hold pride of place. He was famous for the range of his interests, and his astonishing knowledge of, and personal skill in, at least seven or eight of them, and for the number of his very distinguished friends.

Even to one who knew him well - or thought he knew him well - for thirty years or more, Holford remains a mystery. He lived several lives and did not usually allow one of them to mingle with others. It has been said that any deeper relationship between two people is exclusive to them. Holford acted on this. Each friend received his due, and a number of friends did not know of Holford's other friendships.

He was a genius according to several definitions: the infinite capacity for taking pains; and part of the Oxford Dictionary definition 'native intellectual power of an exalted type'. One is a little more doubtful of the later portion of the same definition. 'Extraordinary capacity for imaginative creation, original thought, invention or discovery.' He had however an extraordinary capacity for mental concentration, and thereafter for suggesting imaginative rearrangements of things already known.

If one had to put Holford's claims to genius in a few words it would be - to one person - his peculiar power of seeing what was most important in any problem concerning one of his interests, of knowing how much of it was acceptable at the time to a particular group or audience, and of expressing it with wit, charm and modesty that was infinitely persuasive. He could also understand immediately the real aims and motives of almost anyone talking to him. He was a consummate actor, and for all these reasons, a committee man of genius, especially when his fellow members were people of eminence and intelligence. To this dazzling and fascinating performance in committee - more than to any other single factor - he owed his rapid rise and prolonged influence.

Holford's 'native intellectual powers of an exalted type' included the wonderful power of concentration, which could be sustained for hours, and such quickness of mind that it is doubtful if he ever made a really spontaneous remark. He had an excellent memory and could write a paper or minute, sometimes on a very important subject, almost straight off without subsequent correction of more than a few words or at most a sentence or two. Once, when justly rebuked by the Prime Minister of Australia for a delayed report on Canberra, Holford settled down at 10.00 pm, and by noon the next day the author saw twelve or fifteen pages of the report ready for typing. The first two or three pages, all he had time to read, could hardly have been improved.[1]

Holford was very good-looking and he retained his youthful appearance into his sixties. He was a draughtsman and painter of high talent, had a good musical ear, was a good dancer and (as already noted) an excellent actor and mimic; he had most beautiful handwriting, was a tolerable singer, and his interests covered architecture, town planning, drawing and landscape architecture, the history of these subjects, especially in Italy, and indeed all visual arts. He spoke good Italian and tolerable French and could read German.

All this may seem too much. No man could be like that: he must, many will feel, have had some vices. For the more obvious vices (if anything is a vice nowadays) there is not a shred of evidence, and Holford's life was so closely observed for long periods, by men and women of insight and intelligence, that it is virtually impossible for him to have had secret indulgences. After he met Marjorie Brooks, his future wife, he never, in the common phrase, looked at any other woman. Several looked at him. The Holfords had no children, but so many people stayed with them or lived in flats in their houses in London or at Brighton that it sometimes seemed that Holford had no privacy outside his bedroom door. He is said to have been a very religious man saying his prayers each night at least until his marriage.[2] In later life, the author never heard him mention religion or anything connected with it, but he may have kept such things to himself.

It is, therefore, a relief to know that his character and behaviour contained plenty of human failings, some of them endearing. It was almost impossible to go through a door behind him, and he always took the hardest chair in the room. Yet he could exaggerate – as related later – his youthfulness when appointed to the Lever Chair, and his dislike of spectacles. He did eye exercises of the kind mentioned by Aldous Huxley, and his eyes lasted marvellously; but one night at a dinner at the House of Commons the seating plan was written in blue ink on blue paper, and Holford had to be guided to his place. His observation was very searching.

He preferred only posed photographs of himself, of which he kept many, and was not pleased when a friend took an unguarded snapshot. He himself asked too little for his services and in consequence rather underpaid his loyal colleagues up the early 1950s. He gave extremely generous help to the unfortunate, and when his various offices became independent, and so under proper financial control, he had to be bullied into taking modest payments from them. He should also have retired from the Chair at University

College seven or more years before he actually did so, as it was quite impossible for him to give proper attention to the department; and it may be that it was a sense of guilt that made him treat his deputy there really rather badly – a very rare thing in his life. He was always pressed to stay on by the Provost, and perhaps yielded too easily.

He was a soft touch for anyone with a hard luck story, but in addition to lame ducks, he helped to their first job or first big job certainly 100 and perhaps 250 architects, planners and others, mostly young. He spent much time on this throughout his life, and may be said to have run a kind of employment agency. He has been accused of being a name-dropper and he certainly did like to feel that he had personal knowledge of those in the news, whether Yuri Gagarin or Anthony Armstrong-Jones. He had, however, the defence which Sir Kenneth (now Lord) Clark used when accused of the same failing in his autobiography; that, when one has well-known people as friends or daily colleagues, it is sheer affectation not to name them.[3] He tried to show that he was as other men, even to trying out a pipe and telling (very rarely) a mildly off-colour story. His asthma put paid to the first of these ventures, and the second he told so dreadfully (in contrast to his normal excellence) that he quietly abandoned the attempt. He bore severe attacks of asthma ('hay-fever') each British summer without complaint. Indeed he never complained of anything.

Close observation of him by many, and their recollections, are far from explaining his character or views. He becomes still more mysterious. He seems to have had no political views and no national or racial prejudices. Though he had a dozen apparently close friends, one doubts whether he had one to whom he told all of his own ambitions, troubles, griefs and longings – even in a modified way. He maintained in quiet strictness the one-to-one relationship with everyone. He chatted, listened, laughed, amused and helped but kept himself at a little distance, a little lonely. One plausible theory is that recognizing his great gifts and immune from all temptations (save perhaps a sedulously concealed ambition) he felt it his duty to help, and to pay back all that had been showered on him. 'It's my missionary grandfather' he said more than once, when gently rebuked for the excessive help he gave.

From his mid-forties honours poured down on him, and before the final, dark seven years he had received a peerage and all the distinctions of two professions, together with several honorary degrees. Of the four quite-out-of-the-ordinary-men who proposed, founded and held the Lever Chair, Holford was the most widely gifted and mysterious, though he did not seem at all mysterious to those who knew him only slightly. What forces drove him so implacably and with brilliant success from the age of 18 to 65 Richard Gray who probably knew Holford better than anyone else in the last twenty years has written:

> the forces that drove him ... were without doubt
> consciousness of his own endowment, the

*challenge of competition, the fun of winning, the
social prizes, exquisite consideration for other
people, passionate love of the visible world and the
man-made world, dedication to the causes he took
under his wing, and the desire to lay all this at the
feet of his loved ones.*

In the mass of material Holford left there are no certain guides yet
discovered. The more one reads the more mysterious becomes that
seemingly light-hearted, darkly handsome, fascinating, slightly
Italian-looking man. Sometimes, about 3 am, one wonders momen-
tarily whether he ever existed.

William Graham Holford: 1907-75

William Graham Holford was born in Johannesburg in March 1907,
the son of William George Holford a consulting engineer and mine-
manager. He had been wounded as an officer in Brabant's Horse in
the Boer War. The house of his birth, 42 Abel Road, Berea,
Johannesburg no longer exists. It was the centre of an area
inhabited by smart middle-class business and professional people,
and the parents had a full social life.[4] A number of the surviving
houses now advertise lodgings for people working in central
offices.

Holford's very special powers and character arouse a natural
curiosity about his ancestry. This has been traced on both sides for
four generations by the family and his friend and partner Richard
Gray.[5] The Holford forebears came from the Manchester area (as did
Lever's) or at least his grandfather, the Reverend William Holford,
son of George Holford, was born at Newton Heath in 1831. He went
to South Africa as a missionary in 1855, and was so impatient to get
there that he left the Church of England and became a Wesleyan. He
married Ellen (one of the eleven children of Joseph Walker
(1797-1870). Holford's father William George (1866-1927), the mining
engineer, married Kathleen Maud Palmer (1875-1966). She was one of
the six children of John Palmer who had married Louisa Davies of
Port Elizabeth. Her grandfather and great-grandfather were both
captains in the Royal Navy.

So, as far back as the early 1800s, there is evidence of Holford's
ancestry of zeal, determination and a tough power of survival –
whether as naval officers who rose to the rank of Post-Captain
without known influence, or as a missionary in the 1860s in South
Africa where some farmers were alleged to keep their farms clear of
Africans by going out to shoot them before breakfast.[6] There is,
however, no well-known family sequence of great mental powers or
introduction to great opportunities as with the Darwins and Cecils
(though Holford's father at least showed talent as painter and
draughtsman).

Holford spent his first year or perhaps a little longer at Abel Road, and the family – father, mother, William and his brother Neil, a year younger – then moved some 15 miles from Johannesburg to the Apex mine where his father had been appointed manager. Mrs Holford missed the social life of Johannesburg as it was difficult to return there very often. Holford Senior then found the mine owner was dishonest, and expected him to write annual reports giving unjustified accounts of the mine's prospects. This was common practice in those rougher days. The Holfords returned to live in Johannesburg, where Holford Senior as an independent consultant had financial ups and downs. But Holford's mother was determined that her sons should be well educated, and they were.[4]

From 1914 to 1920 Holford attended the Park Town School in Johannesburg, which had a high reputation, and from 1920 to 1924 he was a pupil at the Diocesan College near Cape Town, one of the best-known schools in South Africa. The school was founded by the first Bishop of Cape Town and resembled Radley College in its strong Anglican traditions.

For the first three of his four years at the school Holford showed no special powers and obtained only tolerable marks in exams.[7] A fellow pupil[8] writes that Holford was not an athlete at a school dedicated at that time to sport. Holford had been banned from games for a year after an illness. He also had a sharp tongue and because of these two characteristics he was left alone by his peers, and seemed to prefer this. In his last year, however, Holford passed the Oxford and Cambridge Matriculation Examination, and with credit in all seven subjects. The Vice-Principal wrote what can be regarded as a mildly glowing testimonial. It did not mention athletics. Holford had by then begun to show talent as a draughtsman and several of his school-boy paintings survive.

He left school when he was nearly eighteen and spent some months with a firm of chartered accountants and then in a bank. One of his stories of youthful pranks was that there was a boom on the Johannesburg Stock Exchange in early 1925, and he drew all the juniors of the bank into a speculation which came unstuck, and caused him to move. He also said that in the bank he learnt to add up the three columns of pounds, shillings and pence simultaneously, and practised shorthand by having his father read Sir Joshua Reynold's *Discourses* to him. He moved to an architect's office, and had several of his watercolours accepted for the South African Academy exhibitions. According to his own account, he wanted at that time to be a professional artist, but his father, to whom he was very close, was much opposed to this idea. 'As the next less disgraceful career with opportunities for drawing was architecture, it was decided that I should be an architect.'[9] Presumably this was before he entered the architects' office of Cowin Powers and Ellis in Johannesburg. Holford was then shown a prospectus written by Reilly for the Liverpool School of Architecture and was captivated by it. Reilly was always clever at recruiting students. It was decided that Holford should become a student there.

In later years he used to imply that he spent several months or even a year with friends in Devon – sometimes adding 'for his health' – before joining the Liverpool School of Architecture in September 1925. There is no truth in this, although there were close family friends in Devon. The most probable explanation of this and some other stories is that Holford enjoyed now and then putting out some exaggeration or small fairy tale about his past, either to tease friends, to see how far the tale would travel before coming back to him. Alternatively, and perhaps more probably, these tales were one of the few escapes he allowed himself from what to others seemed merciless self-discipline extended over forty years. Also, his sense of humour was several layers deep.

There is a great deal of first-hand information about Holford in his years at Liverpool. He was good-looking, and though of no great height (5 feet 8½ inches) he was extremely well-proportioned and surprisingly strong for his size – as he proved in the spirited rough-houses that occasionally broke out in the studios. The impression he made was immediate. Maxwell Fry then a student two or three years ahead in the school, writes of him that he was immediately noticeable: 'in the right sense of the word beautiful ... a finely drawn head, with deep thoughtful but not unkindly eyes ... and his reserved manner ... showed him even then to be a man aware of the responsibilities of his destiny, whatever it was to be.'[10]

Other fellow-students put things differently, but it is clear that between the ages of sixteen and eighteen Holford had developed great powers in almost all activities. Robert Gardner-Medwin, later one of Reilly's successors in the Chair of Architecture, was in the year below Holford and writes '... Bill in his second year had already established himself not only as having the outstanding talent in a year remarkable for talent, but also as an outstanding personality. We sensed, even in those early years, that Bill was 'going places'.[11] The impression he made on his lifelong friend and the fourth Lever professor, Gordon Stephenson, was also great. He seemed to Gordon Stephenson a *gentleman* (Stephenson's italics) and man of the world. Holford was by far the outstanding all-rounder in the School of Architecture and in the university. He played tennis and Rugby football, though not in the first teams, took part in Union debates, edited the student magazine for a year, took part in Union dramatics as well as the special shows which the School of Architecture was expected to provide at the Architects' Ball. He himself wrote in about 1960 that he had also some speaking parts at the Liverpool Playhouse and with Sir Frank Benson's company on tour. He must also have taken part in singing parties of various kinds.[12]

Despite all this, Holford and Stephenson emerged as the best designers and draughtsmen of their year. Holford had by then developed the wonderful powers of concentration that served him so well later on. Moreover, he accepted without question the classical Beaux-Arts methods of teaching. He confined himself to doing very well. Otherwise he could not possibly have done so much and written

weekly letters to his family that ran to twenty, and on one or two
occasions to forty or fifty pages. On learning of these letters, one
feels uneasy about them. Although perhaps homesick, Holford
quickly had many friends at Liverpool, and a healthy nineteen-year-
old rarely writes twenty- or thirty-page weekly letters home. He must
have been able to sleep very deeply for comparatively short nights.

As Holford's charm was always acknowledged to be very great
and he was an excellent dancer, one would have expected him to
have had an extensive acquaintance among young ladies and
caused a number of them to fall in love with him – the more so as
students of the School of Architecture had the reputation of being a
high-spirited lot who enjoyed feminine company. But acquaintance
seems to have been the right word for Holford's relations with young
women. There are no stories of romantic sighs or wild parties. His
companion at most dances was the only young lady in his year, who
looks rather severe in the group photographs, and she at length
married someone else. Despite good looks and charm, Holford seems
to have escaped – perhaps avoided – all the joys and despairs of love
affairs at least until he reached Rome. He thus avoided the greatest
disturbance of concentration that afflicts young people. So, one
recalls, had Lever, but for a different reason (p. 28).

By this third year Holford's skill at the design problems which
formed so large a part of the school's work was acknowledged.
He was one of the three best draughtsmen and designers in the
school, but according to Robert Gardner-Medwin, Holford did not
take Reilly's weekly design studies and subsequent criticisms too
seriously. In common with five others in the fourth year Holford
spent six months in New York offices – in his case that of York and
Sawyer. The six shared a house on Coney Island and Holford said he
made enough money to travel to California before returning to
Liverpool. (It actually came from his brother's godfather.) He found
time in his last year to attend Abercrombie's course in civic design,
and passed most of the written exams, but did not fully complete the
course, doubtless because of his winning the Rome Scholarship.

In the 1920–35 period the big architectural prizes attracted greater
attention and publicity among British architectural schools and
younger architects than either before or since. The Tite Prize, the
Soane Medallion, the Victory Scholarship and most of all the Rome
Scholarship, attracted great competition and received much publicity in the professional journals. Nowhere were they treated more
seriously than at Liverpool. Reilly was a competitive man and
expected his students to win all the prizes, and they certainly did win
a lot.

The Liverpool finalist competitors for the Rome Scholarship in
1930 were Holford, Gordon Stephenson, Lawrence Wright and four
others. They were up against tough competition since other finalists
included Hubert Bennett, a distinguished architect who was later
knighted. One of the many stories about Reilly was that he heard
through his intelligence service that the judges were about to give
the prize to a non-Liverpool student, and that he used his season

ticket to rush to London and so bully the jury that Holford was given the scholarship. That Reilly went as near bullying the jury as he could is very probable, but he probably could not do much. The chairman of the jury was Sir Reginald Blomfield, a very tough and somewhat fierce man, and it contained fifteen other distinguished architects, most of whom must have been well aware of Reilly's reputation for advancing the interests of his own students by every means open to him. So it is probable that justice was done, though it is possible that Reilly (for whom Holford could do no wrong) tipped the balance if the prize hung between two candidates. It is doubtful whether interviews of candidates by the jury began before the following year, but the general record of each finalist was scrutinized in 1930, and here Holford was bound to score. The photographs of several of the designs have been examined, and Holford's scheme, firmly classical in plan, has stepped forward very cautiously in its elevations in a Californian Spanish way slightly reminiscent of the work of Sir Herbert Baker and Curtis Green, who both were on the jury.

The Years in Italy

Italy, where Holford spent most of three years, had an immense influence on him. As Lord Esher said in his memorial address, Holford was 'an intensely European man with the lean and aristocratic look of a doge of Venice ...'. He loved Italy and the summer asthma which was such a curse to him in Britain does not seem to have been a burden in Italy. He learnt to speak Italian so well that he could be mistaken for an Italian, which pleased him.[13] His Italian period is well documented by his own letters, writings, drawings, and photographs and by the records of the British School at Rome, examined by Richard Gray in 1978.

Holford arrived in November 1930 and travelled in the next two and a half years all over Italy, studied Italian piazzas in great detail, and wrote an essay published in the RIBA Journal for February 1933 called 'The Great Baroque masquerade" which was widely admired, (the present author was convinced by that single writing that he would hear more of W. G. Holford).

Reading among the letters Holford wrote in Rome and the enthusiastic reports on his work, one feels he was born out of his time and country. He should have been an Italian working as architect, painter and writer in Italy in 1530 or perhaps 1630. Despite all his later work, his Italian years were probably his happiest, partly of course because he there met and at length married a fellow Rome scholar (in mural painting), Marjorie Brooks. She is described by Mrs Crooke, wife of the librarian at the school in 1930, as being 'radiantly lovely'. Being a blonde she had (she said) 'a lot of trouble with the Italians'. Holford was free of the crushing burdens of work which he later assumed – which indeed he appeared temperamentally unable to refuse.

Holford's journeys round Italy, usually alone, enabled him to realize that he was not as other men. To his future wife from Padua he writes:

*I think the time will soon be ripe for me to go
South again. You understand, don't you, how it is
with me? I think I was born on a bridge between
North and South. Every now and then I have an
inner feeling that makes me go away by myself
and consolidate things and think. When I am with
other people, particularly those I like very much I
am very much with them and part of them and
their world and they have a great effect on me.
But when I am by myself I see things from my
own point of view entirely, and express myself
that way. I can always be alone in a crowd and
with people I don't care about ... I meet all sorts of
people and see them, somehow, in proper
perspective. Then the time passes and I become fit
for human society again. This sounds rather
horrid and very selfish. It probably is, but it seems
natural to me and so I do it ...'[13]*

Several aspects of Holford's basic character and views – mentioned by several later observers – were thus established by the age of twenty-five. He was a solitary person, often an observer rather than a whole-hearted participant. Usually at meetings and on social occasions the real Holford stood back, though his intelligence, charm, quick wits, excellent memory and powers of observation made it appear that he was taking a full part in what was going on. He concentrated yet could preserve detachment: afterwards he could describe the scene and the views, even with a little mimicry, as though he were describing last night's film: amusing, interesting but not a thing that deeply concerned him. In Italy he continued rather oddly to play Rugby football, perhaps urged by St Clair Oakes, a 1931 Rome Scholar. They played for the Lazio Club, and Holford, so he says, once played for Italy.

He also met in Italy Ian Richmond an archaeologist, appointed Director of the British School at Rome at twenty-eight, a man who was one of the first of the four or five men whom he probably took as models for work and behaviour.[14] Ian Richmond's main work was on *The Walls of Imperial Rome*, published in 1930, and he later collaborated with Holford on a study of the plan of Verona. In November 1930, when Holford first arrived at the British School, S. D. Adshead had published an article in the *Town Planning Review*[15] which made some comparisons between Camillo Sitte and Le Corbusier. The article described in some detail the importance of *places*, or urban paved spaces of various kinds, and the placing of monuments and fountains round the sides of the *places* rather than in the centres. Holford doubtless read this article at the beginning of his Italian years, and it may have begun his lifelong interest in enclosed urban spaces.

Apart from measured drawings, which were highly praised, and many sketches and paintings, Holford's two main achievements in Rome were his study of piazzas (forty sketch maps and hundreds of photographs) and writing his essay called 'The Piazza'; and the writing of *The Great Baroque Masquerade*, published in early 1933.[16] For a man of twenty-three to twenty-five both studies show great maturity and the supporting drawings endless patience and great skill.

The journal *Country Life* published an article which attacked somewhat confusedly some of the views in *The Great Baroque Masquerade*, and Holford replied in a more light-hearted way then he allowed himself in later years.

> The British School at
> Rome.
>
> 16 Feb. 1933

The Editor,
COUNTRY LIFE.

Dear Sir:

It is an unusual thing for anyone to take me as seriously as you have done in your leading article of Feb. 11th: hence this reply. I see the point of your argument perfectly, and sympathise with your feelings, but it is clear that you could not understand mine, or perhaps did not want to.

I appreciate the Baroque as much as anyone, a great deal more than most; it was appreciation of its obvious pleasure-giving qualities that led me to write the article you complain of. But I cannot see in it the seeds of any vital new movement either in architecture, in decoration, or in general life – only the lovely decayed flowers of an old one. I think we must go deeper down, and I stand by that belief.

So when I asked for appreciation of the Baroque, I did not mean the blind appreciation which leads to emulation, and to the endless repetition of what was once vital but has now been flogged almost to death. Let the Baroque stand in its own completeness, but separate. Thus, one can appreciate it for what it was.

I really believe you do it more harm by deriding what you call the 'elevating honesty' of the pathetic modern attitude, than I ever did by pleading that we go further back than the Renaissance for our essential values in architecture. Why cannot your historical sense and appreciation of the past exist together with a real live faith in the future? You pick the flowers till there is nothing left to pick, because you cannot see the necessity of planting fresh roots.

D. H. Lawrence once remarked in a letter, 'No old world tumbles except when a young one shoves it over. And why should one howl when one's granfather is pushed over a cliff?'

Good-bye Grandfather, now its my turn.

> Yours etc:

The letter was not published.

Holford was granted a third year of study at the British School (1932–33). He seems to have started late as he, Gordon Stephenson plus a Czech and a Hungarian worked on a planning competition for Antwerp until January 1933.[17] During the spring of 1933 Holford continued his systematic travels in Italy studying piazzas, from Bergamo to Naples. He had previously travelled to most places in Italy and to Sicily, and paid several visits to Venice, the Italian city which he came to regard with most affection - perhaps with more affection than he felt for any other city.

Holford left Italy in the summer of 1933. It is noteworthy that his stay in Italy coincided with the full flood of Mussolini's fascism, then working up to the Abyssinian War, and Mussolini's voice had boomed out from a balcony in most large piazzas in Italy. Yet the subject is almost unmentioned in Holford's Italian letters. He had no nationalist or racial feelings, and was quite objective in descriptions of Mussolini's planning and Hitler's sports stadia. He was completely international in his outlook, and treated each person as an individual. He disliked any oppression, but he appeared to dislike even more any form of propaganda, noisy protest or direct action: whether against Fascism, Nazism or apartheid, or for 'modernism' in architecture or the Spanish left-wing government before Franco. In the 1930s, when nearly all young people were left wing (as all generous-minded youth should be) and read all the Left Book Club books, Holford remained sympathetic but detached. So far as one could tell, he regarded all politics and politicians in general, as necessary evils, though he admired individuals in politics, and was extremely good at spotting the real aims and motives of anyone, politician or not. He would give support to action that seemed good to him but signed no manifestos. One also notes that amongst all the emotional anti's and pro's of the 1930s, and much hot air over the International Brigade and the Soviets as champions of freedom, the Holfords were one of the few who had a Jewish refugee architect to stay in their own house for several months. He remained a friend, and gave much help in the final tragic months of Holford's life.

Holford returned to Liverpool in the summer of 1933 and Reilly - just about to retire because of ill-health - showed his continuing power to help favourite and gifted students. Despite the Great Slump of 1930–33 and consequent fall in university incomes, he had managed to appoint Gordon Stephenson as a junior lecturer and demonstrator in 1932; and his final *coup* was to have Holford appointed a senior lecturer in 1933. To appoint an ex-student with no teaching experience directly to a senior lectureship was then (and now) very rare, and the announcement caused consternation among the staff, as the next in line for a senior lectureship was a competent man who had also been a gallant and severely wounded pilot in the 1914–18 war,[18] and this, perhaps irrelevantly but understandably, was much mentioned. It was the first of Holford's leaps up the ladder to great influence, and fame.

Before the Second World War

In August 1933 Holford married Marjorie Brooks. Both had great, indeed overflowing, vitality. Marjorie was the more extrovert, a talented painter with a special gift for furnishing and decorating houses and sometimes shops. She had been much courted in Italy, not always with honourable intentions. She was also firm-minded, and told the author that she once made a long journey from Rome (typically, paid for by Holford) to propose herself as a companion or wife to a painter she much admired. She was rejected. She had high spirits and liked vigorous dancing, and was not unduly perturbed if she and her partner ended up on the floor.[18] Holford, an equally good dancer, remained always a little detached. He never rolled on the floor. The marriage of this outstanding pair was to include tragic elements, which increased as the years rolled on and in the end brought Holford to total and final exhaustion.

The Holfords set up house in Liverpool at 80 Bedford Street – which now has the Department of Civic Design next door. They began to take a full part in Liverpool's social and artistic life, including painting scenery for the Playhouse repertory theatre. Holford took over Reilly's lectures in architectural history and transformed them by his scholarship and charm of his voice and delivery.

Besides lecturing, Holford started a practice at 80 Bedford Street and entered for several architectural competitions with Gordon Stephenson. The two Holfords at once began to share their house in the way that continued, accommodation permitting, throughout Holford's life. At one time Stephenson, the Bulgarian, plus an impoverished painter and his child, and occasional student helpers all lived at '*80 Beds*' ... 'It is a wonder Marjorie put up with us.'[17] The house was kept together by Amelia, a famous character and friend, who cleaned and cooked and guarded '80 Beds' until she was killed by a bomb in 1941.

At this period the Modern Movement, sometimes called Functionalism, had enormous appeal for most young architects. Stephenson had spent nearly two years in the office of Le Corbusier one of the high priests, perhaps *the* high priest, of modernism. To be not in sympathy with the new enthusiasm for concrete boxes for houses, filled with bentwood and steel furniture, was, for a young architect a sad business. One felt very out of things; and to point out the serious defects and alarming cost of the first 'modern' buildings was to risk quite vicious abuse. There is little doubt that Holford, soaked in the Italian Renaissance, was not really sympathetic. Of course, he put up a wonderful show, knew all about the work of Gropius and the Bauhaus, Picasso and other modern painters and listened carefully to all the refugee architects from Nazi Germany – modernists like Mendelsohn, Chermayeff, Rosenberg and the rest, and to British converts, of whom Connell and Ward and Maxwell Fry were among the most prominent. What is certain and still survive are the only two houses[19] Holford himself designed in the 'modern' style – a semi-detached pair at Icklesham in Sussex, one of them for his mother-in-law. They are not a success in external appearance. Not at all. They are comfortable and well-proportioned within. It is difficult not to believe that, subconsciously, he disliked if not detested the whole functionalist approach to architecture, or at least to its abolition of ornament and subtlety, and so his hand and mind could not be forced to design well in that manner.

The Lever Chair

Holford had been only about two and a half years in the School of Architecture when Abercrombie decided to move to the Chair at University College London, and Holford made the second of his leaps up the ladder. He applied for and obtained the Chair of Civic Design, at the age of twenty-eight. There can be really no doubt that Reilly, although now retired at Brighton, was a prime agent in arranging for this success. For instance, Walter Gropius – a German refugee of international reputation – wrote a letter in support of Holford, though it is doubtful whether he had met him more than once. But Reilly had done a great deal towards arranging for Gropius to come to Britain,[20] and Gropius may have regarded the letter as a small repayment of a debt to Reilly. There was even more consternation this time over the appointment and not without reason.

Wesley Dougill was then Senior Lecturer in Civic Design, had been a Henry Jarvis Scholar at Rome (thus holding the next best award to the Rome Scholarship), had won other prizes, was editor of the *Town Planning Review*, a member of the Council of the RIBA and aged forty-three. According to all normal university rules he should have succeeded Abercrombie. It says much for Reilly's abiding influence in London and Liverpool, and the impression that Holford had made on his colleagues in two and half years, that he was preferred to Dougill. It is certain that in terms of what Holford had already done as student and lecturer, and of what he was to do for the University of Liverpool in the next forty years, it was the right choice. In the narrower duties of the Professor of Civic Design he did not do very much, chiefly because of the coming war.

The main reason why Holford applied for the professorship is probably the obvious one. Like other newly-married men of twenty-eight he wanted more money and to get on in the world. There was a chance he could obtain the appointment and appointments were then few. Lionel Budden, Professor of Architecture, was not due to retire for sixteen years, Liverpool was Holford's British home-town, the only one he knew; and he possessed a house of distinction near the centre of the university. He retained this house for thirty-two years. The fact that he knew nothing of British town planning as it was in 1936 would not have troubled so self-confident a man. In any case, neither of his predecessors had known anything more when they first took up their appointments. There were, however, three other reasons that may have had their influence. His study of Italian town plans and especially of piazzas had given him a great and perceptive interest in aspects of town planning, especially in urban enclosed spaces, practically and emotionally. The professorship would give him an opportunity to pursue these and allied studies. Again – as Richard Gray has suggested – Holford may have wished to use his talents in a field less rigid than the modern movement in architecture. Seven out of ten of the brighter young architects were modernists in 1936. Holford, as has been said, knew all the patter and was a member of MARS (the Modern Architectural Research Group – a propaganda society for modern architecture founded in 1933. It held a well-publicized exhibition in 1938, and faded out quietly during the Second World War). But after the Icklesham houses, all his own designs for buildings or parts of buildings show that he had no desire to be a modern architect in the manner of Le Corbusier, Mendelsohn and Gropius and their followers in Great Britain. On the other hand, he had no wish to be seen to stand out against his own generation of architects in their new-found enthusiasm, and was perhaps conscious of having been in an architectural and planning backwater in Italy for three years. It was Germany, until the Nazis were fully in power, and in Paris, where the new ideas were to be found. To be Professor of Civic Design gave him a distinguished position on the side lines, where he could do what he wanted and avoid the architectural battle. Since the fiery Sir Reginald Blomfield was the leading opponent of 'modernismus', some lusty thwacks were being exchanged.

Lastly, despite his brilliance as a draughtsman, it is very probable that Holford was not deeply interested in the total process of architecture: in preparing and reconciling plans with external appearance, preparing working drawings and specifications and supervising the whole lengthy process of construction. In nearly forty years of friendship with Holford – including periods of close working together – the author remembers Holford preparing a number of detailed designs of parts of buildings and of pavings, but cannot recollect his being at all closely involved with the totality of designing and constructing a building.

Reilly, in retirement at Brighton, of course heard about the impending appointment before almost anyone else 'and picked up his pen to scribble before even reading the papers' on 23 December 1935. It was a revealing letter, of which some passages deserve quotation:

> ... *I do congratulate you. It is a tremendous tribute to your personality. Although Town Planning in the modern sense has been going on for the last thirty years, your whole life in fact, you have no experience to put forward. It is just you. As with*

Eden [Anthony Eden later Foreign Secretary]
every one who meets you is convinced both of your
ability to tackle any job and of your character to
undertake it for the general good and not for mere
personal aggrandisement ... You will now have
time for quiet thinking.

It is a magnificent moment of course for you to be
turned into the new job, for it is the moment when
everyone is beginning to realize our towns have to
be rebuilt whether from a housing or a traffic
point of view. Unless this rebuilding is to be as
haphazard as the old and almost as useless,
someone has to think out, visualize, illustrate and
explain the solutions to the vast problems
involved.

... The Abercrombie stuff is no longer enough, in
fact by giving a fake sense of security does actual
harm ... he and his school would never commit
themselves to anything but generalities. You have
got to be the real designer who provides specific
ideas like Corbusier, Gropius and in the earlier
days, Adshead. When he had the Chair the
Department of Civic Design was a real thing,
greatly contributing to the lustre of the School.
Now it will be so again ... folk will be flocking to
your Department ... for inspiration and teaching
... the Town Planning Review *will become a great*
and vital organ ... put forward real solid ideas and
do not sink into being a petty-fogging town
planner ... if you do the job properly and not run
away from it as the last holder of the Chair did
people will not forget you as an architect any more
than they have Corbusier. Like him you must
always remain first and foremost ... Dougill might
become a Reader ... in Town Planning Procedure,
the stuff you do not know and do not want to, and
he does ... As you are going to look at Town
Planning as the advanced architecture it really is,
you will yourself make some contribution to the
School of Architecture work as Adshead made ...

In 1909 Reilly had made up his mind that civic design and town
planning were the design and building or rebuilding of cities with
grand avenues, squares, circles, vistas and monuments; with
perhaps similar activities, but more trees, in the suburbs. He was not
a man to change his mind with advancing years. If Abercrombie –
then approaching the peak of his international reputation – had read
this letter he would probably have been amused, and even have

quoted Dr Johnson's remark about a Scots Presbyterian Minister of very narrow views 'when a man reaches X's age, it is time for his ideas to have become settled'.

Holford's inaugural lecture *Rus in Urbe* was delivered in the old Arts Theatre of the university where, in the upper gallery thirty years before, some of Reilly's students had held up notices above the lecturer's head HE WON'T BE LONG NOW, and suchlike. The text of the lecture – or rather a long draft for it (7,500 words) – has recently been found among the Holford papers at the University of Liverpool. It discusses, in a way that foreshadows the aims of National Parks, how the countryside may be preserved and town-dwellers given more access to it. It also suggests that a definite boundary should be made between town and countryside, on the lines of the later green belts, and declares that motorways are bound to come.

The years 1936–39 were not a period of which Britain can be proud. There was slow recovery from the 1930–33 slump, but unemployment was very high and Britain and her allies did nothing to stop the rising strength of Germany. It was the time of Munich and the Brownshirts, of Guernica, *The Shape of Things to Come*, and cowardice by the Government. Britain's own rearmament went on at a snail's pace. The streams of German refugees, mainly Jews, should have rung alarm bells in every house. But they did not. The stories of Nazism at first horrified, and then began to seem unreal and even boring. The trouble with at least some of the German refugees was that they not only needed help, but thought they had an absolute right to plenty of it.

The Government did however cast around to see if something special could be done for the areas of very high unemployment, then called Special Areas. One decision was to establish two new and large industrial estates (called Trading Estates for some reason). One of these was in Wales, and the other in the Team Valley near Newcastle-upon-Tyne. The engineers for the Team Valley Estate were Sir Alexander Gibb & Partners, and Holford was appointed as planning consultant and to prepare the layout.

This was Holford's first big commission outside the academic world. It was probably his first commission on his own of any size or kind. The recommendation may have come through the RIBA where Sir Percy Thomas – consultant for the Welsh Estate at Treforest – was President. Certainly Holford soon met Hugh Beaver, a partner in Sir Alexander Gibb's, and they made a big impression on one another. Hugh Beaver – later knighted – may have been one of the three or four men on whom Holford seemed to model himself at different stages in his life. He certainly had great influence on Holford's career, as he recommended him to Lord Reith when Reith was in charge of physical reconstruction and so started the train of events described in the next chapter, by which Lever professors (past, present and future) and their former students had a major share in the preparation of the post-war planning system.

The way in which Holford tackled the Team Valley job was to set the pattern for all his outside work. His first floor drawing room became his office and he had one assistant, David Spreull. Presumably he had an arrangement with his secretary in the nearby Department of Civic Design for the typing of letters. With this equipment he set out to tackle a job that became technically complex because of the need to control the river Team and the presence of old mine workings.[18] In the end the cost was, for those days, great. A resident director, Colonel Melville, proved an excellent liaison officer between the Government, various consultants, contractors and industrialists who might rent factories; but Holford and Spreull designed the central administration building, and standard factories of various types, several of which could be extended to a great size by adding standardized additions.

A quotation which largely applies to Holford at this time and in the future runs as follows:

> He had no wide knowledge of affairs. He had no knowledge at all of business. He had, as I soon found, a marked dislike of office routine. But he had genius, and having that a man can afford to dispense with a great deal of the equipment that most of us find necessary for a prosperous journey through life … in Lloyd George's case it has manifested itself as an extraordinarily quick and subtle understanding of human nature combined with outstanding courage.[21]

Holford soon obtained as wide a knowledge of affairs as he needed, and in time this covered a wide field indeed, but when and how he did it remained another puzzle. His general reading must have been largely done between 1930 and 1936. Thereafter, he was seldom seen with a book, but he could absorb the contents of a paper or a plan at tremendous speed and remember the important points for as long as he wished. He could also act his way through gaps in his knowledge in a manner wonderful to behold. An air of infinite, kind wisdom, and a short question, as though he just wanted to confirm a minor point, would tempt those whom he was meeting to summarize the situation again and even go on to explain exactly what was wanted from Holford; and no one (except his own partner or assistant sitting on the edge of his chair) could guess that Holford had sometimes entered the room entirely ignorant of what was to be discussed. He was a superb actor.

He also, as time was to show, possessed outstanding courage and self-control in big things, but would go to ridiculous lengths to avoid personal unpleasantness. He was not a very good judge of character in recruiting minor employees (including secretaries) and would then allow himself and his affairs to be victimized to a grotesque extent rather than sack the person concerned.

Team Valley and his unexacting duties as professor occupied only part of Holford's time as the Second World War came nearer. He

lectured far afield, became a friend of Julian Huxley (and did some
work for the London Zoo) and later on did some broadcasting. This
turned out to be almost his only failure in projecting his personality
and views. His broadcast voice - as sometimes happens - lost the
charm and spell-binding quality it had in conversation or in a lecture
hall.

Marjorie Holford continued her painting, including more sets for
the Repertory Theatre in Liverpool, but not surprisingly she had
arranged for a studio round the corner in Abercromby Square where
she could escape from the working-drawings, visitors and refugees
in her own home at 80 Bedford Street. At times the house must have
been more like an office and lodging-house than a home.

On the outbreak of war Holford like many others of his age - thirty
two - wondered what to do. He considered taking part in some
construction works in Belgium (or so he says in one note) and he told
the author that his almost perfect Italian and tolerable French took
him near some branch of Intelligence. In fact, his relationship with
Alexander Gibb & Partners soon involved him and the first
available helpers (R. T. Kennedy and David Spreull) in designs for
Royal Ordnance (munition) factories.

It is impossible for an architect of Holford's age to read without
bitterness of the chaos in preparations for war even after it had
broken out. The small team in small rooms in Queen Anne's Gate
waded among hundreds of incomplete drawings and at one time
produced in a single day outline drawings for a new factory at
Woolwich Arsenal. Holford shared a small bed-sitting room with
Kennedy, near Victoria Station, and when Kennedy thankfully
went to sleep, Holford was still sitting up in bed dealing with
correspondence.[22]

Holford was then invited to help build a munition factory at
Kirkby near Liverpool and in less than three months had a staff of
150 men. Despite the unusual nature of the work, Holford presided
over it as though he had years of experience. Kennedy returns more
than once, in his account of working with Holford, to the three
remarkable Holford qualities which struck everyone: his capacity
for work up to a genuine sixteen hours a day; his power to preside
unruffled over complex and costly programmes of work of which he
had had almost no previous experience; and his kindness to all, and
specially to juniors, on both technical and personal matters. There
were times when his colleagues muttered that he was a soft touch for
any hard-luck story, and so, to some extent, he was.

Holford's great contribution to the preparations for post-war
planning - chiefly in the Ministry of Town and Country Planning -
is described in the next chapter, where it can best be shown in
relation to the process as a whole, and to the work of other men and
women. This short account of his life continued with all he did other
than as a planning adviser to the Government full-time or part-time.

Despite bad weather and the problems of collaboration between several hundred newly gathered professional men, contractors' staff and clerks of works, and a big labour force, the Kirkby Ordnance Factory was finished in little more than a year, and the Holford organization was then asked to take care of the building of, finally, twenty hostels, each for 1,000 women and girls, twelve near Ordnance Factory No. 7 outside Warrington and eight around another ordnance factory at Swynnerton in Staffordshire. Despite what could have been for an ordinary man a full-time job with Lord Reith, Holford agreed to take this on, chiefly to oblige Kennedy and two or three other helpers who were likely to be out of a job.

Once again a large staff – more than 200 architects and supporting staff – were quickly recruited, and the Holford team became entrusted with the design, layout, building, landscape design and furnishing of these buildings for 20,000 people. It was a really astonishing example of what Britons can (or could) do at a pinch, for each hostel contained almost everything that, say, Scandinavian tourist hotels contain today: sleeping quarters, baths, dining halls, drying rooms and laundries, sick bays and all, even hairdressing rooms. Moreover, the hostels were practically the only buildings then being built that were to a high – though austere – standard of design – including mural paintings, executed free of charge by architects and other employees in their short spare time (there was not much to do on Sundays as howling gales swept over the Risley Moss). They were much praised and were visited by the King and Queen.

Holford's part in all this was to attend key meetings in London, then travel northwards on Friday nights, visit the hostel construction in Staffordshire or near Warrington on Saturdays, and go on to his house at Liverpool which had survived a bomb 100 feet away. He would talk there to W. A. Eden – then in charge – about surviving civic design activities, and returned to London on Sunday evenings. He did this week after week, and those who remember wartime trains in winter will appreciate his stamina. He also had the burden in 1941–42 of his wife's pregnancy and complications that led to its termination. There were no children of the marriage, and Holford was very fond of children. One way and another he needed all the fortitude which post-captains RN and an African missionary grandfather had contributed to his genes.

The tremendous effort of 'the hostels' had a truly British end: the munition-making 'girls' flatly refused to live in them, or nearly all of them. No official explanation was forthcoming at Warrington, but the unofficial explanation was that the women resolutely refused to live 10 or 15 miles from their families, and all men, so columns of blacked-out buses and even trucks moved them to and fro. There was a happy ending. The hostels were completed just as the Royal Navy and the US Army Air Force (as it was then called) needed extra training camps and staging posts. A US Air Force colonel could hardly believe his eyes and ears on finding that the stricken British could provide luxurious accommodation for 6,000 men, within a week.

On one of Holford's last visits a blow-hard admiral (recalled from retirement to command a training establishment), made a short speech of appreciation of the excellent accommodation. When he'd finished Holford asked him quietly whether he should say a few words in reply, on behalf of the builders. The admiral turned and fixed the medium-sized youthful civilian with a glaring eye. 'Reply? – *Good God*, no!' This story, told by Holford immediately to two of his staff, is perhaps the last occasion on which Holford was known to tell a story against himself.

A last memory of that hostel – by then named HMS *Blank* – was of a pretty Wren walking at dusk among the many buildings, calling out in a singularly sweet voice: 'Darken Ship! Darken Ship!' until the sound died in the distance.

In the war years, usually at lunch time, Holford used to attend the meetings of PEP (Political and Economic Planning) – an all-party group that prepared short reports on current problems. Here he appeared, as always unobtrusive and shy but alert, heard proposals for after the war, and met or re-met such men as Julian Huxley, Max Nicholson, Michael Young and the Elmhirsts of Dartington Hall and various eminent civil servants. He also acquired the lease of a mews house in Little Chester Street, just west of Grosvenor Place and Buckingham Palace, in which he and his wife lived for ten years.

Having escaped the bombs which hit his portion of the Ministry on 23 February 1944 – he was on fire duty the following night – Holford's next big non-governmental job was for the City of London. The City had suffered horribly during the wartime bombings. About 26 million square feet of floor space had been destroyed – nearly one-third of the total that had existed in 1939. In 1944 the City Engineer had prepared some preliminary proposals for re-building and new traffic routes, but because of the City's importance, as the pivot of Britain's financial and commercial life, and the grievous destruction of historic buildings, the Common Council decided that a further report should be prepared by private consultants of high standing. The City appointed Charles Holden and Holford. Holden was an architect of great reputation, chiefly for his London underground stations and headquarters. In 1945 he was aged seventy. Holford was thirty-seven. It is doubtful if Holden knew or cared anything much about town planning, but he was an elder statesman of wisdom who knew some of the important people in the city. His party in the plan was to work out the sight-lines needed to preserve views of St Paul's Cathedral from traditional view-points: from the Victoria Embankment eastwards to London Bridge.[23] Holford and a small team working with him did all the rest.

The work was largely done in the year of 1946 and included measuring all the pre-war floor-space in the City and all that had been destroyed; and inventing a technical device called the 'Plot Ratio', which allowed quite large amounts of floor area to be provided on a given site whilst still ensuring that the daylight in each room would be up to a tolerable standard. Holford familiarized himself with the City of London and developed a deep affection for it, by walking around it on Sunday mornings and eventually knew the position and name of almost every street and alley.

It was as well that he did so. Early in 1948 a planning enquiry was held in the Guildhall to decide among other things whether around 270 of the City's golden acres should be subject to compulsory purchase to ensure a proper new layout. Almost every owner of property in the City had filed an objection, and it seemed at times that the entire English Bar had been briefed. 'Not that I resent being here,' said one barrister, 'I am very glad to be here!' and fifty or more colleagues chuckled in agreement. Sir Walter Monckton (later Lord Monckton) appeared for the City Corporation and called virtually only one witness, Holford. For several hours a day for most days of the long hearing Holford sat alone on the platform with some notes on a small desk. He was cross-examined by over forty barristers, plus solicitors and objectors in person. He was never ruffled and never, it seemed, at a loss. Once or twice he asked permission to have a point verified during the luncheon break. It was a tremendous performance, and when, at the end, Sir Walter Monckton paid a warm tribute to him there was a long loud murmur of agreement from all over the Guildhall.[24] Not many of the proposals were carried out, apart from one or two new lengths of road. But Holford was to do further work in the City.

From the end of the war the great question was what Holford was going to do next; and so perhaps set his course for the next thirty years. He had already, at the age of thirty-eight, achieved a commanding position. He was head of the Research Division of the Ministry of Town and Country Planning, the division which – staffed almost wholly by temporary civil servants (and containing three Lever professors) – was to lay the foundations, on the technical side, of post-war planning in Britain. He was held in high regard by W. S. Morrison, Minister from 1943 to 1945, and by the two senior officers of the Ministry. He was soon to add greatly to his reputation by the City of London Plan, and of course Liverpool University asked, very reasonably, when he was going to return to his duties as Lever professor. Other suggestions were made, including one that he should become head of an organization resembling that of Albert Kahn in the USA which carried out a huge volume of work. Such a Holford organization could speedily have been built up and might have obtained a vast amount of work. Holford was horrified by the idea. Nothing, he said, revolted him more than the thought of 300 draughtsmen 'with green eyeshades' in a vast drawing office, all dependent on him for work! He then added: 'Anyway, what of the 10,000 architects still in the Services? Are we going to pinch their bread, when the Min. of Lab. has saved our skins?'[25]

The truth was that for two or three years, probably 1944 to 1947,

Holford did not know what he really wanted to do. It was probable also that even he was exhausted when the war ended, and should have taken a long holiday. The causes of indecision were his feelings of loyalty to Liverpool and his university on the one hand; and, on the other, the fact that Abercrombie was to retire in 1947 from the Chair at University College London; and if Holford succeeded Abercrombie he could both continue with academic life and teaching, and attempt some of the important commissions and new responsibilities which his wartime friends and achievements, and residence in London, would certainly bring to him.

University College had been an early bidder for Holford, having offered him the succession to Abercrombie in November 1945. It was followed by the Ministry of Town and Country Planning. Indeed, in December 1945 the Permanent Secretary wrote to Holford that the Treasury had agreed to Holford's appointment as Chief Technical Officer with the rank of Under-Secretary.

On a number of occasions in his life Holford was undecided – indeed 'dithered' is the better word – over whether to accept or refuse offers – and he refused too seldom – but he did not allow such a human weakness to appear in writing. A letter to the Provost of University College on 1 January 1946 is an exception. It contained in writing pros and cons which he might have considered in his bath. It might be summarized as saying, in thirteen longish paragraphs 'on the one hand this, and on the other hand that' and ended by refusing the Provost's offer. But it did mention the various jobs that had been offered to Holford and perhaps was intended to keep University College interested. They remained interested.

A little later (probably mid-1946) the Ministry renewed its offer. On return from an interview with the Permanent Secretary (by then Sir Thomas Sheepshanks) Holford told a member of his staff that he had refused to commit himself to accepting a civil service post. His eyes then sparkled as they did when he was prepared to be coaxed to describe some odd behaviour by others (this was rarely). He was of course coaxed, and he did a perfect imitation of Sir Thomas, towards the end of the interview, drumming his fingers on the desk and saying 'well, think about it. We can offer you £2,000 any time ... if you can't, I suppose we'll have to think about X, though somehow or other we might have to offer him up to £4,000'. X was the respected chief engineer and town planner of a northern city, with all the good qualities and limitations of a man who'd fought his way up in local government in the hard 1930s. But the idea was altogether ludicrous that he would be worth twice Holford (and more than Sir Thomas himself) in what was, at that time, a key appointment.[26]

Holford's indecision, which did indeed cause the Ministry real difficulties, continued. He was busy on the City plan but his missionary conscience troubled him over his department at Liverpool for which he had done so little and which was now flooded with post-war candidates of high quality. It was kept going with difficulty by W. A. Eden. Wesley Dougill had died. Holford had also been asked by Liverpool University to prepare a five-year development plan, and report on whether the University should remain where it was among slums and war damage or move out to Otterspool or even further. He completed a first plan, with the help of Ward Shennan and a staff of two or three, in 1948–49.[27]

In the end, Holford decided to follow his two predecessors as Lever professor to the Chair at University College. Lord Crawford[28] whom Holford had probably first met on the Royal Fine Art Commission of which Crawford was then Chairman, was strongly in favour of Holford transferring – according to Patrick Abercrombie, who also supported the move. Other names mentioned in connection with Chair were J. H. Forshaw, co-author with Abercrombie of the LCC plan, who was then fifty-eight, and Arthur Ling, later professor at Nottingham. Holford's appointment was agreed in August 1946 and he took up the appointment in October 1947.[29]

The Liverpool influence in the Ministry remained as powerful as ever in that, when Gordon Stephenson, Holford's old friend at Liverpool, moved from being Chief Technical Officer at the Ministry of Town and Country Planning to become the fourth Lever professor, his place was taken by R. T. Kennedy who had worked in Liverpool and with Holford on hostels and in the Ministry for nine years. Holford felt the loss of his Liverpool friends, and perhaps felt guilty at having done so little as Lever professor. He retained as close a connection with Liverpool as he could. He was the university's planning consultant till 1955, kept on his house next to the Department of Civic Design till 1965 and remained a member of the principal Liverpool societies concerned with architecture and the visual arts.

Holford's Inaugural Lecture at University College in November 1948 was called *Civic Design*.[30] This reads much better than it sounded. Holford must have been very tired, as his usual charm and sparkle of delivery were missing. It distinguishes with wit and great insight between architecture and town planning and between the two 'columns' of planning: the administrative on one side shading into law, government, politics and social policy; and design on the other, backed up by architecture, landscape design, civil and traffic engineering and on to geography, geology and many related sciences.

Some of Holford's basic beliefs about civic design and his 1948 confidence in British planning are so well-expressed in the lecture that they demand quotation:

> Later still, if his own genius and the quality of his
> teachers lead him to it, [the youth] he may re-
> discover the simple values which he created by
> instinct as a child. But this time it will be by
> design and not by chance. He will have a
> technique behind him; and when he is master of it
> he can use it to express his ideas about life, about
> nature, about society and about beauty as he sees

it. This he can do without self-consciousness or
stumbling, because he is now, in the adult sense,
an artist.

I think the same kind of evolution is to be found
in the design of towns. Architects and engineers of
ability and experience, and promoters and councils
of rare discrimination, can between them produce
contemporary design of a high order that is simple
and moving. But they cannot do it by a return to
archaic simplicity or by sitting down to admire the
past and devaluate the present. Most of what we
know we derive from history, and the most
valuable derivation is not style and manner but
the applying of fundamental design principles to
changing times and places.

... The artist in us can appreciate almost any
urban scene, however ordinary, in certain
conditions of light or atmosphere or emotion; but
the selection in this case is done by nature or the
onlooker and not presented as a finished work of
art by the town planner himself. Where others can
crystallize and concentrate, he can but spread his
wares at so much to every acre; and the power he
has to create a unified impression by the emphasis
of certain buildings or contours, is not by any
means absolute.

... but all these ... will go for nothing, as far as
town planning is concerned, unless they tend to
strengthen the two central columns of the
structure, town planning admistration and civic and
landscape design. The time is apt for these
improvements. We happen to be, in this country,
in a condition favourable to the operation of the
planning mechanism. Less liable than we were
before the war to the panics inseparable from
mingled possessiveness and uncertainty, we are in
a sense morally fit to experiment in a socially
significant movement of the arts. The United
States, with a shorter experience of self-discipline
and hardship, and a higher index of living, is
more under the sway of the kind of fear that
makes planning ineffectual.

There is, I am sure, more fundamental
confidence in this country than in many other
parts of the world; and for this reason, as well as
for the more advanced legislation which this
confidence had engendered, we are the focus of
worldwide attention in all matters relating to the
planning of town and country. It is a

commonplace for us today to discuss concrete development plans with a parish council as part of the normal business of democracy in action, rather than as an unusual example of an enlightened landlord under the influence of Tolstoy.

I should like to end with a tribute to our own pioneers. To Stanley Adshead and Patrick Abercrombie, two men of exceptional skill and imagination, and two illustrious holders of the Chair of Town Planning, first at Liverpool and then at London, must go some of the credit for our achievements in this field.

One notes also in the lecture that on education he was then against part-time evening courses, as being too much of a strain for students and staff. This was certainly true of the University College students. A lecturer who had given a good evening lecture and hoped for a lively discussion was very disappointed to find that hardly anyone spoke. A member of staff told him not to blame himself '... They are too tired'. Nevertheless Holford refused to follow the example of Liverpool, which introduced full-time courses and gave up evening classes. One can hardly doubt that one reason for this was that it was only in the evenings that he could spare time for academic duties.

It may reasonably be held that the process of atomization which eventually destroyed Holford began, though slowly, as early as 1948. He simply could not refuse any interesting piece of work, (including, to the exasperation of his colleagues and partners) much work which either was unremunerative or was clearly going to result in a loss. There came a time, inevitably, when even his magnificent mental and physical equipment was stretched to the limit, and the grave illness of his wife and his constant care for her then imposed a fatal strain. But in 1948 this lay twenty years ahead. In the meantime, commissions and responsibilities streamed in, and soon, honours.

His appointment at University College was part-time, and quickly his work in the department became small. The department lagged behind, as has been stated, - or at least soon differed from - most other university town planning departments in that the majority of its students were in the evening classes.

In 1948 Holford was appointed to prepare a plan for Cambridge and its neighbourhood. He was already doing work for St Thomas's Hospital and Eton College and on the Liverpool University plan. Holford had the great gift of being able to turn clients and fellow committee members into friends. It was friendship of a special kind, in that most of the new friends were almost as busy as he was and the friendships had to be kept in repair by a dinner party once a year or, more usually, by a quarter of an hour's chat after or before meetings.

Holford made as good use of these encounters as was possible. Relaxed, amusing, courteous, brief, he was welcome to everyone. So were his remarks. He was once met by a colleague at Liverpool as he left the room of a rather forbidding vice-chancellor who had a bleak smile, and was asked how he had got on, and replied 'Oh, I've had my full twenty minutes of winter sunshine!' He was also the complete non-intriguer, and thus eminent men who were in danger of being lobbied greeted him with that extra warmth of one who has made a neat escape. It followed that pre-war friends like (to use their later titles) Lord Cohen and Sir Hugh Beaver, were soon followed by Lord Crawford at the Royal Fine Art Commission, Lord Annan at Cambridge, Lord Birley at Eton, Lord Evans at University College the Huxleys, the Elmhirsts at Dartington Hall, and a score of others including Lord Boyd of Guinness's and Lord Hinton of the Central Electricity Generating Board.

Holford preferred to work by himself, with a secretary and one, or at most two, assistants to help him on work in which he took a special personal interest. When he and his wife moved to Cambridge Terrace in Regents Park in 1950 he was able to arrange things the way he seemed to like. It was a large house on five floors, and Holford was able to have the main L-shaped room on the first floor – the *piano nobile* – for his own work. He had a knee-hole desk with extending flaps, a large eighteenth-century dining table for conferences, and an architect's drawing table of the same period. There was no modern furniture of the stainless steel or bent plywood type in any of their houses, though they had some Gordon Russell furniture, angle-poise lamps and a glass-topped table. Besides occasional visitors who occupied what Marjorie Holford called 'The-Bridal Suite', the house enabled them to resume the communal living that suited them. Two helpers – and highly individual characters – Mr Marjoram and Miss Perkins lived in the basement, and flats at the top of the house and over the garage at the rear were almost continuously occupied, often by young couples like the Haskells; Haskell being an architect and ex-Rome Scholar who helped Holford. For quite a long period the top flat was the London home of Robert and Lorna Matthew. Sir Robert Matthew, as he later became, founded the famous architectural firm of Robert Matthew and Johnson-Marshall. The house was beautifully decorated; in this Marjorie Holford excelled. Some of the distinguished pieces of furniture were lent to them by Lord Crawford, who was a friend for ten years or more.

If the years at Liverpool were the happiest for the Holford's, the fifteen years at Cambridge Terrace were the times of achievement and of honours, with which both of them mixed a lot of fun. They were also years in which Marjorie Holford's successive ailments proved an increasing burden on her husband. Despite her gaiety and charm, she did not suffer in silence – quite the reverse – and the fact that Holford's office was in his home meant that calls for aid and comfort could come at any time.

Holford could not of course manage large contracts at Cambridge Terrace, nor did he wish to; and so in the years after the war he began the dispersal of offices and staff which in time, and to an outsider, appeared bizarre, but had for one of Holford's temperament at least some advantages. He liked to work by himself, and for what he could not do himself he liked to be able to rely on one loyal and fully informed person. He detested hierarchies or the sight of a large office dependent on him. He also detested disputes and having to arbitrate in a dispute, or even to correct a secretary who was behaving badly, and several gave him inferior service. On the other hand, he could not refuse a tempting job even though he knew he could not do it himself. He did not want to become involved in personal responsibility for the design and construction of buildings. He already knew that his genius lay in solving the problems that faced high level committees over a wide range of town planning, architecture, landscape architecture and the visual arts. His solution was, therefore, to recruit what he thought was a suitable man to do a particular job, set him up in a separate office, empower him to enlist the necessary staff and let him get on with it. In his choice of his principal assistants (later his partners) he was either very shrewd or very lucky. Of the nine principal men up to 1960, seven were not only very able but remained loyal both to Holford and one another. Of the two unsuitable men, one was not recruited by Holford, and the other was unluckily offered a job from kindness of heart. The advantages for Holford on this system were several. He avoided large gatherings of dependents and a lot of possible disputes between strong characters. He would, as boss, be compelled to visit each job at times. His tremendous powers of concentration would enable him to absorb on the train both a report about the job and later all that the man on the job had to say, including local circumstances, clients' views and temporary difficulties.

Later, as a perfect committee man, he would usually propose a course of action that was both sensible and in accordance with the views of several of the most influential members of the committee.

His power of concentrated thought was tremendous. Richard Gray has related how, when advising on the planning of the Australian capital of Canberra, Holford would remain motionless for a long period, perhaps for two hours, and would then dictate or write two or three papers on different aspects of the work without subsequent alteration of more than an occasional word.

This method of doing work was successful to start with (especially where there was a standard fee) but as offices multiplied and Holford offered to do work for too little, or failed to send in bills, there was a period when chaos was never far away. At various times there were offices in the City of London, at Harley Street, Cambridge, Canterbury, Liverpool, Glasgow and Edinburgh, as well as the key one in Regents Park. In all there have been sixteen Holford offices. And if or when office number 1 ran out of work, there were of course difficulties in moving staff to offices 2 and 3. In later years, Holford wisely left these things to his partners, who have been able to look after the money and move jobs from office to office without difficulty.

Holford's gift of being able to size up a situation by a few minutes talk or by glancing at the pages of a document had to be seen to be believed. John Cooper, a former partner, has described how he once met Holford at York for an important meeting and was shocked to discover that Holford had never received a fifteen-page report sent a week before about the complex object of the meeting. 'I was only able to give him a copy to scan over during the three or four minutes (before the meeting) ...' Bill Holford proceeded to give such an erudite view of the whole situation that (Cooper felt) 'he had achieved a complete understanding and grasp of the matter that exceeded my own'.[31]

Again Professor Lewis Keeble thinks Holford might, among many possible careers, have achieved the greatest heights as an actor. He has described how Holford used to arrive, with three minutes to spare, before the annual show of work of the Diploma students at the Department of Town Planning at University College, London. Keeble (then Director of Studies) told Holford over a quick cup of tea what the programmes were about. Holford:

> *then proceeded to chair the meeting, give a brief*
> *introductory speech and put in helpful comments*
> *from time to time during the discussion. Nobody*
> *who did not know the true facts could possibly*
> *have suspected that he had not been intimately*
> *concerned with the conduct and production of the*
> *work. Saying this, risks suggesting that he was in*
> *some ways a Charlatan. But indeed not: his*
> *performance rang true. In some miraculous way he*
> *was capable of taking in, absorbing and*
> *epitomizing the work of thirty people carried out*
> *over six months as if he had been intimately*
> *concerned with it from the beginning. Of such is*
> *genius.*[32]

Holford beyond all doubt sometimes had powers that were abnormal. One could put to him a complex problem involving elements A, B, C, D, etc., and suggest tentatively that the best solution was, say, G. Holford would look at the ceiling, for thirty seconds or so, and then say ask 'Have you thought of K? ... it might have advantages.' On the way home, one would go over it all, perhaps to begin with a little annoyed at the rejection of solution G, and in the end would find that in all the personal and technical circumstances, K was the best line of action. This happened several times when the author was working closely with Holford, and seemed quite uncanny. In today's jargon, one would say he seemed to have, on occasions, a built-in personal computer and data retrieval system.

It has been made clear that Holford had a dozen, perhaps twenty, different interests and different sides to his character. He kept the interests in separate packets, so that even his partners did not know of the extent and importance of his work for, say, the Central

Electricity Generating Board.

Other aspects of this remarkable man's character provide plenty of material for psychological speculation. It is the public face and the public actions that are of most consequence; and of Holford's we know more than of Lever's or Abercrombie's. The private aspects and contradictions of his character and behaviour do, however, show Holford as a human being with failings and inconsistencies, and these add to his interest for most people; and perhaps are a little consoling.

Indeed, a great deal is known about the private Holford from friends and eye witnesses who studied him at close range, fascinated and for years. Much of this may one day find a place in a full biography. Here, only a few notes are appropriate and the choice is difficult. No man is a hero to his valet, and one must try to pick out just enough blanks or inconsistencies to show that Holford was very human, and to give contrast to his great merits.

His generosity in help, including financial help, to fellow-architects and young people was outstanding. It can be no exaggeration to say, indeed repeat, that 100 architects and planners owed their first job or first big job to Holford: and that, including ex-students, young Rome Scholars and anyone from Liverpool, the number may well have reached 250. Some forgot this help: quite a lot never did. On the other hand, he could be thoughtless towards those working most closely with him unless they made a direct appeal to him. It is doubtful if he had any thought for the morrow for himself and he probably never thought of others having money worries. He could also indulge in slightly absurd economies, such as wearing a shirt that was a little frayed at the neck, and keeping tiny scraps of food on saucers in the refrigerator in his beautiful houses at Regents Park and Brighton. Innocent enquiry as to whether these bits were for the cat was blankly received.

'I suspect', writes Professor Keeble, 'that, despite his genius in many other ways, Holford was essentially in the administrative and minor organizational sense a quite disorganized person.'[32] This was so, and was at its worst over money matters, in which Holford has no interest, but was – for a number of years – unwilling to leave to others. He disliked asking for money, and asked professionally for too little, and before his assistants (he had no partners until about 1954) had had time to plead with him for a more realistic attitude over this vital matter. Sir John Overall, former Chairman of the National Capital Development Corporation at Canberra, Australia – to which Holford and his partner Richard Gray acted as consultants for many years – writes of 'Holford's modesty in handling of financial matters. His professional fees were moderate at all times.'[33] It is possible that habits of asking for too little was partly the result of the frugality he imposed on himself at Liverpool as a student, when an old friend of his father helped him to complete the course, partly a genuine modesty, and partly it came from a dislike of all controversial matters and his liking to be liked. He was almost universally liked, yet an observant woman employee in South Africa noted, with surprise, that, even when he was a life peer and loaded with honours, Holford could be upset by the thought that even one quite unimportant person disliked him.

This asking for too little seemed, indeed was, important at the time to colleagues who knew Holford could easily double his income and theirs; but it all came right in the end – as has been stated earlier – and then Holford asked too little from his partners. Even from a commission where the fees ran to well over £1 million, and where he himself was closely involved, he would accept only a sum such as was earned by a newly-qualified assistant.

Holford's private secretaries, or some of them, were another trial to his close colleagues. His modesty prevented his realization that his activities had, first, become nationwide, and then spread to four continents. These called for a personal assistant (as she would now be called) at the headquarters in Cambridge Terrace, who had high intelligence and broad knowledge, an excellent sense of priorities and the social poise to handle important people tactfully. A typist could have been obtained as well. Instead, Holford seemed to accept any nice young woman, recruited we know not how, who could type, take dictation and answer the telephone. Once recruited, Holford would defend them loyally, with a hint of reproach to a critic, as though the latter lacked human charity towards a slightly backward child. It is to the credit of several of them that they coped cheerfully and tolerably with twenty subjects beyond their experience or grasp, and with messages from up to six other Holford offices plus University College.

Apart from his help to students and fellow architects, Holford frequently sent money to people who may or may not have had a claim on him; and equally frequently was asked to join in campaigns for this and that. 'I am the unwilling recipient ...' he wrote to (Sir) Howard Robertson about Walter Gropius's request that Holford should express disapproval of a design for a UNESCO building. He remained light-hearted. In 1955 those who were attending a regional planning conference in London were called Communists by a London newspaper, and the American Embassy tried to pull out an American lecturer ten minutes before his speech, Holford being chairman. Holford took this very lightly. To a colleague he said 'Relax George, we'll go to prison together,' and to a pushy reporter 'Yes but that's what you're saying; not what I'm saying.'

By 1955 Holford's close colleagues, by then his partners, worried quite a lot about his burden of work. In 1951–52 his wife had had a most serious illness in the United States, and the treatment had cost a lot. His magnificent constitution had always to bear the burden of severe asthma attacks in any British summer. He did not suffer when in South Africa or Australia, but it was rarely possible for him to be away from Britain in summer. Yet despite strong physique and nerves, his prime requirement after 1955 was the refusal of additional responsibilities, however interesting or flattering the requests might be. This he could not do. When in the late 1950s one of his partners pleaded with him to slow down, he replied that he and his wife had no children, and he would prefer to do all he could rather than 'live on indefinitely as a cabbage'. The thought of Holford living as a cabbage produced a laugh in which he joined, but he made no promises.[34]

In the 1950s Holford was concerned with plans for Cambridge, Corby New Town, and the layout and some buildings for Exeter, St Andrews, Liverpool and Kent universities. The Cambridge plan did not arouse quite as many controversies, feuds, splinter groups and polemics as did attempts to plan Oxford, but it aroused quite enough to prove that academics yield to no one in narrow self-interest, and appear to have plenty of spare time to fill. Holford was appointed jointly by the county, university and city authorities, but when it came to the enquiry the university split off without warning and brought in Sir Michael Rowe to make a sustained attack on Holford's proposals. One young man, who had changed over from Holford's office to what became the other side, lost his head entirely and published a libel which he was compelled to retract. On the other hand, Holford was asked to do work for King's College, which proved to be one of the office's most pleasant commissions, and lasted for several years.

The work for St Andrews University proved that strong feeling over planning proposals is not confined to English universities. The university proposed in 1955 to take half of some immensely long gardens, some of them neglected, belonging to ten or twelve terrace houses. Despite the great Scots regard for education (when the Vice-Chancellor of Edinburgh, then Sir Edward Appleton, entered the later enquiry, all in the room, including the inspector and assessors, stood up until he was seated) the proposal started a feud of astonishing heat, which split the town and it seemed almost split Scotland. The author was lobbied about it in the West Indies. Eventually the proposal was abandoned. The then Lord Crawford, whose home at Balcarres was only a few miles away, was much distressed, as he had been Rector of St Andrews and had proposed Holford for the work. He advised Holford to withdraw from 'the miserable affair'. But Holford was not one for withdrawing and even at the time the sound and fury seemed absurd. In 1974 those same gardens were still largely unused and neglected.

During the 1950s Holford was also President of the (now) Royal Town Planning Institute, consultant for the Federal Capital of Canberra in Australia, and for work in Pretoria in south Africa. He was being drawn (1957) into the great problems of the new Central Electricity Generating Board, which was to own and operate all power stations in England and Wales and distributes the power generated through the grid of high-voltage lines. The work included the siting of power stations, choosing architects and landscape architects and especially choosing the best routes for the grid and supergrid with its conspicuous pylons. Holford was a part-time member of the CEGB for sixteen years, and arranged for valuable help from Michael Shepheard, Thomas Sharp and Sylvia Crowe. He also chose architects, such as Frederick Gibberd, who proved they could work to mutual advantage with the CEGB engineers. This work was held by the late Howard Mason, senior CEGB architect, to have been Holford's greatest, and almost entirely unknown, contribution to the preservation and protection of rural England and Wales. He had also become, in 1953, a member of the Historic Buildings Council and soon afterwards chairman of the council's advisory committee on listed buildings which had the responsibility, among other duties, of advising the council on the allocation of government grants towards the repair and maintenance of some of the most famous houses in Britain. Holford's interest in this part of our architectural heritage is shown by his care, as chairman, of all the papers, and by having them expertly indexed and cross-referenced, so that the case for helping the repair of one great house could be carefully compared with the cases put forward for help for similar houses.

It was also in the 1950s that he undertook two tasks of great difficulty, which were of great personal interest to him. These were proposals for the new surroundings of St Paul's Cathedral (begun in 1955) and for a new Piccadilly Circus (1962 and 1966). The design of enclosed spaces in cities had fascinated him ever since his studies of Italian piazzas in 1930–33. His deep feeling for the subject had several causes: his affection for Italy and the Italian Renaissance; the fact that the studies of forty piazzas were made, when he was about twenty-five, full of vigour, and already in love with Marjorie Brooks who was in Italy with him; and probably because he was a man of cities.

The area around St Paul's Cathedral had been severely damaged by German bombing. Buildings to the north and east had been almost entirely destroyed. The most suitable new buildings and their arrangement were a matter of great concern and some dispute between the Ministry, the London County Council, the City authorities and owners and developers. By 1955 tempers were rising high. After the Second World War there was strict licensing of building and building materials, with preference going to new housing and factories; and there was undoubtedly a prejudice against 'the City' among the leaders of the Labour Party which was in power for six years. The Conservative Government, which had regained power in 1951, realized more fully the national importance of the City's financial dealings and its exchanges and commodity markets, and the justice of City landowners' complaints. The latter pointed out that after the Great Fire of 1666 – which destroyed a far greater proportion of the City than had the German bombs – much of the City had been rebuilt in four years, whereas in 1955, after ten years of peace, acres and acres of ruins and willowherb still extended from the Barbican to the Thames.[35] As building licensing (save for control of the location of factories) came to an end in 1955, the problem of what to do around St Paul's had become urgent, and Holford was called in, probably at the insistence of Mr (now Lord) Duncan Sandys who was then Minister of Housing and Local Government, into which the previous Ministry of Town and Country Planning had been absorbed. Duncan Sandys (founder of The Civic Trust) tried hard to find the best possible setting for St Paul's and took a great personal interest in the plans. He had a model of the cathedral prepared, and various building blocks, and spent time trying out various arrangements himself and sent photographs of the results to Holford. He also asked other well-known architects for their views.

Holford regarded the surroundings of St Paul's as a personal task. In a very real sense, the first scheme was his own work, down to most beautifully drawn suggestions for pavings. The Minister approved of this scheme but when Holford in his turn asked the opinions of two other architects and, in consequence, proposed some modifications, Duncan Sandys disagreed.[36] Subsequent discussions and changes were involved and numerous, but the arrangement and form of the buildings near St Paul's, as actually built were largely guided by Holford's reports and plans. His liking for towers – which Richard Gray has traced as a constant element in Holford's approach to architecture – also emerged in his St Paul's scheme in a proposal for a twenty-storey building (later reduced to fifteen), near the cathedral.[37]

Holford also reserved the Piccadilly Circus problem for his own personal attention during most of the 1960s. It was another example of his capacity to 'take serious things lightly' that he felt he could fit the solution of this most baffling and infinitely complicated problem into such relatively few hours as he could spare from other work.

The circus, with its central statue always called Eros, has a special place in the affections of Britons and of many in what used to be the British Empire. Apart from Sir Reginald Blomfield's buildings at the end of Regent Street, the buildings around the statue have been rather ramshackle for the whole of this century, being at their best when hidden by flashing lights at night.

By 1959 various proposals for rebuilding around or a new layout for the circus had been made and almost wholly rejected for seventy years. After the Second World War the London County Council wished to transform the Circus into a space that would do credit to London and the Commonwealth. This would have meant demolition of the London Pavilion buildings and, at the least, modifications of the three other familiar building groups – the Monico, Trocadero and Criterion.

Great public feeling and great financial interests were involved.[38] Holford was called in and produced his two schemes of 1962 and 1966. The proposals then disappeared for at least ten years into a morass of arguments over traffic, public and private interests, particular rebuilding proposals, restrictions on height and bulk, exhibitions, Green (explanatory) Paper and much else. Both the

Holford schemes had merit. The first was simpler and created a large raised pedestrian space (called a piazza, no doubt in memory of his study thirty years earlier) which included Eros. His second scheme left Eros on a small island, dangerous of access, which was left much as it was, but proposed a new, large and dramatic pedestrian deck, floating above all the traffic, which would have linked nearly all the sites and streets to the east of Eros. Both schemes were eventually whittled away into extinction.

Thus in his two potentially great urban enclosed space schemes, Holford achieved appreciable success around St Paul's and none at all at Piccadilly Circus. At least so far. Piccadilly Circus has not yet been redeveloped. It might however be remembered that, although Holford ceased to be planning consultant to the University of Liverpool in 1955, it was found, when a final review of work done was made in 1974, that three major Holford recommendations (made in 1949) had in fact been carried out.

In the 1960s Holford's career reached its zenith. His wife had been seriously ill in 1951–52, as already stated, and had suffered intermittently from what was then called a slipped disc, but by 1960 her health appeared good, and she could indulge her passion for furnishing and re-decorating houses, did quite a lot of painting and would confess – seemingly with a slight feeling of guilt – to a deep interest in dress design and haute couture. She dressed beautifully for all social occasions with that charming, carefree appearance (so maddening to less fortunate women) of having made no effort at all.

Commissions, new responsibilities and honours were showered upon Holford, and his powers for a year or two appeared limitless. He was President of the Royal Institute of British Architects in 1960–62 and received the Royal Gold Medal in 1963. He was presented with this at a private audience with the Queen, an unprecedented honour. The interview lasted half an hour and was described in a letter to his mother. He did not say in the letter that Her Majesty had asked some shrewd questions about architects and their quarrelsome relations with one another. Holford's recent experience as President of the RIBA no doubt enabled him to make a model reply. He was also Prime Warden of the Goldsmith's Company in 1962–63, and was created a life peer as Lord Holford of Kemp Town in 1965. He was elected ARA in 1961 and as a Royal Academician in 1968.

Somehow or other he fitted in his honorary work for the Fine Art Commission and the Historic Buildings Council, as President of the Housing Centre, Trustee of the Soane Museum, President of the Liverpool Blucoat Society and others. Later he became a Trustee of the British Museum and Treasurer of the Royal Academy. When one examines the full list it seems incredible that he fitted in so much: especially as he seems to have made a valuable contribution to almost all of his committees.

The first sign of failure in Holford's physical condition, perhaps the first step down from the peak, occurred in 1965. In a letter to

Professor Kantorowich he reported that a consultant at St Thomas's had detected signs of a blood disorder, but that he was now much better. Ten years later it fell to the same consultant to tell him he had not long to live. He began after 1965 to talk more frequently of retirement from the Chair of Town Planning at University College.

Holford indeed constantly talked of retirement from his professorship. He was certainly doing so by 1956, as the Provost (now Lord Evans) then returned a cheque for £300 – apparently for outside lecturers – and told him the college wanted him to stay, and that his work on the surroundings of St Paul's enhanced the reputation of the department. An amusing letter survives from 1958 when J. J. Clarke begged him not to resign, on the grounds that if his strength failed, or commissions failed, his academic post would continue to provide an income. Holford said truthfully that the Provost particularly wished him to stay, and as late as 1967 Lord Annan (the new Provost) thanked Holford for all he did for the college. These labours must have been in giving the college extra weight in the great conglomerate of London University or in the outside world.

From the narrow academic viewpoint, it does seem that Holford should have left University College by 1960, and that his continuing as professor without having proper time to give to his duties held up much-needed reforms. He did little there save lecture on the history of town planning to first-year students, but he was probably reluctant to abandon a connection with youth that had lasted for forty years. His odd attitude to money continued. In 1965 and 1967 he managed to pay £525 and £254 for fees for extra lecturers out of his pocket rather than ask University College for an additional grant that would readily have been given. There is no doubt that these payments were conscience money because he knew he was doing too little. When he finally resigned in 1968 he was, in a human way, rather annoyed to find the item on a college agenda without a previous warning to him.

This and other modesty over accepting money make it quite surprising that he was able to buy and furnish the splendid house at Brighton about five years before he gave up the house in Regents Park in 1966. Both Holford and his wife loved Brighton and the flat in Eccleston Square that succeeded the Regents Park house was only a few minutes' walk from the Brighton trains at Victoria Station.

Despite the appointments yet to come at the British Museum and Royal Academy, the 1960s began to contain disappointments. He could not complain that the design of the British Embassy at Rome was given to Sir Basil Spence, since Holford had never claimed to be a great architect. He never did complain, but Marjorie Holford admitted he was sad. He had loved Rome, went back when he could and still spoke excellent Italian, and would undoubtedly have tried to make the Embassy his *magnum opus*.

He was also shaken to find that a centre for environmental studies was to be established in Britain with an initial endowment from the Ford Foundation, without his being consulted or even informed.[32] He became a member of the governing body of the centre, which in due course took over his own house in Regents Park; yet the occurence may have been taken by him as a sign of declining influence. He was very sensitive over such matters, though to almost everyone else he appeared still on a pinnacle, firm, and broad enough for one. He travelled to South Africa and Australia and occasionally to his Liverpool and Edinburgh offices, gave the Romanes lectures at Oxford and had received honorary degrees from Oxford, Durham, Liverpool and Exeter.

Most lives are tragic towards the end. To those with inside knowledge, Holford's last five years were as deeply tragic as his gifts and achievements had been outstandingly high. At the end of 1969 Marjorie Holford suffered a severe stroke. Holford devoted his energies to achieving her partial recovery by his own personal exertions, which were unsparing and almost unbalanced. After some weeks, friends implored him not to undertake a useless martyrdom, to sell his house at Icklesham and obtain proper professional help. These pleas were ignored until they could be ignored no longer. Holford did the cooking and housekeeping and even tried to organize distinguished old friends (some of whom had their own troubles) to come on a rota basis to look after his wife when he had to be absent. He then staggered nearly everyone by accepting the directorship of the Leverhulme Trust Fund. His own explanation was that the firm no longer needed him, it would be a new challenge and take his mind off his wife's state and of course the remuneration would help.

It really was an extraordinary last act for a man of so many interests; and there was no neglect of those duties. For three and usually four days a week he travelled from his flat near Victoria to New Fetter Lane by underground at about 8 am and returned at 7 pm, to avoid the rush hours. He boasted that he and perhaps two others examined all applications for grants, asked for expert opinions when needed and, subject to the Trustees, allocated all funds. The Leverhulme Trust Fund's administrative costs were, he said, markedly lower than those of any comparable foundation in proportion to annual revenue and grants made. He sometimes looked very tired and ill, and when old friends, seeing this, told him that he was wasting his great gifts, and should do nothing himself save that which subordinates had tried hard to do and failed, he showed no resentment, but just seemed puzzled.

By 1974 he was clearly unwell, but could still briefly relax, as when he was almost shanghai'ed to Paris for four days by Eugene Rosenberg – the distinguished architect and former refugee who had stayed with the Holfords in 1938. They visited exhibitions and old haunts, ate and rested. Holford seemed much refreshed.

In early 1975 Holford was told he had not long to live. He did what he could for his wife, saw quite a lot of friends at St Thomas's Hospital and, as Lord Esher said at the memorial service in St Paul's 'he died what used to be called a Roman death'.

Holford had great and many gifts and was at least in some respects a genius, and his help for others continued for forty years. His defects, minimal in proportion to his merits, arose from an inability to refuse work and a compulsion to be modest, to be liked and to avoid controversy. Women apart from Marjorie meant nothing to him. One wonders sometimes whether anyone meant a great deal to him, or whether anyone understood him – all of him. He had no close and lasting friendships after he and Gordon Stephenson went different ways. He walked by himself. A young former Rome Scholar who had worked with him and was a devoted admirer writes that he suspects Holford 'was a lonely, private, unfulfilled person'. One doubts whether this extraordinary man, so generous and kind and witty and so seemingly light-hearted, was often happy.

NOTES AND REFERENCES

1   The author's recollection of this incident, which occurred at the Holford's house at Cambridge Terrace about 1960, was firmly imprinted on his memory by his feeling at the time that he would have been much disturbed by such a complaint, seemingly justified, from a Prime Minister. But as Holford's partner Richard Gray has recorded, Holford could take serious things lightly and embarrassing things gracefully.

2   Information from Richard Gray.

3   Sir Kenneth Clark, *The Other Half* (John Murray, 1977) xii.

4   Neil Holford interview January 1980.

5   Ancestry has been traced for four generations. On the paternal side to an exciseman in Lancashire about 1800 and on the maternal side to Captain Palmer R. N., married in 1799.

6   Holford had several stories of this kind about his grandfather's times in South Africa, and there is little doubt that farmers could only hold their farms by brutal methods against large and small bands of native raiders, thieves and squatters.

7   Richard Gray visited the Diocesan College in 1979 and obtained, *inter alia*, copies of Holford's marks in the chief exams and of a letter of recommendation from the Vice-Principal.

8   Dr W. N. Vellacott, letter, November 1978.

9   This is the way Holford told the story to the author, and to others in the author's hearing.

10   E. Maxwell Fry CBE, ARA, letter, September 1977.

11   Professor Robert Gardner-Medwin, 'Notes on Holford', February 1978.

12   As any student might, he bought a *Liverpool University Students' Song Book* early in his first term, but he must have used it, as at one time he persuaded twenty-four fellow students to sign it. Only four of these were in the School of Architecture.

13   Letter from Holford to Marjorie Brooks, his future wife, February 1932.

14   Richard Gray feels reasonably sure that he had identified several of these models, all men of great distinction, including Sir Hugh Beaver and W. S. Morrison, later Lord Dunrossil.

15   S. D. Adshead, 'Camillo Sitte and Le Corbusier', *Town Planning Review* Vol XIV (1930–31) 85.

16 *RIBA Journal* Vol. No. XL (January 1933) 153-72.

17 They all camped out, sometimes with Marjorie Brooks as well, in one, occasionally two, mock Tudor semi-detached houses, in the most respectable suburb of Hoylake. The houses belonged to Stephenson's mother and a cousin. As the team worked nearly twenty hours a day towards the end, and spoke, when provoked, five languages at least, Stephenson's relatives must have been very tolerant people. 'Occasionally Charles Reilly would turn up with his ivory-knobbed walking stick and broad brimmed black hat *pour épater les bourgeois* in the little street ...' Gordon Stephenson, 'Notes on Bill Holford', 1978.

18 David Spreull, letter about Holford, 1978.

19 He had previously shared with Gordon Stephenson and FRS Yorke a success in the Gidea Park competition for small houses.

20 Statement by Gordon Stephenson, 1978. Stephenson was on the staff of the school at the time, knew what was going on and lobbied, as much as a junior lecturer could, in Holford's support when the latter applied for the Chair of Civic Design.

21 John Griff, *Lloyd George: The People's Champion 1902-1911*, quoting the 1st Viscount Devonport (Eyre Methuen, London 1978) 101.

22 R. T. Kennedy, notes about Holford, 1977.

23 Holden's suggestions are reproduced on pages 298 and 299 of C. H. Holden and W. G. Holford, *The City of London: A Record of Destruction and Survival* (The Architectural Press, London, 1951). The author is indebted to this book for most of the information about Holford's work in the city.

24 *The Architects' Journal* 5 February 1948 and the author's diary.

25 Conversation with the author about 1946. The impression he gave was that dislike of heading a huge organization was uppermost in his mind. Yet the fact that, comparatively young, he had not been in the armed forces, did not escape his 'missionary conscience' during the war. He mentioned the matter more than once to the author who - having been discharged from the RAF - was perhaps thought a suitable confidant. He never deviated a yard or an hour from his intended route or engagements because of bombs, whether in the Liverpool raids, the mini-blitz of 1944, or the flying bombs later on.

26 In retrospect the story seems improbable, but the author is quite certain of the figures and facts. X is still alive. Sir Thomas was then receiving £3,000 and the Chief Engineer of the London County Council £3,500; and to tempt X to move to London something extra might have been needed. One would like to know what the Treasury would have said to the proposal to pay a local government engineer more than a Permanent Secretary.

27 *Proposals for the development of a site for the University of Liverpool* (Liverpool University Press, 1949).

28   Lord Crawford and Balcarres summarize *Who's Who.*

29   Records of University College London.

30   The lecture was printed in full in *The Town Planning Review* Vol XX No. 1 (April 1949).

31   John Cooper, recollections of Lord Holford, 1978.

32   Lewis Keeble, *Lord Holford - A Memoir* (1978).

33   Sir John Overall, *Recollections of Lord Holford,* (February 1978).

34   Similarities between Holford and Isambard Kingdom Brunel (1806–59) will strike anyone who knew the former and has read Rolt's biography of Brunel. Brunel was short, had brilliant dark eyes and sensitive hands. He took a gay part in charades and private social occasions. He was a talented draughtsman and painter. He seemed unable to refuse work, and sometimes kept going for twenty hours a day. He had a beautiful wife, for whom no expense was spared, and a luxurious house in Duke Street, Westminster, in which he had his own private office. Seemingly there was no other woman in his life. He was at the height of his fame at thirty-seven. He had some contempt for honours, and doubts about religion, coupled with a profound pessimism. 'Turning a deaf ear to the warnings of his doctors and the appeals of his friends he once more took command ... He knew his disease was mortal.' L. T. Rolt, *Isambard Kingdom Brunel: A Biography* (Longman, London, 1957) 4, 98, 101, 145, 284, 294, 332 and 325. Holford was the luckier in that his wonderful strength and medical science supported him, more or less, to the age of sixty-eight. Brunel died at fifty-three, but had descendants through his daughter, and three permanent memorials to his genius: Brunel University, the Clifton Suspension Bridge and, one hopes, the wonderful ship *Great Britain* now being restored at Bristol.

35   C. H. Holden and W. G. Holford, *The City of London: A Record of Destruction and Survival* (Architectural Press, London, 1951).

36   R.T. Kennedy, notes about Holford, 1977.

37   As the author has always been strongly opposed to high buildings for residential and especially for commercial purposes (which may be regarded as stealing views, light and air from neighbours and the public without compensation), it is odd that he never discovered Holford's liking for towers. He was a little shocked by Holford's support for the National Westminster Bank tower in the City of London, but it was only in 1979 that he heard from Richard Gray of Holford's passion for towers and of his talking with some glee of 'breaking the height barrier'.

38   City of Westminster Information Office, *Piccadilly Circus Profile* (1975). An excellent summary of events and proposals.

8

PREPARATIONS FOR POST-WAR PLANNING

It has been claimed in the introduction to this book that the Lever professors and their former students made the major contribution to the technical preparations for post-war town and country planning in Britain. The following short chapter is an account of how the contribution came to be made during a period of four or five years, and is limited to that subject. There is no claim that the account is a history or even summary of all war-time work towards physical reconstruction and post-war planning. In particular, the administrative and legislative actions are described elsewhere (e.g., J. B. Cullingworth as in note 7, for this chapter.).

As was made clear in Chapter 5 there was little real planning between the two wars, if one defines 'real planning' as the effective guidance, in the public interest, of the use of land and the layout of roads, buildings and open spaces. The 1,440 local authorities in England and Wales, with whom town planning powers then rested, were too frightened of big claims for compensation to enforce adherence to a plan even when one had been prepared, and the 138 joint committees did no better.[1] The Prevention of Ribbon Development Act of 1935 had come too late to prevent the disfigurement of many towns by their approach roads being flanked for several miles by houses, just one house deep, on either side. The best defence that many local authorities could find against unlimited sprawl into the countryside was – as stated earlier – to lay down a density of one house to 5, 10 and even 100 acres, so making building development uneconomic.[2] [3] So the resolution to prepare a plan taken by more than 900 authorities out of 1,440 did not mean very much.[4] Nor did the publication of the Barlow Report[5] in January 1940 mean much at first to the general public or senior officials in the Ministry of Health (then the Planning Ministry), although, as stated on p. 117, it provided the agenda for the major investigations of the next few years.

The Need for Reconstruction

When the bombs began to fall heavily on cities in September 1940, attitudes changed very quickly. The first need was to assess the damage being done to buildings and services, and to arrange that necessary repairs or, in the case of buildings, worthwhile repairs, did not obstruct the huge programme of building and civil engineering works needed for war purposes. To ensure that this was done Lord Reith was appointed as Minister of Works and Buildings in October

1940.[6] He in turn appointed Hugh Beaver (borrowed from Sir Alexander Gibb & Partners) as Director-General of the new Ministry. Once the immediate situation and the war building programme had been provided for, Lord Reith turned his great energies to the future, and before the end of 1940 he presented to the War Cabinet a paper called *Reconstruction of Town and Country*, in which he pointed out the ineffectiveness of pre-war planning and set out the need for co-ordination between planning, industry, agriculture and transport. He then set out the desirable objectives of town and country planning and asked for a central planning authority on Barlow lines.[7] In January 1941 the Cabinet Committee on Reconstruction was set up under the chairmanship of Arthur Greenwood: of this Lord Reith was a member.

It is necessary here to distinguish between the non-physical and the physical aspects of 'Reconstruction': a word then used to cover all the political actions likely to be needed before or soon after the end of the war. The former group included labour and employment, health and social security, education and, to some extent, agriculture and food. There was also the question of how best to look after city children, most of whom had returned home within a few months after the evacuation of September 1939. These things were successively the responsibility of Arthur Greenwood, Sir William Jowitt and Lord Woolton – the latter an unwilling recruit after he had achieved permanent fame as Minister of Food, 1940–43, when he ensured that the poorer half of the population and their children were better fed (though unexcitingly) and healthier than ever before.[8]

The physical side of reconstruction included all works and buildings, and town and country planning in its widest sense; including how to deal with the great 'compensation' obstruction to planning, guidance of development in rural areas, National Parks, New Towns and the essential town planning interest in the design and layout of roads. These things were successively the responsibility of Lord Reith, Lord Portal, W. S. Morrison and Lewis Silkin.[9] Problems and policies about housing, roads, agriculture, water resources and minerals were to be dealt with by discussions – sometimes rather sharp – between the Planning Ministry (under its various names) and the ministries, such as Health, Transport and Agriculture, which had previously been responsible for these vastly important things. In the 1980s, when post-war rebuilding is the subject of much adverse criticism, and town planning is largely regarded by the ordinary citizen as obstructive and boring, it is difficult to remember or credit the really passionate interest in literally building a new Britain that existed during the Second World War. Yet it was so. Newspapers published and explained rebuilding plans in some detail, and exhibitions were crowded.

It was also in February 1941 that Lord Reith set up his own Reconstruction Group to undertake research into reconstruction and town planning problems: Holford was among the first to be invited, probably because he had been known to Hugh Beaver for his work on the Team Valley Industrial Estate and on Ordnance factories. Others in the group were John Dower, H. C. Bradshaw and Thomas Sharp. In April Reith appointed a 'Consultative Panel' of twenty-two members including industrialists, trade unionists, geographers, Frederic Osborn, the New Towns expert, and Patrick Abercrombie.[10] The 'staff experts' were Bradshaw, Dower and Holford, with H. G. Vincent as the administrative guide. Vincent and E. S. Hill became the two civil servants to whom the new professional and academic recruits were to become most indebted. Vincent gave general guidance on who was who among the various ministries, and on the best lines of approach; and Hill advised on the translation of technical matters into legislation, and on what was suitable for legislation or was best left to technical handbooks.

Holford was almost certainly regarded from the beginning as leader of the small full-time team, by virtue of being Lever professor and of being recommended by the Director-General. It is therefore rather sad that in the early months he was far from full-time, because of his work on Ordnance factories and hostels. Thomas Sharp, then forty years old and a man of high reputation as a town planner, wrote that the first weeks were 'of utter frustration'.[11] In almost every branch of wartime activity at that time recruits to new organizations or units went through similar periods of despondency. Sharp, a man of strong feelings, who had already waited twenty years for real planning, took this period badly. In fact he became ill, and when he recovered he became secretary to the Scott Committee,[12] which enquired into suitable uses for land in rural areas and the related problems of conservation. The setting up of this committee was quite largely a consequence of the work of Abercrombie, Clough Williams-Ellis and the Council for the Preservation of Rural England in the inter-war years. Sharp is believed to have written most of the committee's report which, together with the Barlow and Uthwatt reports,[13] were the principal enquiries on which British post-war town and country planning was based. Sharp later made a study of village planning, and then became chairman of a small technical group which examined site planning and layout in relation to housing. He wrote most of their report, which was published in 1944 as a supplement to the *Housing Manual*.[14] Gordon Stephenson (later the fourth Lever professor) wrote the remainder.

John Dower, another member of the first small team, was, like Sharp, an intelligent and rugged individualist who refused to be unemployed. He took National Parks as his subject and produced a report which was at once so good and so personal that the civil service mandarins simply did not know what to do with it. After considerable delay, they took the almost unprecedented decision to publish it as a Command (Government) Paper with John Dower named as the author.[15] Various explanations for this decision were passed around at the time. All that matters now is that it was a magnanimous, and correct, decision; and the report largely determined the present National Parks and the ways of looking after land within them.

During 1941 and 1942 the Reconstruction Group (which had been joined by J. H. Forshaw, a Liverpool graduate and Architect to the London County Council) examined three groups of problems: prevention of wartime actions that might hinder proper reconstruction; existing planning machinery and the new legislation needed; and the relative costs of different layouts and kinds of building development.

In 1941 Patrick Abercrombie and J. H. Forshaw were asked to prepare a post-war plan for the London County Council area – that is, the 120 square miles of the inner built-up area of London, which at that time was the administrative area of London, exclusive of the City. This plan[16] and its successor the *Greater London Plan*,[17] prepared by Abercrombie alone (helped by five former students), were, as was stated in Chapter 6, probably the most influential plans that were published during the war, and the New Towns around London were one of the results. Much of the work on these plans was done within the Ministry by a separate team working under Abercrombie's direction. There was close contact between all technical officers and Gordon Stephenson wrote Chapter 8 of the *Greater London Plan*.

After the heavy raids on Coventry, Donald Gibson, then City Architect of Coventry, was given the chance to prepare plans for reconstruction of that city. Gibson was a graduate of the Department of Civic Design. Thus the two most influential plans, and the most publicized plan of those prepared during the war were prepared by the second Lever professor and two Liverpool graduates. In the same year, Adshead was appointed to prepare a reconstruction plan for Southampton, and Denis Winston, one of Abercrombie's former students and a later professor of town planning, went to Northern Ireland as Chief Architect.

It was also in 1941, when heavy raids continued till May, that the Royal Institute of British Architects formed its own reconstruction committee, and since Reilly was a member there is no surprise to find it also contained six of his former students, as well as Patrick Abercrombie. Far more importantly, in this crowded year, Reith appointed Mr Justice Uthwatt to chair a committee which was to examine the whole problem of compensation and betterment as it affected public control of the use of land. The committee published an interim report in June 1941 and a final report in September 1942. Directly and indirectly these reports were of great consequence but the Lever professors and their students were not concerned. Some of the Uthwatt recommendations are given in a note.[18]

The Uthwatt proposal for a Central Planning Authority was not accepted, but, as has been stated in Chapter 5, town planning powers and the pre-war town planning section of the Ministry of Health, headed by Pepler, were brought over to Works and Planning, together with S.L.G. Beaufoy and L.P. Ellicott, both former students of Adshead. Pepler, who had been principal town planning officer and adviser to the government during the inter-war years, might have been expected to be a little upset to find that, when at last real town planning was about to take place, he was passed over, at sixty years of age, as the Minister's chief adviser in favour of a thirty-five-year-old. But Pepler was not like that. He was entirely unselfish towards any proposals that helped the cause of town planning, and was perhaps glad to find young and tough successors to carry on the battle which he had been fighting, more or less alone, since 1914. He acted as an exceedingly well-informed elder statesman and, when need arose, as a shock-absorber between the new recruits and senior civil servants.

The New Ministry

By late 1942 Holford had more time to give to the Ministry and he was accompanied to Lambeth Bridge House, where the Ministry then was, by Gordon Stephenson and later by R. T. Kennedy who had been Holford's deputy on all the hostels' work.

By then, Lord Reith had been succeeded by Lord Portal. It is impossible not to feel sorry for Reith. He possessed very great powers and great energy. In his sixteen months at Works and Buildings he had set in hand two of three great 'planning' enquiries (Scott, Uthwatt, Barlow) and he had chosen excellent men for the key jobs in his ministry: Hugh Beaver as Director-General, T. P. Bennett as Director of Works, Holford as chief town planning adviser, and Abercrombie for the two big London plans. Three of these were to be knighted within five years and Holford in ten.

Reith had already been removed by Churchill from the Ministry of Information when it was still a grave of reputations – having had nothing but defeats or muddles to announce. He was now sacked again. It was said he had annoyed Churchill by offering to take on more and more responsibility. Reith was certainly shaken by being dropped[19] and rightly so. Lord Portal did not do much, at least about planning. After less than a year, in January 1943, it was announced that W. S. Morrison was to become Minister of Town and Country Planning under an Act setting up this new ministry. The Ministry, as its name suggests, gathered to itself all central town planning powers, responsibility for legislation and the civil servants previously concerned with planning. Construction works were returned to Works and Public Buildings, taking Lord Portal with them.

The function of the Ministry was to secure 'consistency and continuity in the framing and execution of a national policy with respect to the use and development of land ...'[20] This very civil service definition, with its slight Gibbonesque rhythm, was sometimes chanted in chorus in the Research Division. What did it mean? - save it was preferable that an Act, or other important action, should not too obviously block or contradict its predecessors?

Early in 1943 the Ministry, by then housed in and near St James's Square, took the form it was to keep until after the major post-war planning Act - the 1947 Act - had been passed. There was the Research Division whose job was 'to assemble and present the factual and scientific data upon which all planning policy must be based'.[20] This was headed by H. G. Vincent, a permanent civil servant, who would now be ranked as an under-secretary. Holford was the principal technical officer, and almost all of those in the division were recruited from the universities and professions for their special knowledge of subjects affecting the use of land.

There were soon four main groups of men and women. These comprised, first, the professional town planners and architects with the Planning Technique Section who tried to think of better layouts for buildings and access to them, both in town and country. Their studies included building density, daylighting, open spaces and preliminary studies for New Towns. They had to think out its own solutions to most of these problems. There had been little previous study. Le Corbusier's *Voisin* scheme for the centre of Paris, and indeed all le Corbusier's work, had some influence; and so had Clarence Stein's work in the United States. The importance of motor traffic was foreseen, aided by Alker Tripp's small book *Town Planning and Road Traffic*,[21] which went to four editions in two wartime years. On the other hand, the Royal Academy's plan for London in 1943 tried to put the clock back fifty years - indeed to Haussmann's Paris of the 1870s. Architects (some on leave from the Services) came in from bomb-weary London to stare at the gorgeous coloured drawings with mingled joy and derision.

In the second group of the division there were central services, comprising statistics, maps, the library and information. Thirdly, there were individuals or small groups working on special problems that would clearly be of great importance to planning in particular localities: for instance, Stanley Beaver's work on surface minerals (sand, gravel, quarries) and - as have been mentioned - Dower on National Parks and Thomas Sharp on rural areas and villages.

Lastly, there were the regional officers, two for each of ten of the eleven Civil Defence Regions of England and Wales. These were of two kinds: research officers and planning officers. Research officers, usually geographers or economists, reported on employment prospects for their regions and prepared papers on particular local problems. They came to London about every fortnight to exchange ideas and advise on proposals that might affect their regions. The job of the regional research officers was difficult and usually thankless. Careful papers on the outlook for West Cumberland or West Cornwall in the 1950s were apt to be pigeon-holed in 1943. Only an impending Parliamentary Question from a trouble-making MP would bring Mr X hot-foot from Wales or Nottingham, sometimes right to the Minister's room. X would work all night and be proud of it. Two days later he would be nothing again, and the Private Secretary would have forgotten his name. It was not surprising that it was a regional research officer who now and again tried to start some kind of palace revolution.

Somewhat earlier, the regional planning officers (professional town planners), had been appointed to discuss impending legislation with local authorities and advise the Ministry on local views. Once the new local planning authorities (counties and county boroughs) were established after 1947, both kinds of regional officers faded away into a short-lived system of Regional Controllers.

By the end of 1943, the influence of the Lever professors was firmly established in the Ministry. The previous, the existing, and two future Lever professors were working there, three of them in the Research Division. Almost the only technical problem that was examined outside the division was that of urban estate management during the future rebuilding of many thousands of destroyed offices and commercial buildings; and of how sound development and management practices would be affected by the coming legislation. This matter was examined by a group under the chairmanship of the Deputy Secretary, Laurence Neal, but as the secretary (the fifth Lever professor) was borrowed from the Research Division, liaison was maintained.

In one sense the Research Division was the most important in the Ministry, as it was responsible for the suggestion and examination of new ideas, using such facts and scientific evidence as were then available. The new ideas had of course to be subject to decisions on whether they were politically acceptable and practicable, and if so, on how to introduce them to local authorities and embody them in legislation. These things were looked after in the rest of the Ministry.

During the preparation of the *Greater London Plan* Abercrombie's small team worked, as has been stated, within the Ministry, and there was close collaboration with Gordon Stephenson and the Planning Technique Section. The plan's influence on ideas for New Towns, and in other ways, was very great.

One of the best-known products of 1943–44 was the proposal that, in the rebuilding of old towns and the planning of new developments, the population should be grouped in units of about 10,000 people, called Neighbourhood Units. Such a unit could be planned to have its own schools and small shops, and some community buildings within easy reach of all homes; and open spaces, roads and footpaths were to be planned to provide for convenient local movements, which would also minimize danger from traffic. This sensible proposal had great influence on post-war residential layout in Britain and elsewhere.

The year 1944 opened noisily with the bombing of the Research Division's home, as recorded on p. 177. New accommodation was found and the pace of preparations for post-war planning quickened.

The Control of Land Use was published[22] and this coalition paper proposed, *inter alia*, that compensation and betterment should be looked after by a Land Commission, and so laid the foundation of the 1947 Act. The Dudley Report on the *Design of Dwellings*[23] was also published, and was followed by the *Housing Manual* to which, as has been stated, the Ministry contributed a section. In 1944 Reilly, who had first thought of a Civic Design Department, was asked to take part in post-war planning by preparing a plan for Birkenhead. Reilly though seventy years old in 1944 appeared in his temporary office in Birkenhead before 9 am, beautifully dressed, and worked steadily till 6 pm.[24]

Between 1943 and 1950 ten Acts of Parliament were passed concerning town and country planning and closely related fields.[25] Among the more important were the 1944 Act, the 1945 Distribution of Industry Act, the 1946 New Towns Act, and, above all, the 1947 Act which laid down the main framework for post-war planning. Between them these Acts ensured that only major local authorities would be the new planning authorities, and that they would have the right to buy bomb-damaged or decayed areas (the blitz and the blight) for redevelopment by themselves or others. The location of new factories was to be guided by the Board of Trade, and the organization for New Towns was announced. There was also to be a once-and-for-all purchase of development rights in land for £300 millions, but this last proposal came to nothing and this part of the legislation was at length repealed.

In 1944 Britain's new ideas on town planning began to move to what were then colonies. It may be that the number of well-fed, well-paid Americans moving to West Indian bases or to West Africa prompted the government to try to do more for the colonies concerned. 'Development and Welfare' teams were sent out; and included as town planners and architects, Robert Gardner-Medwin for the West Indies,[26] Maxwell Fry for West Africa and R.P.S. Hubbard for Malta. All were Liverpool men. Substantial sums were later to be spent on basic services and housing, education and tourism. Several former students of Lever professors later went to the West Indies. David Spreull, Holford's first assistant, was town planning officer of Jamaica for nearly twenty years. Yet after forty years of effort it remains doubtful whether most of the West Indies, so isolated and with so few natural resources, can ever be anything but poor as the Western World sees poverty.

Post-War Planning

The landslide electoral victory for Labour in 1945 meant that W. S. Morrison was succeeded as Minister for Town and Country Planning by Lewis Silkin, later Lord Silkin. In the two previous years the results of the Reith enquiries had been incorporated into legislation or into preparations for the 1947 Act. Silkin was a forceful man who had had five years as Chairman of the London County Council Town Planning Committee. No time was lost. The New Towns Committee was set up with Lord Reith (brought back from the wilderness) as Chairman. The committee worked very quickly, but its final report was published only two days before the New Towns Act received the Royal Assent.[27] The planning of the first New Town at Stevenage was begun in the Planning Technique Section even before the Reith Committee began work.

The Designation (decision on location and boundaries etc.) of Stevenage as a New Town had a stormy reception from local residents, but the town went ahead. Clifford Holliday was appointed Chief Architect and was soon joined by Peter Shepheard. Both were Liverpool graduates. Holliday later became Professor of Town Planning at Manchester.Shepheard, now Sir Peter Shepheard, became President of the RIBA and later Professor of Architecture and Environmental Design, and Dean of the Graduate School of Fine Arts, in the University of Pennsylvania. Five other former students of Lever professors were soon to hold senior New Town appointments.

Of the eight new Towns around London only two were on sites recommended by Abercrombie in the *Greater London Plan*. These were Stevenage and Harlow, but a third, Basildon, was almost on a site proposed by Adshead in 1931.[28] In addition to his work on the London plans, Abercrombie prepared plans during the war for Plymouth, Hull and Bath, as has been mentioned in Chapter 6; and Minoprio and Spenceley, two of Reilly's favourite pupils, became consultants for Worcester.

In 1945–46 the work of the Planning Technique Section was mainly concerned with the Ministry's first handbook of technical guidance, which was suitably concentrated on the problems of war-damaged city centres. It was called *The Redevelopment of Central Areas*[29] and was published, after much delay, in 1947. Although it was 100 pages in length, inclusive of illustrations, it contained a great deal of information in a concentrated form. Its device for measuring floor space in relation to site area, called the *Floor Space Index*, and its proposals for measuring the amount of daylight that would probably be received by a building of given form, were two of three important technical devices invented during 1943–46. The third was the *Plot Ratio*, invented by the Holford group in the City of London. The handbook was widely used in the post-war decade.

Another Ministry initiative in 1945–46 was to appoint consultants to study the special problems of regions which had suffered greatly from unemployment in the inter-war years, and to make proposals for improving their basic services and, if possible, economic prospects. Pepler, who had retired from the Ministry in 1946 and was to be knighted in 1948, was appointed to prepare a plan for the North-East of England;[30] Longstreth Thompson for Merseyside; R. H.

Mattocks and J. S. Allen for West Cumberland; and T. Alwyn Lloyd and Herbert Jackson for South Wales and Monmouthshire. Nothing much came of these reports, of which two were published.

Local authorities were busy trying to solve a dozen extremely difficult local post-war problems, and had not much time for studies that bunched them with neighbours. For the same reason, most of the inter-war and wartime joint planning committees slowly faded out, though the Clyde Valley joint committee to which Abercrombie became consultant, lasted for some years. The bigger local authorities also disliked 'regions' in any form, though they had to put up with Regional Controllers for a few more years. It was widely said that the dislike of regions by the main local authorities, Counties and County Boroughs, was partially due to the activities of regional commissioners in 1940-41. These gentlemen had been appointed to carry on civil government in their part of the country in the event of invasion, or anything else that disorganized communications with London. As no invasion occurred, time hung heavy on their hands, and some began to make speeches and attend receptions at which - so the story went - they expected precedence over the previous sovereigns of local government: Lord Mayors and Chairmen of County councils. At the end of the war this was not forgotten. Regional Controllers (1945-50) were civil servants, who presided over a group of other civil servants each of whom had been seconded from a particular Ministry - Health, Transport, etc. - to try to look at problems 'regionally', and so speed up post-war decisions. It proved a cumbrous system and was soon abandoned.

The four regional reports did little more than state what everyone knew, and had no great influence. At least one of the regional reports was also badly written. The author of this book was told by J. D. Jones (now Sir James Jones) that the Ministry wanted him to rewrite it. He refused on the grounds that the report was largely rubbish, and would have no influence, however well it was rewritten. J. D. Jones was kind but firm; and the author decided that he would perhaps be wise to resign from the Ministry, and did.

The Break up of the Research Division

At the end of the war, the Ministry obtained valuable recruits from the Services and others who had been in work immediately concerned with winning the war. Two of these were Colin Buchanan and Hugh Casson. Yet despite hard work in preparation for the great 1947 Act,[31] and its new planning system and on handbooks, there was a feeling in the Research Division that its main job was done. In addition, academics were being called back to their universities, and the doubts of others about their future were not banished by Holford's own behaviour. Holford had never pretended to be the administrative head of the division, a man who decided what was to be done and saw that it was. He was there, doing his own work, yet always ready with advice and help or to argue a Research Division case on ministerial committees. This he did with consummate skill. But by 1946 he was himself being pulled three ways.

His work on the City of London plan was exacting. Liverpool University wanted him both to prepare its development plan and to return to his duties as Professor of Civic Design: and not without reason, as he had been away for seven years. And the Ministry wanted to keep him as their Chief Technical Adviser, as he had really been since 1942. The 1946 *Whitakers Almanac* lists Pepler as Chief Technical Adviser and places him above Holford. In the 1947 and 1948 editions, Holford reappears as Chief Technical Officer, but this must have been an error, or reflected only the Ministry's continued hopes.

Towards the end of 1946, Holford did not so much resign as simply fade away, and Gordon Stephenson took his place, under three different titles in less than two years.[31] In 1948 Stephenson left the Ministry to become the fourth Lever professor. He was succeeded by R. T. Kennedy, who had worked closely with Holford from 1939 to 1946; and he in turn was succeeded by former students of Adshead or Abercrombie until 1960; and even in 1965 five former students were still in senior posts.

As far as this book is concerned, the end of preparations for the new kind of town and country planning may be said to have taken place in 1947. By then, most of those gathered by Holford were leaving the Ministry. The main job of enquiry and invention and the writing of technical recommendations had been completed: making the new machinery work was largely an explanatory and administrative responsibility. It seemed likely that there would be few interesting professional jobs in the Ministry in the following ten years, and these few – being at the top – were already booked. It was also clear that the returning administrative civil servants did not like such a concentration of power in the hands of a band of amateurs, that the Research Division would be abolished and any surviving sections would be put under close administrative supervision. Dame Evelyn Sharp (now the Baroness Sharp), who soon became Permanent Secretary of the Ministry, was aware that the technical civil servants had previously been treated badly, and tried to bring about improvements.[32]

The truth, however, was that the preparations were (largely) completed, and the more adventurous spirits wanted to go out into the world and take responsibility for making plans of their own of the new kinds. Those technical men who were in the Research Division in 1946 did not do badly later on. Seven became professors and four have been knighted. Moreover, whatever may be thought of British town planning in 1981, both the system and its results received high praise, almost throughout the world, for fifteen or twenty years after the Second World War. On the technical side its proposals had been very largely the work of Lever professors and their former students. Lever would have been very pleased.

NOTES AND REFERENCES

1   Gordon Cherry, *The Evolution of British Town Planning* (Leonard Hill Books, 1974) 101.

2   G. Cherry, *op. cit.*, 103.

> '... the idea of rural zoning was taken up, and several rural schemes were proposed for controlling building in the undeveloped countryside, at densities ranging from one house to two acres to one house to 100 acres.'

3   A local authority's decisions on density were not liable to claims for compensation. Thomas C. Coote, letter to the author, February 1978.

> ... I recall Abercrombie and Adshead meeting to discuss countryside zoning on town planning maps, on which all land had to be allocated for some 'residential' purpose - none left blank. So we devised Rural Zones of one house to three acres and even tried 1 to 10 acres in the hope that it would be accepted by the Ministry.

4   G. Cherry, *op. cit.*, 100.

> 'In England and Wales 402 local authorities were wholly or partly subject to planning by virtue of resolutions prior to the 1932 Act; by March 1938 a further 530 local authorities had made Resolutions.'

5   *Report of the Royal Commission on the Distribution of the Industrial Population* (The Barlow Report), (Cmd 6153, 1940).

6   He had been unemployed since leaving the Ministry of Information, and was suggested by Ernest Bevin, Minister of Labour and National Service, 1940-45. Alan Bullock, *The Life and Times of Ernest Bevin: Vol. II Minister of Labour 1940-45* (Heinemann, London, 1967) 71.

7   John B. Cullingworth, *Reconstruction and Land Use Planning 1939-47* (HMSO, London, 1975) 54.

8   *The Memoirs of the Rt. Hon. The Earl of Woolton* (Autobiography), (Cassell, London, 1959) 259.
Frederick James Marquis became Lord Woolton of Liverpool in 1939. In his early days he had lived for some time in the University Settlement at Liverpool and had become a keen sociologist. He contributed two articles to the *Town Planning Review*, one in 1910 (Vol. I, 66) 'Some Sociological Aspects of Town Planning' and one in 1912 (Vol. III, 244) 'People's Palaces' with S.E.F. Ogden. In 1939 he became Director-General of Equipment and Stores in the Ministry of Supply and went on to become Minister of Food from 1940 to 1943. It was for his triumphs in this most exacting post that he became so well known. In November 1943, on the request of the Prime Minister he became Minister of Reconstruction until 1945.

9   Lord Reith, Minister of Works and Building 1940-42 (later changed to Works and Planning). Lord Portal, Minister of Works and Planning

and First Commissioner of Works and Public Buildings 1942–44. Rt
Hon. W. S. Morrison (later Lord Dunrossil), Minister of Town and
Country Planning 1943–45. Rt Hon. Lewis Silkin (later Lord Silkin),
Minister of Town and Country Planning 1945–50.

10   Frederick J. Osborn (ed), *Planning and Reconstruction Year Book
1942* (Todd Publishing Co., London, 1942) 163.

11   Thomas Sharp, reminiscences of William Holford in a letter to author,
December 1977.

12   *Committee on Land Utilisation in Rural Areas* (The Scott Report),
(Cmd 6378, 1942).

13   *Expert Committee on Compensation and Betterment Final Report*
(The Uthwatt Report), (Cmd 6386, 1942). and also Barlow Report.[5]

14   The *Housing Manual 1944*, prepared jointly by the Ministry of Health
and the Ministry of Works (HMSO, London, 1944).

15   John Dower, *National Parks in England and Wales* (Cmd 6628, 1945).
The Report began by defining a National Park as:

> *an extensive area of beautiful and relatively wild country in
> which, for the nation's benefit and by appropriate national
> decision and action, the characteristic landscape beauty is
> strictly preserved; access and facilities for public open-air
> enjoyment are amply provided; wild life and buildings and
> places of architectural and historic interest are suitably
> protected; while established farming use is effectively
> maintained. (F. J. Osborn (ed) Reconstruction Year Book 1946,*
> Todd Publishing Co., London, 1946, 504).

Dower recommended ten such areas as future National Parks, but the
report was also concerned with the controls to be imposed within those
areas, the facilities to be provided, the machinery, powers and the
techniques required and the necessary co-ordination with other
planning purposes and other departments. The National Parks Committee, set up by Silkin in 1945, made its report in 1947 and recommended 12 National Parks and 52 Conservation Areas. This led to the
setting up of the National Parks Commission and the 1949 Act.

16   John H. Forshaw and Professor Patrick Abercrombie, *The County of
London Plan 1943* (Macmillan & Co. Ltd, London, 1943).

17   Abercrombie, *Greater London Plan 1944* (HMSO, London, 1945).
London, 1945).

18   In its final report *op. cit.*,[13] the Uthwatt Committee adhered to the idea
of a Central Planning Authority, and one proposal was that a Minister
of National Development should control planning as well as
reconstruction works. The committee also recommended that the state
should acquire the rights of development of all land outside built-up
areas on payment of fair compensation and the compulsory purchase
of all war-damaged, or obsolete and unsatisfactory areas which needed
reconstruction as a whole. It suggested that there ought to be clearly

defined 'Reconstruction Areas' in which no rebuilding should take place except under the licence of the Central Planning Authority, until Reconstruction schemes were prepared. It recommended that a ten-year life be placed on obsolete buildings. Its most important proposal was that of a Central Planning Authority which should take over the planning proposals of the Ministry of Works and Planning.

The Uthwatt Committee also proposed solutions to the long-standing problems of compensation and betterment and, although its recommendation that development rights should be paid for at 1939 prices was later dropped, the report was nevertheless most influential.

Lord Woolton (*op. cit.*, 275) said of the report:

> *As a piece of social justice it seemed indisputable and it pleased immensely that section of society ... who believed that land, which they claim to be the basis of the wealth of the nation, should belong to the people and not to those whom fortunate chance had enabled to possess it ...*

19 About a year later, the *Architects' Journal* published three articles on planning and building. The first contained a summary of events in the earlier war years and in this Lord Reith was deservedly praised. The last two articles outlined a great programme of works after the war ended. Lord Reith apparently took these proposals as official, and wrote for more details in the evident expectation that he would be asked once again to guide one or another aspect of the reconstruction programme. *Architects' Journal* Vol. 98 (August 1943) 92, 125, 143.

20 Minister of Town and Country Planning (W. S. Morrison), Town Planning Institute's Town and Country Planning Summer School 1944. H. Myles Wright, *The Planner's Notebook* (Architectural Press, London, 1948) 342.

21 Alker Tripp, *Town Planning and Road Traffic* (Arnold, London, 1942).

22 *The Control of Land Use* (Cmd 6537, 1944).

23 Design of Dwellings Sub-Committee of the Central Housing Advisory Committee: Report (The Dudley Report) *Design of Dwellings* (1944). This report was chiefly concerned with the design, planning, layout and equipment of dwellings and also standards of construction.

24 Josephine Reynolds, who worked with Reilly at the time.

25 The Principal Acts between 1943 and 1950 were:
1943 Town and Country Planning (Interim Development) Act
1943 Amending Act on Ribbon Development
1943 Minister of Town and Country Planning Act
1944 Town and Country Planning Act
1945 Distribution of Industry Act
1945 Requisitioned Land and War Works Act
1946 Acquisition of Land Act
1946 New Towns Act
1947 Town and Country Planning Act
1949 National Parks and Access to the Countryside Act.

The White Papers, Reports, Handbooks, etc. included:
1943 Harrison Report (Chairman of the Acquisition of Land Sub-Committee of the Sub-Committee on the Uthwatt Report)
1944 The Control of Land Use White Paper
1944 The Dudley Report – The Design of Dwellings
1944 Housing Manual
1945 Dower Report – National Parks in England and Wales
1945 1st Whiskard Report
1946 2nd Whiskard Report
1946 3rd Whiskard Report
1947 Report of National Parks Committee
1947 Handbook 'The Redevelopment of Central Areas'.

26   Letter from Professor Robert Gardner-Medwin, November 1979.

27   The New Towns Act passed in 1946 provided for the Designation of sites for New Towns by the Minister of Town and Country Planning and by the Secretary of State for Scotland. It also provided for the setting up of Development Corporations and set out their powers.

28   Professor Stanley D. Adshead, 'South Essex Plan Review' *Town Planning Institute Journal* Vol. XVIII (1931–32) 122–26.

29   Ministry of Town and Country Planning (HMSO, 1947) *The Redevelopment of Central Areas*

30   Helen McCrae, *George Pepler* (unpublished) MS p. 131.

31   The 1947 Town and Country Planning Act came into general operation in July 1948. Pepler said of it:

> The old system of planning which planners found so
> frustrating was made necessary by the compensation
> provisions of previous Acts. The new Act both largely removes
> this burden from the shoulders of planning authorities and
> consequently introduces a new system of planning.
> *(Journal of Town Planning Institute* Vol. XXXIII 1946–47 p. 51).

The Act had three main features. Firstly, it set up a completely new planning system by repealing most of the previous planning legislation and making planning obligatory. The planning authorities were now the counties and county boroughs and this drastically reduced the number of planning authorities. Secondly, compensation was no longer to be the responsibility of the planning authorities as a Central Land Board was established and £300 million set aside for compensation. Both Board and proposed fund were later to disappear. The third basic principle of the Act was that it provided Exchequer grants to assist local authorities to purchase and develop blitz areas.

32   In 1946 Stephenson was appointed Chief Research Officer and a year later he became jointly Chief Senior Technical Officer (with L. P. Ellicott, a former pupil of Adshead at University College). In October 1947 he was appointed Chief Planning Officer in the reorganization following Holford's departure, but he resigned two months later to become the fourth Lever professor.

33   Letter from Dame Evelyn Sharp to Gordon Stephenson, August 1947.

EPILOGUE

Fifty years after the passing of the first Town Planning Act British town planning had become an established profession with substantial achievements to its credit, and, as was then thought, a very bright future. The Town Planning Institute had 2,600 members in 1959 (compared with 1,026 in 1939) and nearly 1,000 student members. Five hundred of its members were then working abroad. It had come a long way since the thirty-five founder members had first met in 1913. In 1959 the Institute felt confident enough to apply for incorporation under a Royal Charter. (In 1971 it was granted permission to use the prefix 'Royal'.) When it did so the President, Senior Vice-President and six members of Council were graduates of Liverpool and former students of Lever professors.

Unfortunately, in 1959 there was little sign that the Department of Civic Design's work had benefited its home town. The physical changes in Liverpool since 1909 had been few and some were for the worse. The last trams had disappeared in 1957, the sites of the many buildings destroyed by wartime bombing were still nearly all empty, and the air was still dirty. (The Clean Air Act was passed in 1956.)

Various half-hearted plans for rebuilding or a new road system had been discussed and then shelved and the proposal for a great Mersey bridge – like those now spanning the Severn, Forth and Humber – was blocked by differences between local authorities and miscellaneous other objectors. New building had been largely confined to local authority dwellings, which were greatly needed but not always of the best form or quality. Some have now been demolished and others are empty.

The year 1959 was, inconveniently for this story, the year before the dawn of better things for Merseyside. In 1960 Graeme Shankland was appointed to prepare plans for a new central Liverpool. Very exciting they were, and they had the effect of bouncing Liverpool's men of influence into thinking about their city and its needs. After a dozen reports by Shankland and Walter Bor, the city's planning officer, things gradually improved: the air was cleaned; a new and second Mersey tunnel almost abolished cross-river traffic congestion; and at length Liverpool has been able to boast not only of the Beatles and the Liverpool Sound but of quite a number of good new buildings, including two cathedrals, and a multitude of cleaned buildings.

The university had made a quick start (guided by the third and fifth Lever professors), after building licensing ended in 1955, on redevelopment of the 85 acres of land allocated to it near Abercromby Square. A new Department of Civic Design, designed by Gordon Stephenson (the fourth Lever professor), had been opened in 1952 and till the mid-1960s publicity for Liverpool's rebuilding tended to concentrate on what the University had done. The university area was even called 'Liverpool Action Area No. 1'. There was little else to photograph.

It was however also in 1959 that the Department of Civic Design decided, like the Town Planning Institute, that it too had come a long way in the fifty years since Reilly had persuaded Lever to pay for the world's first university studies of town planning, and that its achievements and those of its professors and graduates deserved modest jubilee celebrations. Gordon Stephenson had radically changed the teaching in the department after he arrived in 1948. Part-time courses were abandoned and a two-year full-time Master's degree course was established, which was thrown open to graduates in geography, economics and sociology as well as to architects and engineers. (Later on, students were also admitted if they had obtained a first class degree in almost any subject. These did as well as students whose first degrees had been obtained in subjects more closely related to town planning.) In this it followed the recommendations of the Schuster committee on the training of planners.[1] The department had always attracted students from abroad and this continued after the Second World War. Student numbers were usually between thirty and forty, and in the years 1957–59 there were twenty foreign students from fifteen different countries.

The *Town Planning Review* was also re-organized after 1948, and set out to persuade men of international reputation to become contributors. It was successful in so doing, partly because of the high reputation in which British town planning was then held abroad. Apart from current achievements and possibilities, the *Review* persuaded eminent scholars to describe town planning as it had existed and made progress in ancient Egypt, Greece and elsewhere. It may reasonably be claimed that no journal in the field of town planning and associated subjects has since equalled the *Town Planning Review* for the years 1949–53 in the quality of its authors and writing and the range of subjects examined.[1] The *Review* still sells more copies abroad, in twenty countries, than it does in Great Britain.

In 1952 the department had moved, as already stated, into a new building at the corner of Abercromby Square. This again was a pioneer venture, since so far as is known it was the first building anywhere to be designed exclusively for town planning studies. The building also stands on, for it, historic ground. The site is about 75 yards from that of the house which Reilly had occupied in his later and most famous years as Professor of Architecture, and almost adjoins the house which had belonged to Holford since 1933 and was to be occupied by him on his Liverpool visits until 1965.

In 1953 Gordon Stephenson was invited to succeed Frederick J.

Adams as Professor of City Planning at the Massachusetts Institute
of Technology. This was a compliment to both himself and the
department, as the opportunities for city and regional planning in
the United States then seemed great, and the finance available for
research was likely to be generous. For good measure, Mr Clarence
Stein, the pioneer of new towns and neighbourhood units in
America, made an offer to take the *Town Planning Review* as well
across the Atlantic so that Gordon Stephenson could continue to edit
it.Despite the *Review's* big overdraft, Sir James Mountford, then
Vice-Chancellor of Liverpool University, did not think that this was
a good idea at all, and nothing further came of it.

In the event, Stephenson did not take up the appointment at MIT.
After being consultant to the University of Western Australia for a
year, he became Professor of Town Planning at Toronto for six years
before returning to Australia. He was succeeded as fifth Lever
professor by Myles Wright. Continuity with the former Research
Division of the Ministry of Town and Country Planning had been
maintained. In 1955 three former members of the division were in the
department and a fourth gave occasional lectures.

In May 1959 Mr Henry Brooke (now Lord Brooke of Cumnor), then
Minister of Housing and Local Government, accepted an invitation
to attend a lunch, and open a small exhibition in celebration of the
jubilee of the Department of Civic Design. The exhibition reviewed
urban development since 1909, mainly by means of aerial photographs, of which several thousands had been examined in order to
show fifty years of successes and failures of British town planning.
After being shown in Liverpool, the exhibition went on a short tour
to other planning schools.

The actual jubilee day, 15 May, was brilliantly sunny and as the
Exhibition Room of the department communicated with the
adjoining courtyard through open french doors, the relayed
speeches could be heard by students gathered there, in what they no
doubt felt were ideal conditions. Mr Henry Brooke's speech was
politely received. It was, truthfully, rather dull. The department had
sent to Mr Brooke's Private Secretary some carefully prepared notes
on current planning problems of consequence, in the hope that the
Minister might speak on some of them at the jubilee. Not a bit of it.
The Private Secretary (or Mr Brooke) decided that important
speeches were for the House of Commons or the Lord Mayor's
Banquet, not for a small celebration in a provincial city.

The third, fourth and fifth Lever professors attended the
ceremony. It was sad that Sir Patrick Abercrombie had died two
years too early to join in the jubilee celebrations of a department in
which he had been the first full-time member of staff before
becoming Britain's greatest town and country planner, and
probably the last of the great planning individualists. The
professors of town planning at Manchester and Newcastle-upon-
Tyne (both Liverpool graduates) also attended the jubilee, which

was marked by a leading article in *The Times*[2], and special articles in *The (Manchester) Guardian*[3] and the professional journals.[4] The *Town Planning Review*, as was to be expected, published a special issue, which contained excerpts from its twenty-nine published volumes.

The Times in its commentary estimated that up to 1959 the Lever professors had between them prepared plans for over fifty towns, cities and regions including (in Britain) London, Edinburgh, Bristol, Sheffield, Plymouth, Bath, Doncaster, Hull, Stratford-on-Avon, Cambridge, York, Warwick and Scarborough; as well as the Universities of Liverpool, St Andrews, Exeter and Kent. Outside Great Britain, their plans had ranged from Dublin to Addis Ababa and from Halifax (Nova Scotia) to Lusaka, Durban and Western Australia. It is safe to prophesy that never again will the holders of a single appointment have so great an influence.

The year 1959 was a fortunate one for the jubilee of the Department of Civic Design, and, for another reason, a suitable one at which to end this book. The department's monopoly had ended. In addition to Liverpool and University College, London, two other British universities had begun to offer town planning courses in the years before the Second World War; and after 1945 – in the golden years for British planning – hardly a year passed without the announcement of a new planning course, or even several. The heads of the older schools (clearly interested parties) protested in vain that Britain was training more town planners than the country would need, or indeed could stand. And so it has proved. In 1981, the aspiring British town planner can choose between more than 120 courses in town planning or closely associated subjects in universities or polytechnics, without any certainty of a job at the end of his or her studies.

In 1959, however, very few graduates from the new courses had obtained senior positions. The former students of the Lever professors still held a comfortable majority of senior positions in Britain and the Commonwealth – as professors, consultants, the chief officers in the Planning Ministry (and in Scotland from 1947 to 1952), and senior officers in the largest local authorities. Thirty one held responsible positions abroad in eighteen countries, where four (possibly five) held professorships; and a few years later O. Weerasinghe and Hamzah bin Sendut were to become respectively Chief of the Physical Planning Section of the United Nations in New York and Vice-Chancellor of the University of Penang. And despite competition from the graduates of newer courses and institutions, Lever professors' students continued to hold senior Ministry positions until 1965 or later.

For another reason 1959 is a suitable date at which to end the story of the Lever professors and their work and influence. All the professors up to 1959 had also been consultants, and were thus able to base their teaching on current problems and the latest methods for solving them. Abercrombie could not imagine a good teacher who was not also a practitioner. This continued for another decade at Liverpool and elsewhere; yet the end of combined teaching and practice could perhaps be foreseen. In 1959 the majority of town planners in Britian were necessarily in local government service, but collaboration between local authority planning officers and those planners in private practice continued, and relations were cordial. Things changed.

By 1970 a proportion of local authority town planners were advocating the principle of the 'closed shop', though at that time many members of the Town Planning Institute thought it a little unprofessional, and certainly rather low class, to declare as their ultimate aim that no one save a local authority employee should do any town planning in Britain. Another decade got rid of any little scruples of that kind. By mid-1980 certain local authority town planners, for the most part members of the Royal Town Planning Institute, took 'industrial action' – that is they threatened to strike and so block the entire town planning process in their districts – if private consultants were employed.[5]

This action leads to three sad reflections. If such threats and action become common, local authorities, which in area, population and financial resources are, unavoidably, of second, third or fourth rank, can never invite men and women of high quality to examine a local planning problem, even though it might be a once-in-a-lifetime problem, and one capable of examination and report in six months or a year. These smaller authorities would be doomed to have second, third or fourth rate advice for ever. Secondly, the Royal Town Planning Institute was founded by consultants, or those who combined teaching and consultancy, consultants have provided seventeen of the Institute's sixty-four presidents and nearly all of those of national or international fame. The export of highly skilled professional services still brings Britain valuable foreign exchange and opens the way to other exports. But work abroad must almost certainly depend on high reputation and on work accomplished and in hand in Britain. The actions described will destroy the British base of British planning consultants.

Most sadly of all, there has been no report that the Council of the now Royal Town Planning Institute has rebuked those of its members who have introduced or threatened to introduce such practices into what was once a profession of high standing.

NOTES AND REFERENCES

1   Articles in The *Town Planning Review* 1948-54 included:
    (i) Historical Articles
    H. W. Fairman 'Town Planning in Pharoanic Egypt' (TPR, Vol XX, 1949, 33)
    H. Frankfurt 'Town Planning in Ancient Mesopotamia' (TPR, Vol. XXI, 1950, 99)
    V. Gordon Childe 'The Urban Revolution' (TPR, Vol. XXI, 1950, 3)
    R. W. Hutchinson 'Prehistoric Town Planning in Crete' (TPR, Vol. XXI, 1950, 199)
    R. E. Wycherley 'Hellenic Cities' (TPR, Vol. XXII, 1951, 103)
    R. E. Wycherley 'Hellenistic Cities' (TPR, Vol. XXII, 1951, 177)
    R. W. Hutchinson 'Prehistoric Town Planning in and around the Aegean) (TPR, Vol. XXIII, 1952-3, 261)
    R. W. Hutchinson 'Prehistoric Town Planning in and around the Aegean) (TPR, Vol. XXIV, 1953-54, 5)
    (ii) A Series on Planning Schools
    Professor F. J. Adams (1) Massachusetts Institute of Technology (T.P.R. Vol.XX, 1949, 144).
    Professor W. G. Holford (2) University College London (T.P.R. Vol.XX, 283).
    Professor G. H. Perkins (3) Harvard (T.P.R. Vol.XX, 1949, 315).
    Professor T. J. Kent Jnr. (4) University of California (T.P.R. Vol.XXI, 1950, 18).
    Professor J. A. Parker (5) University of North Carolina (T.P.R. Vol.XXI, 1950, 145).
    Professor J. S. Allen (6) Durham University (T.P.R. Vol.XXI, 1950, 253).
    Professor Gordon Stephenson (7) The University of Liverpool (T.P.R. Vol.XXII, 1951, 8).
    H. K. Menhinick (8) Georgia Institute of Technology (T.P.R. Vol.XXIII, 1952-3, 292).
    (iii) There was also a series by Clarence Stein called 'Toward New Towns for America' (T.P.R. Vol.XX 1949)
    (iv) In addition there were articles by such men as Lewis Mumford, Sir George Pepler, Robert J. Gardner-Medwin, S.L.G. Beaufoy, J.J. Clarke, F.J. Osborn, J.H. Forshaw, T. Alwyn Lloyd, Thomas Sharp and Gordon Stephenson.

2   *The Times* 18 May, 1959.

3   *The Manchester Guardian* 15 May, 1959.

4   John S. Millar: University of London. Fiftieth Anniversary of the Department of Civic Design *Town Planning Institute Journal* Vol. XLV 1958-59, 250 *Architects Journal* Vol. 129 May 28, 1959, 793-4

5   *The Planner News* August 1980, 4, published by the RTPI

INDEX